TIRSO DE MOLINA & THE COUNTER REFORMATION

Frontispiece Portrait of Tirso de Molina in the Biblioteca Nacional, Madrid

TIRSO DE MOLINA
& THE DRAMA
OF THE COUNTER REFORMATION

by

HENRY W. SULLIVAN

© Editions Rodopi N.V., Amsterdam 1976
Printed in the Netherlands
ISBN: 90–6203–399–7

To
FRANK PAUL CASA
Teacher and
Friend
*

ACKNOWLEDGEMENTS

The debts that this monograph has incurred are principally of a personal, inspirational nature. The original idea around which the third chapter is built was the insight of my old friend, Professor Ion T. Agheana of Dartmouth College. The potential importance of probabilism for the *comedia* enunciated itself more gradually; in Oxford lectures by Professor P. E. Russell in the early 1960s on Jesuit culture and in increasingly illuminating detail during conversations with Mr. Jonah N. Fortner of New York City and Professor Antonio Regalado of New York University in the early 1970s. To Professor Regalado, I also owe the clear realization that skepticism had become a real force in sixteenth-century Spain. My thanks also go to Dr. Premraj Halkhoree for permission to film his doctoral dissertation of 1969. The research for this book was conducted principally in the Biblioteca Nacional, Madrid, the British Museum in London and the Newberry Library, Chicago, and my thanks go to the staffs of those libraries. I am deeply indebted to Professor Frank P. Casa of Michigan for his inexhaustible patience in suggesting improvements in the original MS and to my wife, Professor Mary E. Ragland, for inducing me to omit much material that only hampered the main lines of the book's development. I should also like to express my gratitude to Professor Richard H. Popkin for his generosity in allowing me to draw heavily on his work on skepticism. Finally, I should like to thank Mrs. Leonore Scherrer of Chicago, who typed the final MS in exemplary fashion.

Amsterdam, July, 1976.

CONTENTS

Acknowledgments 4
Contents 5
List of Plates 6
Introduction 7

I THE CULTURAL AND INTELLECTUAL BACKGROUND OF
SPAIN IN THE COUNTER REFORMATION 13

> The Council of Trent and the *comedia* — The Controversy 'De Auxiliis' — Moral Probabilism and Casuistry — Philosophic Skepticism and the Criteria of Knowledge — Further Applications to the *comedia*

II TIRSO'S THEORY OF DRAMA 71

> The Mimetic Theory — The Hybrid Drama of the Moderns — Tragic Elements in the *comedia* — The Pragmatic Theory — Tirso's Aesthetic Voluntarism — Active Participation

III THE PERSONALITY OF THE TYPICAL
TIRSIAN PROTAGONIST 101

> Ego versus Situation — Ego versus Self — Ethical Voluntarism

IV THE BAROQUE IN TIRSIAN DRAMA 121

> Definition of the Baroque — Tirso and Velázquez — Tirso and the Play-within-the-Play — The Aberration of the Senses

V TIRSO'S PRISMATIC USE OF LANGUAGE 149

> Tirso's Anticipation and the Compression of Time — Tirso's Use of Prophecy and the Ominous — Tirso's Imagery — Tirso's Wordplay

Conclusion 169
Selected Bibliography 173
Index 185

LIST OF PLATES

Frontispiece Portrait of Tirso de Molina in the Biblioteca Nacional, Madrid

Fig. 2 *Las hilanderas* of Velázquez (1647-57)

Fig. 3 *The Rape of Europa* by Titian (c. 1560-61)

INTRODUCTION

The newness of this study stems from its attempt to place Tirsian drama against the background of neo-Scholastic theology in Spain. This 'ideothematic' approach seeks, by revealing an identity between contemporary ideas and dramatic themes, to illustrate how the classical Spanish theater played a central role in the nation's cultural and intellectual life. For it is my broad contention that the catastrophe of religious division in the Renaissance created a spiritual need throughout Europe that was supplied by the drama. The acute crisis of conscience in Counter-Reformation Spain created both the conditions favorable to the elaboration of a modern, vernacular theater, and supplied this *comédia nueva* with many of its most characteristic themes as playsubjects. A proposition as modest as this would hardly rise above the level of a truism, were it not for the generally serene picture that we in the present day have tended to form of Spanish church history. The unbroken continuity and conservatism of Catholic thought, coupled with Spain's historical adherence to the Catholic faith, have combined to establish a broad impression of doctrinal uniformity that is positively deceptive with respect to the Counter Reformation.

Now this is not to say that, behind a façade of obedience to the Catholic church, Spaniards privately subscribed to a series of heterodox or schismatic opinions; quite the contrary. It was precisely the strain involved in Spain's unswerving loyalty to traditional beliefs amid the turmoil of a changing world that gave to its art and literature that sense of beauty breaking the bounds of control which we commonly term the Baroque. Strain showed, for example, in the free will debate which came dangerously close to causing a new schism in Spain around the turn of the century, but the uniqueness of Spanish thought in the Counter Reformation lay in the skill with which the resilience inherent in Catholic orthodoxy was employed by theologians and other thoughtful men to resolve new problems without genuine precedent within a neo-Scholastic framework. In reading Elizabethan tragedy or the specifically controversial plays of northern dramatists such as the Dutchman Vondel or the German Gryphius, we do not hesitate to point out elements that are clearly atheistic, skeptical, humanist, pro-Catholic or pro-Protestant. In Spain, however, we may easily fall into the trap of assuming that Catholic conformity left Spaniards serene and untroubled in their religious consciousness. For above the internecine, doctrinal squabbles of Europe loomed larger issues of common concern to all, such as the scope of human freedom, the possibilities of certain knowledge, or the antidotes to irresistible doubt. Transmuted by art, these ideas found their spontaneous and immortal expression in dramatic poetry. But if an oversimplified view of Spain's late-sixteenth and early-seventeenth centuries succeeds by default in concealing the power and violence of fundamental human questioning in the period or the degree of the individual's anguish, then the modern student literally does not possess the tools to understand what the Spanish *comedia* was about.

For purposes of definition, I am calling the Counter Reformation that period of Catholic revival and attempted reconquest of the Protestant north which ran from the break-up of the final sessions of the Council of Trent in 1563 to the Peace of Münster in 1648. That peace, which brought the Thirty Years War (1618-1648) to a close, and the formal Treaty of Westphalia which confirmed Europe's religious divisions along political lines, really mark the end of the Habsburg effort to reimpose Catholic orthodoxy on their heretical neighbors. From the 1580s onwards, the national theaters of England and Spain soared swiftly; Dutch drama thrived soon thereafter, German drama briefly also, and French drama, at first derivative and second-rate, achieved a later, aristocratic classicism of its own between 1630 and 1680. I hope to demonstrate that this 'coincidence' of real-life drama and thriving poetic drama was no coincidence at all.

In employing what I have termed an 'ideothematic' approach to Tirsian drama, I am only too well aware of what might be called the *Geistesgeschichte* fallacy. This, roughly speaking, is the discussion of literature in terms of pure philosophy or a philosophy in diluted form called the 'history of ideas' (*Geistesgeschichte*). By this reckoning, a literary work embodies or illustrates the ideas current in the period or the 'spirit of the time' (*Zeitgeist*) and is studied as such. Thus, while tying the sense of the literary work to the theoretical or moral preoccupations of the age that created it, the critic runs the risk of ignoring questions of genre, style, artistic value, authorial uniqueness and so on, and may well lose sight of the work as an entity and a totality. How is one to discuss the all-important history of contemporary ideas when analyzing the Spanish *comedia,* then, while avoiding the pitfalls of a simplistic application of the ideothematic approach?

Comedia criticism has been enriched almost beyond recognition since the Second World War by the quantity and quality of attention that the Spanish drama has received. Many of the most fruitful advances in analysis have come from countries other than Spain, such as France and Germany, and notably England and N. America. The British Hispanists, such as E. M. Wilson, A. A. Parker, A. E. Sloman, P. N. Dunn and many others, have shed new light on the *comedia* by the use of what R. D. F. Pring-Mill has termed a technique of 'thematico-structural analysis.'[1] This approach, of which the most conspicuous and systematic exponent is Parker, consists in a process of resolving the action of a given play into its component parts and tracing back the chain of causality by which the events of the dramatic action are precipitated to the theme. By a careful separation of the strands of the storyline into its main plot and one or more sub-plots, a subtler structural interrelation and dramatic craftsmanship were revealed in these plays than had hitherto been suspected. Wilson, Parker and others were able to show that dramatic unity, especially in Calderón, often lay in the themes, sometimes identical, of the main plot and sub-plot. Painstaking analysis of the contribution of each character to the development of the play's action and theme, and of the carefully conceived chain of causality by which the theme was complicated and resolved, presented a corpus of dramatic literature that functioned according to a set of rules of its own. The uniqueness of Spanish dramaturgy, which had hitherto perplexed even its most ardent devotees, was thus unveiled in unsuspected beauty and complexity of design.

The question now arises: 'to what do we owe the pre-eminence of theme in the Spanish drama'? In Shakespeare, for example, character predominates; in French comedy, situation and well-organized plot usually take precedence. My contention is that the Spanish drama departed fundamentally from a conceptual basis. By this, I mean an abstract insight into the human condition conceived as a problem or a question. These 'insight-in-stress' concepts contained inherent possibili-

---

1. This is actually a literal translation of Pring-Mill's own Spanish coinage. The phrase is both a felicitous and an accurate one. See his valuable essay, "Los calderonistas de habla inglesa y *La vida es sueño*: métodos del análisis temático-estructural," in *Litterae Hispanae et Lusitanae,* ed. Hans Flasche (Munich, 1968).

ties for drama, since they were actually predicated in dialectical oppositions to begin with (freedom versus destiny, certainty versus doubt, appearance versus reality, truth versus falsehood). Drawn from Spanish history, hagiography, Italian *novelle,* Bible stories or Greek legends, plot material was any situation or tale that offered thematic possibilities for opening up conflict and interplay of the kind we have described. In this way, theme was born of problematic origins and this problematic dimension belonged, in my view, to the specific stresses of the Counter Reformation in Spain.

The book's first chapter attempts to establish this point in detail with reference principally to the plays of Tirso. I shall emphasize that the problem of human freedom eclipsed all others in magnitude during the period. The gruelling discussion of grace presented as central to this problem is the briefest and clearest exposition that I have been able to arrive at while still doing some justice to the integrity and enormity of the subject. The problem of human freedom is shown in its relationship to the drama as a phenomenon *per se* and to the spread of moral probabilism and philosophic skepticism as modes of thought in life and on the stage. The second chapter treats Tirso's theory of the drama as the Mercedarian himself set it out, demonstrating the variety of his doctrines, his intelligent espousal of the Moderns' cause, his plea for artistic liberty and the Scholastic origins of what I have termed his 'aesthetic voluntarism.' The third chapter pursues the theme of freedom and human scope of action as exemplified by the typical Tirsian protagonist, both in his or her grappling with external situations and inner conflicts within the psyche. It is shown that Tirso's protagonists obey an ethical voluntarism restrained by discretion. The fourth chapter discusses the Baroque as an artistic phenomenon that expressed the paradoxical plight of Counter-Reformation man and contained in its ponderous strains and artfulness the essence of spiritual doubt and anguish. Here, skepticism is seen raised to a principle of art itself. In the fifth and last chapter, the implications of Tirso's dramaturgical Baroque are analyzed in terms of style and language. In his prismatic use of language, the same fracturing, splitting and compressing processes are seen at work as in Tirso's delineation of character and his love of theatrical illusions. In these last four chapters, form is thus shown evolving out of content as defined by the first chapter.

I hope by setting out the applications of the ideothematic approach in successive chapters that its validity will be clear. While it is obviously insufficient to say of a given play 'this theme expresses that idea,' it is eminently possible to show the manner in which theme (chapter I) can be applied to the more traditional categories of theory (chapter II), character (chapter III), situation (chapter IV) and language (chapter V). The study is rounded out with a conclusion that attempts to reconstruct Tirso's *Weltanschauung* in general terms and to draw together the strands of our preliminary conclusions in a final synthesis of the man and his dramatic art.

TIRSO DE MOLINA
& THE DRAMA
OF THE COUNTER REFORMATION

I

THE CULTURAL AND INTELLECTUAL BACKGROUND OF SPAIN IN THE COUNTER REFORMATION

> "Alcázar y iglesia santa..."
> *El amor médico,* I, ii.

The purpose of this chapter is to show how the feelings of confusion created by the major intellectual dilemmas of Counter-Reformation Spain found a badly needed outlet in the popular theater of the day. Modest and self-evident though such a contention may be, by no means every student of the *comedia* would concede its validity, or even approve the logic of connecting Spanish stage entertainment to the grand agonistic debates inherited by the seventeenth century from the century before. What were these debates? Did they touch the people? Did popular confusion find an expression in the *corrales*? Why was such an outlet badly needed? In these early pages, it will be my aim to answer those questions and related ones, to show the vital link between the *comedia* and the intellectual matrix of the society that produced it and thus clear the way for a particular discussion of the theater of Tirso de Molina in subsequent chapters.

We have said that the Spanish *comedia* flourished in the Counter Reformation. This period, which may conveniently be said to run from the break-up of the Council of Trent in 1563 to the end of the Thirty Years War in 1648, had as its goal both internal religious reform and the restoration of Catholicism in Protestant northern Europe. Conceived in a spirit of conscious and energetic reaction against the schismatic forces of the Reformation, the offensive campaign sought not only the extirpation of heresy but, indirectly, a return to the medieval world-order that had prevailed before Luther. Hence while the Counter Reformation achieved some notable successes (e.g. the reconquest of

South Germany and Poland by the Jesuits), it was unlikely, given the magnitude of the intellectual problem, to succeed in its overall attempts to contain the movement of European thought away from a theocentric medieval world-order towards an evolving anthropocentric one.

The implications of this for Catholic Europe were considerable. For if Western civilization was shifting its focal center from God to man, a reactionary movement that refused to recognize this fact of life was bound to involve its adherents in a profound crisis of conscience. The individual, his loyalties divided by the claims of two irreconcilable imperatives, would be thrown into an insoluble conflict. Where human freedom and individual conscience called, the devout Catholic collided with a medieval value-system and a reactionary public policy; where God and traditional loyalties called, he was obliged to suppress the murmurings and insights of a new and inalienable sensibility.

A resultant state of paradoxical doubt, of paralyzed confusion is a recurrent motif of Spanish literature in the Counter Reformation, and it gave great stimulus to a theater which frequently probed deeply in its formulation of problematic situations, but usually reached timid, "safe" and reconciliatory conclusions. Such a spirit stands in direct contrast to the contemporary Elizabeth and Jacobean drama, where the implications of a tragic situation were freely pushed to their logical, catastrophic limits. The Spanish *comedia* could consequently serve a double function in its society: a) homeopathically to purge a doubt-filled collective conscience of its feelings of confusion, and b) to leave the spectator restored in himself at play's end by concluding on a note of reaffirmation. Thus the *comedia* operated as a very effective safety-valve for all sectors of society and its success was correspondingly great. Significantly, the guardians of doctrinal orthodoxy — the clergy — provided the theater with its most dogged and ferocious opposition throughout the seventeenth century.

That the appearance and full bloom of the *comedia* in the Counter Reformation was not merely an historical coincidence may be induced at a surface level from comparative chronology. The first permanent theaters in Madrid opened in 1579 (the *corral de la Cruz*) and 1582 (the *corral del Príncipe*). Both Cervantes and Lope de Vega were writing for the stage by the late 1580s and in the next decade the *Fénix* had impressed upon the *comedia* the distinctive form that it retained for nearly a century. By the time of Westphalia in 1648, however, the most vigorous and inventive phase of the national theater was over; Rojas Zorilla died a premature death, Tirso, long silent, finally died; the theaters were closed for extensive periods owing to deaths in the royal family; numerous actors' troupes disbanded without steady employment, and rich or regal patrons removed the theater to the courts . . .

The real causes of the *comedia*'s decline, however, lie deeper. As the Counter Reformation spent its force and the division of Europe along religious boundaries became a political *fait accompli,* the *comedia* forfeited its principal *raison d'être.* Spain, in a mixture of resignation and impotence, let the Protestant north go its own way, directed its energies to France and the dilemma of having to opt for or sustain one of two value-systems lost its urgency. The *comedia* presaged this cultural failure too, for while the mood of Spain in the first eighty years of the sixteenth century had been one of confidence and energetic expansion, as the Counter Reformation wore on and the tide of history ran its inevitable course, this mood changed to a worried sense that things were going wrong, to introspection and *desengaño.* The *comedia,* which had always been an outlet of Spanish popular feeling, now tended to reflect the deepening gloom and pessimism of Spanish society in the seventeenth century. The drama was a mask behind which the Spanish populace concealed its feelings of disappointment as well as of confusion.

In Spain, then, the theater became a part of life, a legal national narcotic, a target of prolonged criticism, the most abundant theater in contemporary Europe. The *comedia* was apparently a by-product of the Counter Reformation and its decline mirrored the eventual decline of Spain. To understand the *underlying* causes of this symmetry, however, it is essential to bear in mind that Spain actually inspired the Counter Reformation directly in two important ways. Spanish armies and New World bullion gave power to the secular arm of the Catholic revival, while the Jesuit Order founded by Ignacio de Loyola took the lead in spiritual and intellectual combativeness. And both these sources of inspiration resolve into a single one, if we consider the then theocratic nature of the Spanish state.

A theocracy is by definition a form of government in which God is recognized as the actual ruler and His laws are taken as the statute-book of the kingdom. The theocratic concept found a late, explicit expression in the *De legibus ac Deo legislatore* of P. Suárez (1612) and the *Política de Dios y gobierno de Cristo, nuestro Señor* of Quevedo, a work that went through nine editions in 1626, the year of its first appearance. But the ideal medieval monarch had always theoretically ruled as God's anointed viceroy on earth and Spain displayed a continuing fidelity to this medieval heritage. When Ferdinand and Isabella formed foreign and domestic policies based on the interests of the Christian religion, they merely perpetrated the Castilian tradition of holy crusade against Islam; the deep-seated feeling of Spaniards that they were a chosen people and the bastion of Western Christendom. Charles V and, above all, Philip II continued to make Catholic interests the basis of their *Weltpolitik,* regarding Protestantism as a calamity and (in Philip's case) a pestilence to be resisted at any cost. Throughout the sixteenth century in Spain, then, Christianity continued to provide a unique link between national life and ideological programmes.

The theocratic composition of Spanish society influenced the directions of its intellectual endeavour just as surely. The Renaissance in Spain was a wondrous flowering of traditional disciplines and notably theology, in which the achievements of the Salamanca school put Spain in the van of Catholic and thus, to a degree, of all European thought. Her intellectual vigor also extended to maritime exploration, technological inventiveness, the exploitation of new crops and mining techniques, to pre-excellence in music, literature and the arts. On the other hand, the revival of Scholasticism closed out most genuine philosophical novelty (*novedades*) and put a brake on most areas of Renaissance speculation. As Neil McInnes has written: "The characteristic Spanish thought during the Renaissance was neither humanism nor natural philosophy but a reaction against both, a last determined defense of Scholasticism. This movement reached its apogee in the Council of Trent... and ended with the death of Suárez in 1617. It was centered in Salamanca and Alcalá, and later at Coimbra in Portugal, and was dominated by the Jesuits. It provided the philosophy of the Counter Reformation and in Spain it succeeded in annulling the influence of Erasmus."[1]

A "determined defense of Scholasticism" also tied Spain to a defense of the whole gamut of Thomist thought, even where St. Thomas had been writing on subjects other than theology. Since Aquinas had succeeded in synthesizing Christian doctrine and Aristotelian thought, an attack on one was an attack on the other; any new theories in the areas of (Aristotelian) physics, astronomy, cosmology or physiology were bound to be regarded as heresy and were so treated. The lives of

---

1. See Neil McInnes, "Spanish Philosophy," in *The Encyclopedia of Philosophy* (New York and London: Macmillan, 1967), vol. VII, p. 513.

Miguel Servet, Giordano Bruno and Galileo bear witness to the fate of original thinkers at the hands of dogmatists such as Calvin or the Italian Inquisitors. But just as the attempted political containment of Protestantism ultimately failed, so did the efforts of Spain and her allies to preserve the edifice of medieval science. Consequently northern Europe slowly forged ahead in disciplines where empirical observation, unobstructed experiment and free speculation were essential, activities either discouraged or proscribed by the Inquistion. Thus, after a brief but brilliant rebirth of intellectual power, Spaniards paid the same price for their fidelity to the past in the intellectual sphere that they eventually paid in the political sphere. This loss of control is most clearly seen in France's taking over from Spain her intellectual supremacy as well as the hegemony of Europe.[2]

To sum up, the victory of the theocratic and reactionary forces in Spanish society over all genuine philosophical innovation stamped a cultural seal on the most varied intellectual endeavours of the seventeenth century, including imaginative literature. This was so pervasively true of the *comedia* that the very universality of agonized conservatism in these plays has actually blinded us to its presence. If the Counter Reformation had in fact produced schismatic and heterodox dramatists in Spain, their work could be used to throw the main philosophical pre-suppositions of their conservative *confrères* into some meaningful and illuminating relief. But, as things stand, we must try to glimpse the whole forest before we can see individual trees.

It should already be intelligible that the dramatists whose work has survived ought not to be viewed as the "conformists" in an "Age of Faith" that they are so often represented to be, but instead highly sensitive and thoughtful men who frequently captured the essence of human questioning and tragic conflict with extraordinary skill. Their

---

2. The passing of intellectual supremacy from Spain to France is best represented by the direct legacy of Francisco Suárez, especially his *Disputationes metaphysicae* (1597), to René Descartes. Descartes knew parts of the *Disputationes* by heart and carried a volume of them with him everywhere. See the article "Suárez" in *The Encyclopedia of Philosophy,* vol. VIII, p. 31, and Martin Grabmann, "Die Disputationes Metaphysicae des Franz Suarez in ihrer methodischen Eigenart und Fortentwicklung," in *Mittelälterliches Geistesleben* (Munich, 1926), vol. I, pp. 525-60. See also the remarks on Suárez in Etienne Gilson's *Etudes sur le Rôle de la Pensée Médiévale dans la Formation du Système Cartésien* (Paris: J. Vrin, 1951).

curiosity often led them to the creation of ingenious hypothetical situations, where the irreconcilable forces predicated in the very notion of Counter Reformation were set on a collision course. Then, either because the dramatist could not contemplate or dared not express the ultimate implications of his drama, he resorted to an even greater ingenuity in resolving the play's *impasse* than he had employed to devise it in the first place. This characteristic phenomenon of much Golden Age drama, where the *comedia's* hierarchy of values is sorely tested but ultimately respected (a source of disappointment to some modern readers), has been aptly termed by Professor Frank P. Casa a "retraction."[3]

It is insufficient however merely to assert as we have done, that spiritual, intellectual and moral confusion existed in the Spain of our period and that such confusion surfaced in the *comedia*. The conflicts behind these confusions must be spelled out and some idea conveyed of the sheer power and magnitude of the issues involved: these included the very fundaments of religious belief, the nature of the Creator, the crucial question of the nature of man's relationship to Him, man's attitude to the universe, to his own historical past, to the traditional criteria of truth, knowledge and moral conduct, all issues that became doubly charged with passion since they aroused the most belligerently and irreconcilably opposed views. To construct a logical sequence leading into the controversies of the Spanish Counter Reformation, therefore, we must begin with a brief overview of the Catholic reaction to the ideas of Luther as codified by the Council of Trent and the resurgence thereafter in Spain of certain problems which Trent had not been entirely able to resolve. The main controversies concern three areas: the theology of grace (the *De auxiliis* controversy); moral theology (probabilism); critical philosophy (philosophic skepticism and the criteria of knowledge). Later on, I will try to show what bearing these intellectual currents have on the *comedia*. Since our subject is Tirso proper, I have limited my choice of illustrative examples mainly to his theater, though many similar passages could be adduced from the work of his contemporaries. This has been done to avoid prolixity and, while making general points, show how Tirso was typical of his generation.

---

3. Professor Casa outlined his theory in a paper entitled "Retraction in Golden Age Drama," given at the Univ. of Illinois at Chicago Circle on Feb. 23rd, 1973.

The Council of Trent and the *comedia*

Though in the first stages of the Reformation many parties advocated a conciliatory policy towards Protestantism, and Protestant bishops attended the early sessions of Trent, it was a militant and reassertive Catholic spirit that eventually prevailed. This spirit was largely Spanish and formed part of that general hardening mood (especially in Trent's third phase after Philip II's accession) which was the Council's most important single historical consequence. Spain pushed most strenuously for a firm attitude at the Council and was most profoundly influenced by the sombre humor thereafter perpetrated and by the closing of intellectual perspectives that Trent entailed. This bears directly on the history of the drama since Trent also established the atmosphere of muted discussion in which the *comedia* provided a breathing space.

Secondly Trent, though it laid down strong dogmatic decrees, could not and did not resolve all the problems before the Council in definitive form. These residual problems or "loose ends" left by the Council reappear in a variety of subsequent debates and many are treated in the *comedia* (e.g. grace, the Eucharist, duelling, clandestine marriages). But it is really the interaction of these two realities, the reassertive mood and the nagging questions, the attempted moratorium placed on unresolved problems, that lend the *comedia* its own special character. Beneath the festive and carnivalesque exterior of the *comedia,* we may often discern an oblique and subtle treatment of themes of the greatest transcendence and urgency. Apart from matters touching theology and canon law, the theater broached the abuse of royal power, tyrannicide, wife-murder, homicide, incest, etc. Were such subjects treated daringly in serious treatises, the printed works would undoubtedly have been placed on the Index; appearing in comic guise in contexts suggested by situations rather than stated in specific "unorthodox" passages, controverted problems could be treated in a novel manner and still escape the vigilance of the censor. Part of the appeal of the *comedia* undoubtedly lay in its offer of the forbidden fruit that tasted sweetest.

The Council of Trent (the nineteenth ecumenical council by Catholic reckoning) assembled in Tyrolean Italy for the first time in 1545. The work of Trent was constantly complicated by diplomatic pressure from European rulers, by the ongoing chess-game of war and power politics in the background and by no means least a succession of Popes of widely differing temperaments. In consequence, the Council actually met at three different periods: 1545-47; 1551-52; and 1562-63.

Trent had as its main objectives a long overdue reform of ecclesiastical life and sundry clerical abuses, as well as the definitive determination of the doctrines of the Church in answer to the Protestant heresies. The desire for some general ecclesiastical reform had become universal by the end of the fifteenth century, but it assumed schismatic proportions in Germany owing to political forces and the concept advocated by northern humanists and reformers alike of a universal priesthood: that every man is in direct contact with God; Christ needs no vicars, either Pope or priest. Trent had considerable success in its own reforms (e.g. episcopal residence, reform of religious orders, establishment of clerical seminaries, etc.) and in redefining Catholic dogma, but this latter success merely made the religious division of Europe an irretrievable breach.

Trent's most important dogmatic decree (*sessio VI*) concerned the question of justification and grace, in which Luther's views were anathematized. The importance of this question is so great that a whole section of this chapter has been devoted to it, and a supplementary estimate of the impact of the *De auxiliis* controversy on the Spanish theater added in the final section. Suffice it to say at this point that the quarrels on grace were the most exhausting and unremitting of any in the sixteenth and seventeenth centuries combined.

The decrees on the Mass stand second only in dogmatic importance to that on justification, and also have their impact on the Spanish theater. Luther's concept of a universal priesthood cut directly at the priest's role as intermediary between man and God, and nowhere more so than in his sacramental function in the celebration of the Mass. Apart from the aggravated problem of the transubstantiation of the sacraments, the Lutheran view of communion under both species, the non-sacrificial nature of the Mass, etc. seemed to endanger the central mystery of the Eucharist. The traditional views on these matters were vigorously reaffirmed at phases two and three of Trent, and Spanish theologians (Soto, Cano, Laínez, Salmerón) often intervened decisively in their formulation.

Since the Eucharist was especially associated with the feast of Corpus Christi, we witness in Spain a remarkable phenomenon after Trent. Throughout the sixteenth century, the choice of Christmas as the religious festival most favored for dramatic treatment in early *farsas* and *églogas* was steadily supplanted by Corpus Christi. After the dispersal of Trent in 1563, however, these *autos* as they were often also called, first took on a specifically sacramental and symbolic character in the *Ternarios sacramentales* (2 vols., 1575) of Juan de Timoneda, whom B. W. Wardropper has called the father of the pre-Calderonian *auto*.[4] Thereafter the genre of the *auto sacramental* was exercised by Lope de Vega, Valdivielso, Calderón and others, and had immense popularity.

Wardropper has denied that the *autos* of the Counter Reformation were a reply to the Protestants or even an arm of combat, but rather an act of affirmation.[5] The question is one of emphasis, naturally, and one may ask when a cherished belief is reaffirmed so splendidly and tenaciously as was the mystery of the Eucharist, whether this is not in itself a spiritually aggressive act? If national myths find articulate definition, this often illustrates that their power to compel has begun to decline. I do not suggest here that the splendors of Corpus Christi were shoring up a flagging belief, but that the *autos*' suddenly acquired sacramental import and the great vogue of this aberrant drama-form clearly responded to the Tridentine defense of the Mass. In Jacobean England, it is true that the masque, a stylized pageant-filled and frequently allegorical drama-form gained a striking vogue, but the ends to which the secular Jacobean masque and the sacramental Spanish *auto* were put could hardly have differed more radically.

Patient analysis of the Spanish drama in the light of the articles of Trent will one day yield a rich harvest of thematic parallels. At present, I wish to draw attention to two more in the area of canon law: duelling and clandestine marriage.

It is common knowledge that the concern for personal honor reached the level of an obsession in seventeenth-century Spain and was the most characteristic single theme of the *comedia*. The obsession with honor in life frequently led to armed combats occasioned by real or imaginary slights, and since certain offenses required expiation in blood, the victorious duelist automatically transgressed the Sixth Commandment: "Thou shalt not kill," and the injunction in Deuteronomy 32:35: "To

---

4. See B. W. Wardropper, *Introducción al teatro religioso del Siglo de Oro: La evolución del auto sacramental: 1500-1648* (Madrid: Revista de Occidente, 1953), pp. 202-03.

5. Wardropper writes: "Hemos visto que los autos no surgieron como respuesta a la reforma protestante ni como arma de combate de la Contrarreforma. Antes forman una parte íntegra de la reforma católica minoritaria. Son herramientas para afirmar, antes que armas para atacar ... La conciencia de la misión católica de España contribuye a hacer más populares los autos" (op. cit., p. 323).

me belongeth vengeance, and recompense." On these points canon law and social honor codes could not be reconciled, and in any case duelling infringed the domain of canonical jurisprudence.

The duel of honor grew out of the trial by "ordeal" and judicial combat of the Middle Ages, in which God supposedly always favored the innocent. Although some ecclesiastics endorsed such duels, most medieval Church authorities and Popes regarded them as a superstition and tolerated judicial combat because of public opinion. When trial by combat, jousting and tourneys declined in popularity in the early sixteenth century, duels of honor multiplied alarmingly. Consequently the Council of Trent, when it outlawed extra-legal duelling, did so in the most severe terms: "Detestabilis duellorum usus, fabricante diabolo, introductus, ut cruenta corporum morte animarum etiam perniciem lucretur, ex christiano orbe penitus exterminetur...."[6] Lords temporal were enjoined to interdict duels of honor in their dominions under pain of excommunication; the corpses of victims, regarded canonically as suicides, were to be denied burial in holy ground.

Though Trent checked duelling in some degree, it is notorious that the custom persisted and Charles IX of France, for example, flouted the Church in 1564 by issuing an edict expressly reserving to himself the power to authorize duels. Calderón's *El postrer duelo de España,* written in 1665 but situated in 1522, expresses in its title a pious fiction as regards either date. In that play, involving Caldéron in a deliberate anachronism, Charles V condemns the barbarous custom and refers it to the Council of Trent:

> CARLOS   Escríbase luego al Papa
> Paulo Tercero, que hoy
> goza la Sede, una carta
> en que humilde le suplique
> esta bárbara tirana
> ley del duelo, que quedó
> de gentiles heredada,
> en mi reinado prohiba
> en el Concilio que hoy trata
> celebrar en Trento...[7]

---

6. *Decretum de reformatione,* cap. XIX, Acta Concilii Tridentini, anno Christi, 1563. Quoted by N. A. Bennetton in *Social Significance of the Duel in Seventeenth-Century French Drama* (Baltimore: Johns Hopkins Press, 1938), p. 13, note.

7. Calderón de la Barca, *Obras completas,* ed. Angel Valbuena Briones (Madrid: Aguilar, 1966), vol. I, p. 1311.

Though Calderón's words here may reflect his own opinion of duels of honor, we know he was no stranger to such swordplay himself and in any case the *comedia* literally abounds with duels, fought either formally or more commonly in self-defense or to rescue the honor of a lady. That this most abundant sub-genre of the *comedia* was dubbed the *comedia de capa y espada* amply demonstrates the integral role of swordplay in developing dramatic situations. Hence, while the dramatists may have paid lip-service to canon law on duels of honor, they reflected an inherent fact of life on the stage and exploited it systematically. Indeed, critics of the *corrales* made this portrayal of duels one of their most consistent targets of attack.

We do not at present possess sufficient evidence to talk confidently about the true attitudes of Lope, Tirso, Calderón et al. towards the morality of duelling. By way of a temporary indication, however, a few words on *Luis Pérez, el gallego* (1629) of Calderón can serve to illustrate the complexity of the problem. In this play, Calderón's most popular success in his lifetime, the playwright looks at duelling from almost every point of view. There are three punctilious heroes, all on the run from justice for having killed or wounded opponents in duels! In the words of Luis Pérez's sister and the *gracioso* Pedro, Calderón may hint at criticism of the eponymous hero's obsession with honor, yet there seems to be a fairly obvious admiration on Calderón's part for the swash-buckling valor of Luis and his companions. Nor is there anything in the play to suggest that the author rejected the moral propositions in defense of duelling set forth by the several personages.

The casuists in Spain (see "moral probabilism"), in innumerable tracts *De justitia et jure, De bello et duello* and commentaries on the Sixth Commandment, sustained a variety of doctrines defending duelling in cases of extreme necessity, some of them somewhat dubious.[8] But, Calderón asks, does one have the right to kill a bridegroom, as does Don Manuel, to forestall a marriage contracted under parental tyranny? Does one have the right to kill a false witness, as does Don Luis, who persists in his perjury under cross-examination? Does one have the right to kill an opponent, as does Don Alonso, in an

---

8. A Protestant probabilist of the seventeenth century, Andreas Stenchelstrup, in his *Dissertatio de duellis* (Hafnia, 1677), p. 64, said of certain Catholic casuists: "*Casuistae Pontificii* varios sibi fingunt *extremae necessitatis casus*; qui tamen non sunt tales; unde nec tutelam nostri inculpatam admittunt" (Stenchelstrup's emphasis).

honorable duel *a macchia* without incurring legal penalty? The theologian Struvius, in his *De vindicatione privata,* upheld a man's right to defend himself against assault by a monarch (!), a magistrate or parent.[9] Both Don Luis and Don Manuel literally cross swords with the magistrate in Calderón's play, and in Luis Pérez's absence from his estate, when the villain of the play attempts to abduct Don Luis' sister, Isabel, Manuel is obliged to kill one of his assailants and wound another.

It is not my intention to draw any firm conclusions at this point regarding Calderón's theories on duelling, homicides in defense of personal honor, etc. It is however obvious that Trent did not bring an end to duels in real life, nor apparently did its decree deter certain Catholic casuists from designating cases where the duel of honor could be licit. The *comedia* clearly demonstrates that the problem was not resolved in theory or practice, and the popularity of cape-and-sword plays and plays like *Luis Pérez, el gallego* show that the Spanish audience warmed to this arrogant lawlessness justified by a tenuous canonical authority.

If duelling played an integral role in developing plot in romantic comedies, love intrigue, in the form of nocturnal serenades, clandestine trysts, elopements, abductions, clandestine engagements and secret marriages, was their very stuff. Among the most controverted aspects on the subject of marriage submitted to the Council of Trent was the validity of marital unions contracted in clandestinity. Some Protestant authorities had denied that marriage was a sacrament at all, and before Trent a majority of ecclesiastics, including some Catholics, were in favor of the validity of clandestine marriage. But while all Catholic theologians resented the inconveniences and scandals of clandestine marriage (*dissensiones, odia, inimicitiae* according to Leitanus), all agreed that marriage was a sacrament that conferred grace. To solve the problem of how to condemn clandestine union without condemning its sacramental character as well (thus playing into the hands of the Protestants), led the Council members to distinctions between the contract and the sacrament, and the fitness or unfitness of the parties (*inhabilitas personarum*). Thus by attacking the form and fitness of the

---

9. Struvius (Georg Adam Struve) wrote a *Jurisprudentia romano-germanica forensis* (Jena, 1670), but I have been unable to find the place and date of his *De vindicatione privata.* According to Stenchelstrup, he maintains this opinion on p. 41 of the latter-mentioned work.

contract rather than the sacramental character of existing clandestine unions, the canonical validity of such marriages could be and was revoked.[10]

As in so many cases, however, the Tridentine decree did not bring controversy to an end. The Council's resolutions provoked an instantaneous attack from the Protestants, and according to Le Bras,[11] the great renovation of Catholic doctrine on marriage, suscitated by transformations in the rite and the attacks of the Reformers, belongs to the latter part of the sixteenth century. He writes: "La plus belle période pour l'histoire littéraire de la doctrine du mariage, avec le milieu du XIIIème siècle, c'est incontestablement entre 1585 et 1635 qu'il la faut reconnaître" (*Dictionnaire de Théologie Catholique*, IX, ii, 2250). These dates correspond almost exactly to the Golden Age of the *comedia*, and the question of marriage and clandestinity received thorough treatment by Spanish theologians and playwrights alike. The three most important treatises in this period were all written in Spain: Pedro de Ledesma's *De magno matrimonii sacramento* (Salamanca, 1592), Thomas Sánchez's *De sancto matrimonii sacramento* (Genoa, 1592), and Basilio Ponce's *De sacramento matrimonii* (Salamanca, 1624). The great work of the Jesuit Sánchez, still consulted, devotes its entire *Liber* III to the theme of clandestinity.

As with duelling, insufficient evidence is available to us at this time to pronounce on the views of the Spanish dramatists towards clandestine marriage. What is certain is the popularity of the theme. Lope's *El mayordomo de la Duquesa de Amalfi* (c. 1606) (treating the same situation and subject as Webster's *The Duchess of Malfi*) contains a case of clandestine marriage, as does Tirso's *El pretendiente al revés*. In the latter play, Carlos and Sirena have met secretly at night for over a year (I, vi), and regard their union as licit. In some twenty-five other plays, Tirso presents the case of a girl who is seduced and abandoned by her lover under promise of marriage and pursues him thereafter in male

---

10. According to the norms established by the *Sacra Congregatio cardinalium Concilii Tridentini interpretum* (instituted in 1564), at a legal ceremony three witnesses were to be present including a priest (*parochus*), usually of the parties' actual domicile, who was to be spiritually as well as physically and materially present. Surprisingly, if the priest were present under compulsion, the marriage was still pronounced valid. See Le Bras, my note 11.

11. See Le Bras' article "Mariage" in the *Dictionnaire de Théologie Catholique*, ed. Vacant, Mangenot et al., especially columns 2233-2252.

disguise. Tirso seems to defend the legitimacy of these contracts *de facto* in the plays' endings, and at Trent, Antonio di Gragnano argued that such unions contained all elements necessary to the sacrament: the form (consent and words of the parties), the matter (the bodies of the spouses) and the ministers (the contracting parties). The clandestine marriage of Pedro and Inés de Castro in Vélez de Guevara's *Reinar después de morir* is crucial to the play's action.

Calderón dramatizes cases of clandestine betrothal in *El postrer duelo de España, Nadie fíe su secreto,* and *Basta callar. El pintor de su deshonra* contains two such cases. According to Professor A. A. Parker, Calderón considers clandestine engagements: "... como elemento censurable en el mundo social que [...] nos presenta...."[12] At the same time, Parker admits that a complete study of the social world portrayed in Calderón's theater is very far from complete, and it seems evident that more attention must be devoted to the whole range of problems thrown up by impediments to marriage in the *comedia,* in relation to the copious contemporary literature of Spanish theologians on the subject.[13]

* * *

When Spain and Catholic Europe joined battle for the reconquest of the North, it was with a vigor untempered by compromise, close to fanaticism. If that surprises us, we must remember that though the controverted issues described above can be formulated in philosophical terms with modern hindsight, in the context of their day they were

---

12. See A. A. Parker, "Los amores y noviazgos clandestinos en el mundo dramático-social de Calderón," in *Hacia Calderón. Segundo coloquio anglo-germano. Hamburg* (Berlin and New York: Gruyter, 1970), 79-87, at p. 87. On the indulgence shown towards infractions of moral law by lovers in the *comedia,* see E. H. Templin, *The Exculpation of "Yerros por amores" in the Spanish Comedia* (Berkeley: University of California Press, 1933).

13. Apart from the major works cited in the text, Antonio de Córdoba, a probabilist and author of a *Tratado de casos de consciencia* (Saragossa, 1581), wrote a *Commentarii in sententias...* (1569) on the best-known work of Duns Scotus, which touches on matrimony, as also did Fr. Francisco de Ovando in his *Commentaria in IVum librum Sententiarum* (Madrid, 1587) and Fr. Miguel de Palacios in his *Disputationes theologicae in IV libros Sententiarum* (Salamanca, 1574-79), 6 vols., the fifth of which (1579) discusses the sacrament of marriage. Also worthy of note are Gutiérrez's *Quaestiones...* (Salamanca, 1617) and the Jesuit P. Gaspar Hurtado's *Tractatus de matrimonio et censuris* (Alcalá, 1627).

inevitably conceived of in religious terms or else touched on questions of immediate relevance for the problems of religious belief. Talk of Reformation and Counter Reformation should not blind us, moreover, to the partial shift in Spain away from the medieval tradition. To paraphrase Professor R. O. Jones, they are segments of one arch which spans the gulf between what we recognize as the Middle Ages and the modern world.[14]

In Spain, Renaissance liberation left its mark. For if the Counter Reformation repudiated revolutionary ideas in its official thinking, it assimilated the force of Renaissance attitudes in its behavior. The sheer energy and corporate enterprise, the business and aspiration that went into the Catholic revival are clearly of their age. The fundamental paradox of the campaign lay in the practical attempts of 'modern' men to reimpose theoretical medieval standards; to act intuitively in heart and limb in ways which the head had in principle ruled arrogant and anti-authoritarian.

These antagonistic impulses placed Spain in her basic posture of dilemma and sent covert divisions into the Spanish soul. Conscience was split into two as the mind hungered with nostalgia for a monolithic past and the soul hungered with impatience for the freedom of the liberated individual. Official Catholic policy had ruled against any changes, and yet it was Spanish casuists who forsook principle for human accommodation, Spanish philosophers who in common with their European counterparts tackled the question of what the human mind can know; theologians like Suárez who bent over backwards to safeguard human liberty in moral choices and the exercise of free will, and in Spain, of all places, where the controversy on grace and justification burst out again with renewed violence.

14. Quoted from R. O. Jones, *A Literary History of Spain. The Golden Age: Prose and Poetry* (London: Ernest Benn, 1971), p. 5. On the subject of the broad movement of European thought away from the medieval tradition, Alberto Bonet wrote: "Si hemos descartado el humanismo como corruptor del método por los artificios literarios, nos apresuramos a reconocerle otra influencia más profunda como elemento transformador de la mentalidad de la nueva Europa. Por él, el yo humano si elevó al primer plano de las preocupaciones como 'objeto de observación y fundamento de acción', según expresión de Höffding. El eje de la conciencia filosófica se desplazó hacia el subjetivismo." See his *La filosofía de la libertad en las controversias teológicas del siglo XVI y primera mitad del XVII* (Barcelona, 1932) p. 103. This is the finest modern study known to me on the problem of freedom during the period in question and I have drawn on it extensively for the ensuing section.

The Controversy 'De Auxiliis'

The Council of Trent scotched the issue of justification, but it did not kill it, and the European debate over the problem of free will and predestination can now be seen in retrospect as one vast drama in three acts. The protagonists of the first phase were, of course, Luther, Melanchthon, Zwingli, Calvin and their disciples, and the Catholic theologians whose first spokesman was Erasmus; this phase ended with Trent. The debate between the Dominicans and the Jesuits in Spain forms a second phase and the campaign of the Jesuits against the Jansenists of Port-Royal in late seventeenth-century France forms the third. In all its phases then, the grace and free will debate raged without taking a breath for nearly two centuries.

The issue of free will versus predestination (or some form of fatalism) is not new today and was by no means new in the sixteenth century. There is a considerable patristic literature on the subject (Origen, Chrysostom, Augustine) and Thomas Aquinas' thirteenth-century views provided the foundation of Catholic orthodoxy. In one form or another the debate is always a current one, since the conflicts of free choice and external necessity are simply data of the human condition. In religious or specifically Christian terms, the dogmatic difficulties lie in the apparent contradiction of two unassailable tenets of Christian faith: that man has free will and that God is omnipotent and omniscient, i.e., he knows all things, including future events. Evidently divine prescience seems to threaten human freedom of action, since what is foreknown would seem necessarily to be preordained. Conversely, man's complete auto-determination appears to challenge the supremacy of God. The absolute efficacy of divine causality had already caused problems to pagan and Islamic philosophers, and the issue has never been settled to universal satisfaction by any Christian theologian. The Manichaean heresy sprang ultimately from the clash of God's omnipotence and man's potential for sinful acts, and the Pelagian heresy from a promotion of free will to the detriment of God's grace.[15]

---

15. Before the appearance of the Manichaean heresy (III to V cy. a.d.), a conflict between the principle of light and good (Ormuzd) and of darkness and evil (Ahriman) had formed the basis of Zoroastrian teaching. But the Manichaean belief that Satan was coeternal with God was deduced as a necessary consequence of the paradox that if God is omnipotent, he is the author of evil acts; since this cannot be

Some mention has already been made of Luther's views on the problem, set out most fully in his *De servo arbitrio* (Wittenberg, 1525), an answer to the attack on him by Erasmus. It was Luther's view on predestination that most shook the Vatican and, as mentioned, the Tridentine rebuttal of Luther was the Council's most important dogmatic article. According to Luther, man is fundamentally evil, his will and nature corrupt. Since man's will is corrupt, all actions proceeding from his will are radically evil and therefore lack any moral or redemptive value. The will in this sense is a slave, hence the title of the treatise. The salvific value of good works is rejected by Luther, who insists on salvation (or justification in Protestant theological terms) by faith alone. Such faith does not mean solely a belief in revealed truths, but confidence in the infinite merits of Christ, the Redeemer, which without any internal transformation or merit on man's part, secure eternal life for the latter. The efficacy of free will is consequently rejected by Luther as a mere title without substance (*titulus sine re*). Luther also argued that Christ's sacrifice was only made for some men, not all; the divine elect would be saved, the repobate would be condemned. He further argued that only with God's grace can the will ever avert sin and, more extreme still, that the apparently sinful acts of the divine elect could not be evil. This so-called pessimistic determinism is the basis of Lutheran theology.

The Council of Trent defined its position against Luther in the following terms. There exists a possibility of salvation for all men, based on the salvific will of God. Human freedom exists under the influence of any form of grace, and though eternal election and eternal reprobation do exist, they do not *propter hoc* destroy this human freedom. Predestination to glory occurs without God's foreseeing man's merits (*ante praevisa merita*), although it implies divine foreknowledge of man's cooperation with grace; reprobation occurs after foreseen demerits (*post praevisa demerita*). In any case, no one can have any natural certainty that he is saved or damned.[16] Regarding this last point, one may comprehend how Lutherans or Calvinists could console themselves in the face of a pessimistic theology, simply by numbering themselves mentally among the elect. What the Council did *not* decide

---

true of a benign God, then Satan, the instigator of evil, must be coeternal with Him Pelagius, the Celtic theologian (c. 360-c. 431), preached that man could achieve salvation and the good life without the special help or grace of God.

16. See Heinrich Fries, *Conceptos fundamentales de teología* (Madrid, 1967).

was how "efficient" grace operated to safeguard human liberty, or the meaning of human liberty if it was not to annul the "efficacy" of grace?

The Spanish attempt to define and describe the operations of efficient grace precipitated the celebrated controversy 'De auxiliis' in the last quarter of the sixteenth century and the first decades of the seventeenth. Though the battle over the distinction between efficient and sufficient grace is usually dismissed as an incomprehensible quibble, it occasioned the most passionate divisions of opinion then, and remains a crucial moment in the history of ideas and the development of human freedom. Before attempting to give an account of the Molinist and Bañecist positions towards which the Spanish debate polarized, a brief, explanatory word on the external history of the controversy is called for.

The first brush came in 1582 barely twenty years after Trent had dispersed, when Domingo Báñez, a Dominican involved in a university debate at Salamanca over the merits of Christ, predestination and freedom, accused his Jesuit opponent, Prudencio de Montemayor, of sustaining a false and heretical doctrine. Montemayor for his part was defended by the celebrated Fr. Luis de León. In the heated and sensational controversy that ensued, both Montemayor and Fr. Luis were denounced to the Inquisition and instructed not to teach the propositions they were accused of.

The second stage was ushered in by the publication of Luis de Molina's *Concordia liberi arbitrii cum gratiae donis* (1588), a work which the Jesuit professor of Coimbra had spent thirty years in preparing and which Báñez had strenuously though abortively attempted to stifle. He did, however, denounce the work to the Inquisition and Molina responded by denouncing the works of both Báñez and his ally Francisco Zumel, a Mercedarian. While the Holy Office consulted various universities of Spain in its dilemma, the Dominicans vilified the Jesuits from the pulpit; Fr. Diego Núñez O.P. and P. Antonio de Padilla S.J. argued their respective cases in two acrimonious public debates in Valladolid amid tremendous commotion. The two views rapidly became the rival rallying standards of their respective orders in what was developing into a war between two theological armies; the Dominicans accused the Jesuits of Pelagian heresy and the Jesuits replied with countercharges of Calvinism. The debate on grace even became a topic of tavern-room oratory.

Clearly in a growing scandal of these proportions, some higher intervention had become imperative; Pope Clement VIII ordered the dispute to be transferred to Rome in 1594 and placed the contending parties under a ban of silence. In 1598, Clement instituted the *Congregatio de auxiliis gratiae,* which lasted amid interminable argument and fury for nine and a half years. In the same year a Dominican commission recommended the condemnation of Molina's *Concordia,* but under immense pressure from the Jesuits and numerous crowned heads of Europe, the Pope wavered and would not confirm the sentence. Clement found himself paralyzed by an issue that seemed to imply a new dogmatic schism within Spanish Catholicism itself.

Finally, presiding over one of the eighty-nine sessions that ensued after 1602, Clement collapsed and subsequently died (1605). Under Paul V, the issue was restricted to the problem of physical predetermination, the real crux of the matter, and on August 18th, 1607, the new Pope delivered his sentence: both adversaries were free to defend their opinion but absolutely forbidden to accuse each other of heresy. Later Pope Paul forbade any writing on the subject without his permission. This "draw" was greeted by the Jesuits, with some justice, as a triumph. Amid cries of " ¡Molina Vítor! ," they celebrated with public festivities, fireworks, music and bull-fights! Few Dominicans and Jesuits agree on the subject of grace even today.

Their disagreement centered on the fundamental issue of physical predetermination, the meanings attached to efficacious and sufficient grace and Molina's doctrine of the *scientia media.* Luther, Molina and Báñez (even Aristotle) would all have agreed that God is the first cause of everything, the prime mover, and that He concurs in the action of all created forces and secondary causes, including men's actions. The actual interpretation of divine causality as described by St. Thomas, however, led to flat disagreement and on occasion to irreconcilable readings of identical, orthodox texts. According to Báñez, God concurs in the production of a free act by man, with a concourse that is previous and physically predetermining, That is to say, that by a physical premotion in the divine sphere, God infallibly causes the consent of man's will in the performance of the intended act. In this premotion or predetermination is also found the medium of the divine knowledge by which God's omniscience infallibly foresees all future acts of intelligent creatures, whether absolute or conditional, since He causes them.

By applying these principles to the supernatural domain, efficacious grace is held to be a physical premotion of the supernaturally equipped will to the performance of a good act. This, the Bañecists or Thomists would argue, by invoking the distinction *in sensu composito vel diviso,* does not destroy the freedom of the act. For though, for example, it is true that a man who is freely sitting cannot at the same time be standing (*sensus compositus*), his freedom in sitting is nevertheless secured by the possibility that he *could* be standing instead of sitting (*sensus divisus*). By this analogue, grace is not efficacious because the free will consents, but instead free will consents because efficaciously premoved to the performance of a good act. Hence there are two forms of grace: efficacious grace (*gratia efficax ab intrinseco sive per se*) which is intrinsically and essentially different from sufficient grace, since the latter only provides the potential to act (the "could" or *posse*), while efficacious grace imparts the action (the "does" or *agere*).

As regards divine election, only sufficient grace is of a universal order, i.e. it is conceded to all men. Efficacious grace is of a specific order and is only conceded to the predestined. Such predestination occurs, say the Thomists, since God determines it by an unconditional decree *ante praevisa merita;* hence in Thomist terms "predestination" means that God destines man to heaven without consulting him. As regards reprobation, the Thomists maintain that God effects this not so much by taking into account human freedom, as by taking cognizance of the non-efficacious, merely sufficient grace conceded to the non-elect. This is the equivalent of a negative antecedent reprobation, i.e. God does not prevent the sins of particular men, such that their destiny will be damnation.

Against this system the Molinists lodge four main objections. The first is the obvious one: that physical predetermination seems to preclude free will.[17] To the Thomist safeguard of the distinction *in sensu composito vel diviso,* the Molinists object that just as a man bound with cords to a chair cannot be said to be sitting freely, so the predetermined will cannot be said to retain the power to dissent. The

---

17. The thrust of the Molinist objection is well quintessentialized by Lessius in the following extract: "Itaque principalis controversia est constituta in hac antithesi. Illi affirmant ad conversionem peccatoris, ad omne opus bonum, imo ad omnem actionem voluntatis requiri motionem Dei praeviam, qua liberum arbitrium praedeterminetur ad consensum; qua motione posita, non potest dissentire. Nos dicimus, talem motionem nec ad conversionem, nec ad opus non bonum requiri; nec facile posse intelligi, qua ratione non evertat libertatem. Reliquae quaestiones fere sunt accessoriae, occasione probationum vel solutionum enatae . . ." *De gratia efficaci* (Barcelona, 1610), cap. II, p. 7. Quoted by Bonet, p. 139, n.

Molinists therefore hold the view that God's concourse in a free act is not previous and physically determining, but simultaneous and "indifferent." Man retains the power to dissent, a capacity called active indifference in their terminology.

The second objection is closely related. How can there be two distinct varieties of grace? How can a grace really be sufficient that requires another grace to complete it? For the Molinists, the consent of the will is all. The two forms of grace are not different; sufficient grace becomes efficacious at the moment of the free cooperation of human will with it. If the free will dissents, then the grace remains "merely sufficient".

The followers of Molina thirdly object that God's predetermining activity as first mover would make Him the originator of sinful acts, the root of the Paulician, Marcionite and Manichaean heresies. The Molinists are helped out of this difficulty themselves by the doctrine of simultaneous concourse, this time applied to a distinction between the entity of the sinful act and the malice of the sin. Hence God's cooperating arm is employed after, and only after, the will of its own determination has decided upon the sinful act. Fourth and last, by destroying the case for the previous concourse of the Thomists, the Molinists cannot recognize that physical premotion is an infallible medium for divine prescience. Hence the importance of the *scientia media* in their system, Luis de Molina's most brilliant contribution to the problem.

Since in the Molinist view, grace can be efficacious in one instance and not in another, according to man's consent, it is said to be in its essence *gratia efficax ab extrinseco*. But the performance of a good act is a joint product of grace and free will, rather more the former than the latter. For it is not free will which empowers grace, but instead grace which makes the good act possible, preparing it and cooperating in its execution. The infallibility of this success (implicit in efficacious grace) is explained by the *scientia media* or 'middle knowledge' of God, by which He knows from all eternity whether any particular will would freely cooperate with a certain grace or not. Aquinas maintained that God's knowledge may be one of vision, viz. a knowledge of that which exists, has existed, or will exist (*scientia visionis*). Alternatively God's knowledge may consist of the purely possible, a knowledge of simple understanding, of things and events which have not existed, do not exist and will not exist (*scientia simplicis intelligentiae*). By the *scientia media,* maintains Molina, God has knowledge of *futuribilia,* i.e. of conditional future contingent events; His knowledge is prior to the decree of His will, but His foreknowledge does not predetermine our free acts. Knowing infallibly what an individual will do under such or another circumstances if offered his grace, God decrees the circumstances and the grace necessary to effect the cooperative action of the individual. If God's will is absolute, the free act supervenes whether it requires the dependence of human free will or not; if the outcome hinges on the conditional will of God and the contingent consent of the individual, God's will may or may not be done. At all events, the infallibility and efficacy of grace is due to the infallibility of God's knowledge, the *scientia media,* not to anything in the grace itself. Although there are differences on the *scientia media* even among Molinists, all agree that God does not know future free acts through any *absolute decree* of His own volition, and the whole thrust of this doctrine is to erect a wall of safety around human liberty emphasizing the importance of man's personal efforts, the value of earned merits and his determination in the success or failure of grace.[18]

* * *

It seems most fitting at this point to say a few words about Tirso's theological stance in this debate from the evidence in his plays. It has been claimed by both Vossler and Menéndez Pidal that Tirso was a Molinist, the coincidence of name even being invoked as corroboration.[19] But this view hardly bears examination and the best theological writings on the subject show that Tirso followed Francisco Zumel, the

---

18. It has been well said that the Jesuit Order was "born Molinist" (Bonet ... p. 105). Such a doctrine was a biological necessity to a society committed to vigorous action and the merit of good acts; Loyola stresses the importance of free will as early as the *Spiritual Exercises.* The modified Molinism elaborated by Francisco Suárez is known as congruism and is a view still widely adhered to. It hardly needs be said that the polemical literature on this whole subject is literally vast, both during the sixteenth and seventeenth centuries and since. The *New Catholic Encyclopedia* (New York: McGraw-Hill, 1967), vol. VI, p. 678, gives a reduced bibliography in the article "Grace, Controversies on."

19. In his lecture series collected as *Lecciones sobre Tirso de Molina* (Madrid, 1965), p. 78, Karl Vossler writes: "A raíz de estas cuestiones nació el drama del *Condenado* con manifiesta tendencia molinista [...] Ni me parece imposible que adoptara su pseudónimo literario en homenaje al autor de la *Concordia liberi arbitri* [sic] *cum gratiae donis,* completándolo con el nombre pastoral de Tirso, cual

Mercedarian and ally of Báñez,[20] though Zumel parted company with the Dominican on the issue of negative antecedent reprobation. Ample proof of Tirso's competence as a theologian is provided by his strict training after the noviciate in the reformed Merdecarian *curriculum*, while the mere number of plays that treat some aspect of the issue of predestination and reprobation vividly demonstrates Tirso's interest in the problem. A word on *El condenado por desconfiado, Quien no cae no se levanta* and *El burlador de Sevilla* must suffice here; the theme deserves a book to itself.[21]

Tirso devotes a number of pages to Zumel in his *Historia General del Orden de la Merced* (folios 134-138), where he describes him somewhat lavishly as: ". . . el más sabio, el más recto, el más reverenciado de los hombres eminentes, de los principes del rey católico y del santisimo

---

modesto poeta cómico y popular partidario del gran doctor Molina." See also Menéndez Pidal, " 'El condenado por desconfiado' de Tirso," in *Estudios literarios* (Madrid, 1920), 85-108.

20. See the articles in *Estudios,* 5 (1949) by Fr. Martin Ortúzar, " 'El condenado por desconfiado' depende teológicamente de Zumel: nueva aclaración," pp. 321-36 and Fr. J. M. Delgado Varela, "Psicología y teología de la conversión en Tirso," pp. 341-77. The first contribution to the subject was that of P. Norberto del Prado, *A un académico de la Española sobre* El condenado por desconfiado (Vergara, 1907). For a Jesuit view, see P. Rafael M. de Hornedo, " 'El condenado por desconfiado' no es una obra molinista," *Razón y Fe* (May, 1940). P. Hornedo later contended that Tirso adopted a neutral view and kept on the fringe of the *De auxiliis* dispute. See his "La tesis escolástico-teológica de 'El condenado por desconfiado'," *Razón y Fe* (1948), 633-46.

21. Apart from the three plays mentioned in the text, the bandit heroine of *La ninfa del cielo* (*comedia*) offers another case of conversion and predestination to glory. When struck down at the play's end, she exclaims:
>No te alteres, que es del Cielo
>en mi predestinación
>inexcrutable rodeo.
>(III, xvii, 970).

The conversion of the prodigal son is dramatized in *Tanto es lo de más como lo de menos*; Dionisio is converted and saved, Doroteo condemned, in the play *La Madrina del cielo,* and there are cases of conversion in *La Santa Juana*, pt. III (III, xvii-xxi), *La Dama del olivar* (III, xx) and *El árbol del mejor fruto* (III, xiii). These do not include the miraculous interventions of efficacious grace in the careers of Pope Sixtus V in *La elección por la virtud* and of St. Bruno, founder of the Carthusian order, in *El mayor desengaño,* both of which explore the workings of divine election. *Santo y sastre* and *La Reina de los reyes* (the latter of contested authorship) are in a lighter vein.

Clemente VIII".[22] In Part II of the same work, on the occasion of Fr. Pedro Merino's election to Provincial of Castile in the Order, Tirso compares Merino to Zumel: "... cuya hechura fue, cuya cathedra obtuvo, y cuyo retrato vivo en lo docto y observante pudo consolar de su partida (i.e. Zumel's death). Está vivo y no permite su modestia alabanzas merecidas de mi que su discipulo, por verdaderas que sean, dirán que incurro en las expresiones que llaman gerales" (folios 382-383). In other words, Tirso is the faithful and affectionate disciple of P. Merino, in turn a punctilious follower of Zumel; Tirso, as Doña Blanca de los Ríos put it, is Zumel's nephew in theology.

Zumel followed Báñez's Thomist views on grace in general, but denied the existence of any negative antecedent reprobation, proposing in its place the universal salvific will of God. As stated, Thomists commonly agreed that only the *auxilia* of sufficient grace are conceded to all men, whereas those of efficacious grace are conceded solely to those predestined to glory. Against the Thomists, Zumel affirmed that all forms of grace and all supernatural gifts are in the realm of God's universal providence, i.e. they are all at men's disposition. If men are not converted and even if they do not persevere in goodness, this is due to an abuse of freedom.

Perseverance itself is, however, an effect proper to predestination. For Zumel, both sufficient and efficacious grace are available, but may fail in particular cases, hence Zumelian providence includes perseverance as an exclusive effect of a predestination termed "special providence."[23] This tempered Thomism explains why the criminal heroes of Tirso's plays, who by all appearances have been negatively and

---

22. This work was studied, still in MS, by Doña Blanca de los Ríos in the library of the Academia de la Historia in Madrid. The great find has been published, three hundred and forty years after its creation, by P. Penedo Rey, ed., *Historia general de la Orden de Nuestra Señora de las Mercedes*, 2 vols. (Madrid: Revista Estudios, 1973).

23. It is hard, however, to see, if special providence recognizes the Thomistic distinction between sufficient and efficient grace and perseverance is in any sense a divine gift, how Zumel overcame the difficulties raised by Báñez's physical predetermination and the degrees of the divine will. P. Varela appears to suggest this when he writes: "[Zumel] Deshace la barrera que Báñez había levantado entre la gracia suficiente y la gracia eficaz, ya que la suficiente lleva algún grado de eficacia intrínseca y la eficaz, con plena eficacia por lo que a ello toca, puede ser frustrable, en el juego con la libertad" ("La conversión ...," pp. 361-62).

antecedently reproved (i.e. predestined to damnation), can in the final outcome be gloriously saved by the universal salvific will of God.

Both the conversion of Enrico in *El condenado* and the second, definitive conversion of Margarita, the heroine of *Quien no cae no se levanta,* clearly illustrate the Thomist (and Zumelist) thesis of the intrinsic efficacy of grace in the realization of a salutary act. The only visible agency in the conversion of Enrico is the force of this grace. In prison (XIII, x), he curses the voice that holds him there and later rejects the entreaties to confession of Pedrisco and the Franciscan friars:

> Juro a Cristo
> que pienso que he de enojarme,
> y que en los padres y en ti
> he de vengar mis pesares.
> Demonios, ¿qué me queréis?
> (III, xiii, 495).

But the voice of his old father, Anareto, the only being Enrico respects and the concrete expression of his persevering devotion and faith in the heavenly Father transforms him and he is converted (III,v).

Similarly, the divine help which effects conversion in Margarita owes nothing to human freedom. As she leaves with her lover (III, x), aflame with illicit passion, she twists her ankle and falls. Margarita fallen on the stage is the symbol of the impotence of human power towards the salutary act. Ultimately, efficacious grace, personified in the Angel, raises her to her feet and metaphorically to glory. This is not possible in either case by mere human cooperation with sufficient grace to make it efficacious, as the Molinists would claim. Both characters need each grace, and when Enrico, thinking he is about to be pierced by the arrows of Paulo's bandits, explains:

> Vénguese en mi el justo cielo;
> que quisiera arrepentirme
> y cuando quiero, no puedo.
> (II, xv, 483),

he implies this distinction. The desire for repentence proceeds from a supernatural motion, but does not actually achieve the act of repentance. In order to complement the influx of sufficient grace which lends Enrico the potential desire to repent (*posse*), there must be a second movement of efficacious grace which brings its realization (the *agere*).

The specifically Zumelist aspect of Tirso's treatment is his rejection of negative reprobation by which God would supposedly deny glory to anyone, discounting their works whether good or bad, since glory in Báñez's system is not a benefit earned as a human due. Tirso does this by rejecting the conduct of Paulo. Paulo's tragedy stems from having lent credence to a dream at the beginning of the play:

> ... el fiscal de las almas miré a un lado,
> Leyó mis culpas, y mi guarda santa
> leyó mis buenas obras, y el Justicia [sic]
> mayor del Cielo, que es el que espanta
> de la infernal morada la malicia,
> las puso en dos balanzas; mas levanta
> el peso de mi culpa y mi injusticia
> mis obras buenas tanto, que el Juez santo
> me condena a los reinos del espanto.
> (I, iii, 456).

He now craves certain knowledge of his final destiny (a right repudiated by the Council of Trent), but receives a false and equivocal reply. The devil disguised as an Angel, tells him his fate will be that of Enrico. Paulo can only assume that Enrico is negatively reproved:

> PAULO Pues al cielo hermano mío
> [to PEDRISCO] ¿cómo ha de ir éste, si vemos
> tantas maldades en él,
> tantos robos manifiestos,
> crueldades y latrocinios,
> y tan viles pensamientos?
> (I, xiii, 469).

Paulo judges Enrico by his works and since according to the 'Angel,' his *fate* is to be identical, Paulo feels that he too is negatively reproved. He despairs of God's mercy (i.e. he fails to persevere in his faith) and turns to a life of crime.

An angelic shepherd encounters Paulo twice in the play and spares no efforts to reassure him of God's mercy:

> UNA VOZ. No desconfíe ninguno,
> aunque grande pecador,
> de aquella misericordia
> de que más se precia Dios.
> (II, x, 479).

In the second encounter, the shepherd offers new guarantees of divine affection through Tirso's use of the image of the lost sheep which has only to return to the fold to achieve eternal happiness. The saddened shepherd is obliged to pull apart the crown prepared for Paulo, reflecting divine grief as he does so (III, xvii). This sadness indicates that divine will has no part in the cause of Paulo's reprobate end. Theoretically, God could have aided Paulo by the special help of efficacious grace (as in Enrico's case), but Paulo's lack of persevering faith in divine mercy prevents this and God respects human freedom.

The theme of *El burlador de Sevilla* is complementary to that of *El condenado*. Paulo's fate shows that there is no salvation without faith, whereas that of Don Juan shows that faith does not suffice without good works. Don Juan demonstrates an excessive and arrogant faith in the divine pardon. This is the sense of Don Juan's response to every warning that he will one day be brought to account in the tag: " ¡Tan largo me lo fiáis! " Don Juan trusts nonchalantly that an eleventh-hour recantation in old age will suffice, leaving him free to indulge his libertine lusts in youth. By condemning him, Tirso not only condemns the doctrinal excesses of faith alone (Luther and perhaps Báñez), but also the facile aspects of an extreme Molinism whereby cooperation with sufficient grace merely requires an act of will on man's part to render it efficacious and thereby secure salvation. On both counts, Don Juan could be called, as one critic has wittily observed, "El condenado por demasiado confiado."[24] The Comendador makes this denial of pardon explicit in the death-scene when the chorus sings:

> *Mientras en el mundo viva*
> *no es justo que diga nadie,*
> *¡Que largo me lo fiáis,*
> *siendo tan breve el cobrarse!*
> (III, xx, 684).

Don Juan is condemned because:

> *Adviertan los que de Dios*
> *juzgan los castigos grandes*
> *que no hay plazo que no llegue*
> *ni deuda que no se pague.*
> (XIII, xx, 684).

Neither Paulo nor Don Juan is damned by negative antecedent reprobation, but through the misuse of free will.[25] Tirso displays remarkable consistency throughout these plays in maintaining a Zumelist stance

---

24. See W. Margaret Wilson, *Spanish Drama of the Golden Age* (Oxford: Pergamon, 1969), pp. 116-17.

25. See Ion T. Agheana and Henry Sullivan, "The Unholy Martyr: Don Juan's Misuse of Intelligence," *RF*, 81, no. 3 (1969), 311-25, for a discussion of the way Don Juan abuses his considerable mental gifts and capacity for insight into those around him.

with integrity and in denouncing the dangers latent in both Báñez and Molina. One can only marvel at the skill and subtlety with which these difficult nuances are dramatized and transformed into vigorous, living theater.

Moral Probabilism and Casuistry in Spain during the Counter Reformation

The confusions provoked in Spain during the Counter Reformation by the conflict between traditional moral principles and the complex necessities of real action in a changing world gave rise to probabilism. Probabilism in moral theology may be defined as a system which holds that when solely the lawfulness or unlawfulness of an action is in doubt, it is permissible to follow a solidly probable opinion in favor of liberty, even though the opposing view is *more* probable. 'Probable' here is understood in its etymological sense of 'provable' (Lat. *probare*), equivalent in modern usage to 'tenable' or 'possible'. This system has the purest Spanish pedigree and virtually no history at all before the period of the Counter Reformation.[26] Its appearance exemplifies yet again the growing intellectualization of the forces tending in the direction of human freedom in sixteenth-century thought, and despite the mantle of silence that seems to have fallen over probabilism in modern times, its importance for our period can hardly be exaggerated. Though it made its first appearance in the works of Bartolomé de Medina O.P. (1577) and other Spanish Dominicans such as Luis López (1584), Domingo de Soto, Gregorio de Valencia, and Pedro Navarro, the system was quickly adopted by the Jesuits and other orders. Among the flood of titles to appear, we might mention Juan de Pedraza, *Summa de casos de consciencia* (Medina, 1578); Gabriel Vázquez S.J., *Commentaria ac disputationes in I^{am}-II^{ae} Summae Theol. S. Th. Aq.* (1597); Juan Azor S.J., *Institutiones morales* (Rome, 1600); Carbone's *Summa Summarum Casuum Conscientiae* (1606); Martín Azpilcueta, *Enchiridion sive Manuale confessariorum et poenitentium* (1607); Thomas Sánchez S.J., *Opus Morale in Praecepta Decalogi sive Summa casuum conscientiae* (Paris, 1615) and so forth. This probabilistic literature multiplied outside Spain as well; in France appeared the *Grande Guide des Curez*

---

26. The first true probabilist was Bartolomé de Medina O.P., who in his *Expositio in primam secundae S. Thomae* (1577) taught that if an opinion is probable it is lawful to follow it, even though the opposing opinion is more probable ("si opinio est probabilis, licitum est eam sequi, etsi opposita sit probabilior").

of the Benedictine Pierre Milhard (1619) and the Jesuit Bauny's *Somme des Péchéz* (1641). There were Protestant probabilists active in England and North Germany as well, the most celebrated being Jeremy Taylor, an Anglican, author of the *Ductor Dubitantium* (1659). I wish here to talk not only about the role of probabilism in the *comedia* and in auricular confession, but also a variety of Jesuit doctrines that partake of the same probabilistic spirit and display a similar tendency towards the accomodation of principle to the exigencies of reality. Specific examples of such doctrines will be adduced from Tirso's theater.

First let it be said that probabilism is a blanket term for a whole range of systems that differ in their degrees of emphasis on the probability of an opinion, but not in their methodological approach: rigorism or tutiorism at the one extreme, probabilism, probabiliorism and equiprobabilism in the middle and laxism at the other extreme.[27] Secondly, we must understand the expression "probable opinion" and the contemporary need for reasoning in such terms. Obviously, certain moral laws which are unequivocal and admit of no exemptions are binding on the individual. On the other hand, where no law forbids an action, there is no obligation on the individual to abstain from performing it. Quite as obviously, this leaves a large area of intermediate ground where the lawfulness of an action is open to considerable doubt. In moral theology, the opinion which favors the law is technically called the "safe opinion" (*opinio tutior*) and that which favors liberty the "less safe" opinion. Writing in the *Dictionnaire de Théologie Catholique* (Vol. XIII, 1936, columns 417-619), Th. Deman characterized the fears expressed by Medina and later Francisco Suárez S.J. over the impossibility of always following the most safe opinion in these terms: "Il est souverainement dur que l'homme soit toujours obligé au plus sûr puisqu'il devrait alors toujours ou jeûner ou restituer etc., chaque fois qu'il doute s'il y est tenu" (col. 474). The roots of P. Suárez's hesitation lay basically in two factors or concerns: man's

---

27. For an explanation of the rarer terms probabiliorism (a phenomenon with some medieval precedents) and equiprobabilism (a compromising formula elaborated by St. Alphonsus Liguori), see *The Catholic Encyclopedia*, Vol. XII under "Probabilism." The terms tutiorism and laxism are discussed in our text. For the subject in general, see Charles Lea, *A History of Auricular Confession*, Vol. II (Philadelphia, 1896), especially Chapter XXI, "Probabilism and Casuistry," at pp. 285-411, and the article by Th. Deman in the *Dictionnaire de Théologie Catholique*, ed. Vacant, vol. XIII (1936) "Probabilisme," from column 417 to 619.

possession of liberty and the insufficient promulgation of the moral rule.

As to following the opinion for liberty, what are we going to regard as a "solidly probable" opinion? This can be determined, according to the probabilists, by intrinsic authority or more problematically by extrinsic authority. Such latter authority is commonly defined as a view held by five or six theologians, reputed for prudence and learning, who independently adhere to it, but only if the point has *not* been set aside by authoritative decision or intrinsic arguments which they have failed to solve. Sometimes one theologian of exceptional authority (St. Alphonsus Liguori, the eighteenth-century theologian, for example) is sufficient to make an opinion solidly probable.

The contention that a single theologian could provide probable authority was first enunciated by Thomas Sánchez in his *Opus Morale* (1615); as Deman observes: "... il admet ... que l'autorité d'un seul docteur probe et savant rend une opinion probable, et qu'on peut conseiller toute opinion probable, fût-elle contraire à celle qu'on tient, poruvu qu'elle soit probable" (col. 484). The inherent dangers of basing moral law on any of several, possibly conflicting opinions, on the authority of a single writer, or indeed of following *any* opinion for liberty — even the least probable — cannot escape the reader, and this degenerate form of probabilism is termed laxism. As early as 1617, the Jesuit General Vitelleschi had said of the principle: 'It is probable, for it has an author to support it,' that it was a rule never to be used. Despite this injunction LaCroix, for example, in his *Theologiae Moralis, Liber* I, n. 66, goes as far as to say that a man is bound to follow the *less* probable opinion and reject the more probable, whenever he can thus secure any temporal or spiritual advantage for himself or for another!

To gain some flavor of the extreme degrees of laxism to which the probabilists went, we may quote the same Sánchez previously referred to on the subject of cannibalism. In the *Opus morale* (*Lib.* I, cap. xviii, para. xi), the Jesuit poses himself the question as to whether it be licit to eat human flesh in order to escape the risk of death, as for example in a town under seige, where no other food is available? He concedes that most authorities have ruled that such action is not licit, but in the twelfth paragraph states as being *more* probable the opinion that there is no intrinsic evil in cannibalism in cases of extreme necessity: "At quamvis hoc sit satis probabile, probabilius credo licere. Quippe non video cur res haec sit intrinsice mala, ac proinde in nullo eventu extremae necessitatis liceat." Many probabilists saw their laxer propositions condemned by the Vatican, and St. Alphonse Liguori called the Spaniard Juan Caramuel y Lobkowitz the "princeps laxistarum." The greatest of all the laxists, P. Antonino Diana (1585-1663), a Theatine monk of Sicily, wrote a work, the *Resolutiones morales,* which contained twenty thousand doubtful cases of conscience, most audaciously interpreted. For this reason he earned the nickname of 'Agnus dei,' since he took away the sins of the world! It is worth noting that Calderón had ". . . los libros del P. Diana" in his library at his death.[28]

Coming to the actual need for the forms of reasoning described above, we may say that probabilism is an expression of skepticism in the realm of moral theology. Absolute certainty is admitted to be an impossibility, and God does not demand impossibilities. In doubtful cases of conscience, we cannot know with absolute certainty whether certain actions are right or wrong, therefore we must remain content with moral certitude or the probability of their being right. The rub comes, as we have said, in the determination of the degree of doubt and the degree of probability; hence such frequently invoked tags as *alii affirmant, alii negant; utrumque probabile*; or later *lex dubia non obligat,*[29] and hence the readiness of some laxer authorities to settle for probable, more probable or even less probable certainty. The application to auricular confession follows logically. If, for example, a penitent ate meat in the solidly probable assumption that Friday morning had not by that time set in, and thus (according to the Church's former teaching) committed a sin, the priest could reduce the doubt of fact to a doubt of law. By leaning on the element of doubt and actually giving the penitent the benefit of that doubt, the priest might lawfully grant absolution. A similar procedure is used today in absolving couples who practice 'illicit' methods of contraception, since the issue is still in doubt and certain reputable authorities advocate the less safe opinion for liberty.

This revolution in moral theology released a tremendous flood of pro-

---

28. We learn from Calderón's will (1681) that he owned a set of Diana's works. He specifies: "Item: es mi voluntad que los libros del Padre Diana se den y entreguen a Gerónimo Peñarrosa." See C. Pérez Pastor, *Documentos para la biografía de Calderón* (Madrid, 1905), at p. 387.

29. Probabilistic maxims also found their way into the parlance of civil law. For example, 4 Coke 15, Dig. 50. 17. 192. both having the ruling: "Benignior sententia in verbis generalibus seu dubiis, est preferenda." This and similar maxims are cited in the *Cyclopedic Law Dictionary,* ed. Schumaker and Longsdorf, 3rd edition (Chicago, 1940).

babilistic literature in the early seventeenth century. It took the form of moral commentaries, guides to penitents and confessors' manuals, in Latin or in the vernacular. Active in its propagation, probabilism particularly suited the Jesuits as a method for offering easy absolution, especially to potentates whom they wished to influence in their campagn to undermine secular government for the benefit of the Vatican, or else to ordinary people disconcerted by the sternness of religious commandments. Probabilism and the casuistical doctrines it spawned eventually escaped the domain of the theologian entirely and this is their importance for the *comedia.* As Deman says of the manner in which probabilism flourished: "Mais, relatives à la conscience morale, [ces doctrines] suscitent l'attention de tous ceux qui, *sans être proprement des théologiens, s'intéressent aux règles de conduite et à la solution des cas de conscience*: par là, nous le verrons, l'influence de ces doctrines fut considérable, déterminant une méthode nouvelle qui se réservera désormais le titre de théologie morale, et favorisant l'éclosion d'une casuistique sensiblement différente de celle que nous avons ci-dessus rencontrée" [i.e. before the sixteenth century (op. cit., col. 481. My emphasis)].

Now among those whom we classify as not being properly speaking theologians yet having an interest in probabilism, we must include the Spanish dramatists of the seventeenth century. The majority of the playwrights of the period were secular poets in the most creative phases of their lives. Tirso, it is true, *was* a trained theologian and Calderón (a member after 1651 of the Third Order of the Franciscans) acquired great theological sophistication as principal poet of the Madrid *autos*; Mira de Amescua, Alonso de Remón O.M. and Lope de Vega in later life were also in priestly orders. This reservation made, we may discern the presence of probabilism in the *comedia* in two main ways: in the mere choice of bizarre and unusual situations that give rise to problematic and doubtful cases of conscience (often referred to as *casos* or *ejemplos*), and secondly in the casuistical phrasing of certain passages, frequently when a character attempts to analyze his options in a soliloquy. These problematic situations obviously lent themselves to gripping and suspenseful treatment as drama and arguably reached their height in the hair-splitting and intangible subtleties of Calderón's treatments, especially those cases which appear to justify uxoricide. A third connection is the appearance of the king at the end of so many plays as an absolving authority in dubious instances of moral transgression. The king in Lope's *Fuenteovejuna,* torn between relief at the assassination of a political menace and the dangers of *any* form of political rebellion, eventually resolves the issue by leaning on the element of doubt (his inquisitors have been unable to force out of the villagers *who* killed the Comendador) and granting a royal pardon ("Pues no puede averiguarse/ el suceso por escrito,/ aunque fue grave el delito,/ por fuerza ha de perdonarse." III, 2444-2447). Similar endings occur in *Peribáñez*, Calderón's *El médico de su honra* and so forth.

Tirso de Molina also has recourse to moral probabilism. In his *Antona García* we have an example of the use of probabilistic reasoning to absolve an offending party. In Act III, ix, when Queen Isabella is finally victorious in the war against Juana la Beltraneja, she forgives the rival faction in the following terms:

> El pleito fue tan dudoso
> entre Doña Juana y mí
> que los que la obedecieron
> por hija de Enrique y dieron
> en seguir su bando ansí,
> no por esto han incurrido
> en deslealtad, ni en traición.
> *Probable fue su opinión;*
> *la nuestra ha favorecido*
> *el cielo,* que está animando,
> señor, vuestra real clemencia.
> (III, ix, 450. My italics)

In other words, though mistaken in their loyalty (and perhaps liable to reprisals or other punishment), the supporters of La Beltraneja have not committed treason, since in a doubtful case of conscience, here concerning constitutional right, they followed a probable (if possibly less safe) opinion.

There are other examples in *Amar por razón de estado* and *La vida y muerte de Herodes*. In the former play, the hero Enrique is enjoined (I, vi) by his tutor and guardian, old Ricardo, to repeat his lesson on the composition of the material universe. Doubtful as to whether the fabric of heaven and earthly creatures are made of the same substance,[30] Enrique invokes probabilism:

---

30. The nature of the composition of the universe was a hotly debated issue throughout the seventeenth century. Enrique's view that heaven and earth are one substance may seem to parallel Spinoza's monistic conception of the universe, except that the Judeo-Portuguese philosopher argued that matter and *spirit* were also one.

> La fábrica de los cielos
> de los dedos de Dios digna,
> eterna en su immensa idea,
> y en tiempo el primer día
> *según opinión probable,*
> es de la materia misma
> que las demás criaturas,
> en cuanto es materia prima;
> (I, vi, 1099. My italics)

The probable opinion of reference here was Galileo's. Galileo took up a fairly definite position on the Copernican theory in his *Istoria e Dimostrazioni intorno alle macchie solari* (Rome, 1613), a work condemned by the Inquisition in 1616. He argued, against received doctrine, that the distinction between the crystalline and incorruptible matter of heaven, and the base, corruptible matter of the sublunary sphere was a false one; that both spheres were composed of the same substance.[31] Tirso protects himself against heresy by qualifying the Galilean view as probable, a caution reinforced by the phrase "dado caso que" which introduces the rest of Enrique's long exposition.

In *La vida y muerte de Herodes,* of the two brothers Herod and Faselo who are rivals for the love of Mariadnes, it is Herod who is eventually designated by old king Antipater as the groom. For this action, Faselo accuses the king of rigorism ("¿Qué est esto, padre cruel? / Riguroso Rey, ¿qué es esto? " II, viii, 1605), and receives the reply that since love is a question of taste, and Mariadnes has emphatically stated where her own tastes lie, Faselo may complain to love: "De gustibus non disputandum." Hircano, Salome and Aristóbulo all walk off stage in succession, each giving the stunned Faselo the same answer: "Sobre gustos no hay disputa." Against such a "tyrannical" opinion, Faselo makes an interesting reply:

> La ley que no las admite (i.e. disputas)
> no es hija de la razón,
> *pues la ciencia y la opinión*
> *más probable las admite.*

---

31. In the words of George de Santillana: "Galileo was the first man who perceived that mathematics and physics, previously kept in separate compartments, were going to join forces. He was thus able to unify celestial and terrestrial phenomena into one theory, destroying the traditional division between the world above and the world below the moon." From the article "Galileo" in the *Encyclopedia Britannica,* 14th ed. (Chicago, 1963).

> Cuando, ciego, amor las quite
> y la acción que tengo tuerza
> su agravio, a vengarme es fuerza,
> tiranas resoluciones
> que quien no admite razones
> da permisión a la fuerza
> (II, viii, 1605. My italics)

Here, against the extreme rigoristic view that resolutions based on inclination and taste admit of no discussion whatever, Faselo argues that such an attitude is irrational, since the most probable opinion does admit it. This lack of a more benign, flexible, probabilistic attitude empowers him, claims Faselo, to resort to the equally irrational course of violent direct action.

An interesting sidelight on Tirso's use of probabilism is provided by his History of the Order, where he devotes an essay to the monastery and Virgin of El Puig near Valencia, an essay extracted and separately published by P. Juan Devesa, O. de M. (Valencia, 1968).[32] Though Tirso had never himself visited the site under discussion, he succeeds, basing himself on previous sources and notably the History of P. Francisco Boil of 1631, in recreating with an almost novelistic vividness the physical location, the monastery's history and the legends surrounding it. These latter were two in number: according to tradition, when Pedro the Cruel was campaigning against the Moors in South-East Spain, his party accidentally discovered a buried statue of the Virgin near the site, supposedly carved by angels from Mary's own stone pillow. Now in a rational, educated and even skeptical mind, such claims could strain the credence of even the most devout Mercedarian. Tirso's procedure as an ecclesiastical historian is ingenious. In the first place, he bases his support for the Marian legends directly on the testimony of Boil, without quoting him *in extenso*. The earlier writer, says Father Téllez: "Discurre luego en la solución de estos aprietos, *de que sale con probables sutilezas,* concluyendo cuerdamente la verdad de los dos puntos principales, que importan en nuestro intento. Esto es: que el haber labrado los Angeles su efigie (i.e. of the Virgin) consta de la referida Bula; y que ésta fuese de el mármol venturoso donde el virgíneo cadáver tuvo

---

32. See Tirso de Molina, *El monasterio de el Puig y su virgen.* Introduction, transcription and notes by P. Juan Devesa, O. de M. (Valencia, 1968). This charming extract from the History reveals Tirso's chronicle prose at its very best: clear, intelligent, melodious and free of all *préciosité*.

reclinada la cabeza, da el crédito que merece el dicho Ambrosio de Morales" (op. cit. at p. 38, folio 72. My italics). Not only then does Tirso refer himself to his predecessor's prudent conclusions, he qualifies these as having been arrived at by "probable subtleties." That is to say, the doubtful case has been dealt with by examining the extreme poles of naive credulity and rigorous denial, and by leaning on the element of doubt to maximize the probability, it has been resolved invoking the *more* probable opinion. It is worth noting that Tirso is careful to attribute this probabilistic solution not to himself directly, but to his source, thus doubly defending himself against possible charges of superstition and gullibility.

The casuistry alluded to on a number of previous occasions is a natural outcome of probabilism. If the sinfulness or not of an action depends on the probable, extrinsic authority of a few writers (perhaps only one or two), then an immense stimulus is provided to devise new arguments exploiting this tenuous authority. Casuistry uses such perverse ingenuity in order to frame some plausible reason that lends an air of probability to any benign or benignant opinion, thus mitigating the deformity of the sin. Though at first, in the 1580 s, the Jesuits were hostile to probabilistic casuistry, they quickly saw its possibilities and have been associated with it ever since. Pascal made their doctrines the brunt of his attack on the Society, in his brilliant *Lettres Provinciales* (1656).

Tirso gives us an example of the use of ingenious *a priori* arguments juggled into a specious logical sequence to prove a particular case (*ad casum*) in the first act of his *Fingida Arcadia*. Here the heroine, Lucrecia Countess of Valencia del Po (in Italy) wishes to forestall her many suitors, although under heavy pressure to come to a firm decision on marriage from her vassals. She gives her guardian, Hortensio, a letter the purpose of which is, by casuistical reasoning, to erect a case for herself such that she can blind the suitors by logic, reject all of them, and keep herself free to marry Felipe-Tirso. We may reconstruct the logical steps of the letter as follows:

Practical case and problem:

1 The soul is governed by two faculties: will and understanding.

2 The latter has as its object the sphere of truth and cannot operate without it; similarly the former cannot operate without goodness, which is its own particular object.

3. This goodness must be perfect and beautiful in all its parts for love to be so; if love lacks either, it is neither goodness nor beauty (Neo-Platonism).

Appeal to scholastic axioms:
1 The latter proposition cannot be doubted, since it is a general opinion ("común sentencia") that good arises from an integral cause (*Bonum ex integra causa*), and
2 anything less than integral perfection, however small the defect, vitiates the good (*ex quocumque defectu*) making it evil.

Practical applications to the case:
1 Therefore, if the female will in its perfect state loves a vitiated good (by the latter's being defective) and, ignoring the defect, submits itself to an imperfect husband, either the love is unreal or it is folly.
2 I, therefore, to avoid appearing foolish (since no one suitor perfectly matches my will and love in all his aspects) do not intend to marry.
3 The various defects in question are severally set down in this letter.

Recapitulation:
1 Though they may seem slight, they are not so, since evil derives from the merest defect (*ex quocumque defectu*) and good from an integral cause (I, viii, 1400).

This parade of casuistical legerdemain does the trick, and Hortensio then disposes of each suitor in sequence by naming his particular fault or "defect."

The theologians of the Society had elaborated a variety of specific casuistical doctrines by the early 1600s to aid their confessors in Europe and also their missionaries in the pagan Orient and the uncatechized Americas. It is not surprising that Tirso should have assimilated some of these influences, since all ideas are common property once enunciated, and we know that Tirso personally held the Society of Jesus in the highest regard.[33] One influential doctrine found in the Mercedarian's theater is the so-called 'direction of intention'. 'Intention' in moral theology is described as an act of free will directed to the attainment of an end, and it influences the morality of an action.

---

33. See the article of P. Ortúzar in *Estudios* V, at p. 328, where he states: "Apoyándose en esta consideración cree el investigador jesuita que el autor [i.e. Tirso] no pudo tener intención de molestar a la Compañía de Jesús. Es evidente el gran aprecio en que tenía *Fray Gabriel a los Padres de San Ignacio y en este punto el P. Hornedo está demasiado parco, pues hay otros documentos más que demuestran ese juicio favorable.*" My italics.

Morally indifferent actions are rendered good by a good intention; good actions rendered even better. But a good intention does not normally redeem a bad action. The Jesuits did, however, argue that the *direction* of intention could mitigate a sin in certain cases. This is not quite the same as saying that the ends justify the means, but it comes very close. As the Jesuits penetrated South China, for instance, they horrified their potential converts by their accentuation of the crucifixion. Since the Chinese refused to eat in the presence of "carrion," let alone worship it, the missionaries judiciously suppressed the need to adore Christ's bleeding corpse. This was arguably a wrong action, but according to the direction of intention (i.e. the winning of thousands of new souls to the true Church) it was pardonable.[34]

At the end of *La mujer por fuerza,* Tirso offers a case of absolution using the direction of intention. Finea, the heroine (in love with Federico), has caused untold confusion, jealousy, embarassment and a near homicide by her machinations and lies. The king, however, rewards her with the hand of the man whom she has so relentlessly pursued, because her genuine love mitigates the 'treachery' of her pretenses. He decrees:

> Hoy mi voluntad es ley.
> Que sea Finea quiero
> mujer del Conde, que es justo
> de sus trabajos el premio.
> Yo no tengo por traiciones
> las industrias del ingenio,
> mayormente cuando amor
> ayuda al entendimiento.
> Todo ha de quedar en paz:
> dale tú la mano, Alberto,
> a Florela; en lo démas
> pongo perpetuo silencio.
> (III, xvii, 547.)

Hence the king, in judicial capacity (the *meum imperium* of medieval times), gives moral judgment in a doubtful case involving reprehensible behavior. Finea's machinations are not held to be treacherous, since her actions have caused no material damage, at the most perhaps mental anguish. The offenses are further mitigated by the direction of the

---

34. The book by Michael Foss, *The Founding of the Jesuits, 1540* (London, 1969) is especially strong on the expansion of the Jesuits in the East. Mr. Foss is a military historian by training.

intention, since love is the propelling force as well as the end desired. Hence Finea is forgiven and the whole affair put under a ban of silence in the style of a prudent confessor.[35]

Other casuistical doctrines justified murder, tyrannicide, killing a false witness, killing in defense in honor, usury, simony, theft in extreme necessity and 'occult compensation' (i.e. theft to recover personal goods, outstanding debts, loans, or payments due). Under the doctrine of equivocation, false testimony, perjury, mendacity and 'useful' lies (the *mendacium officiosum*) could be justified by permitting mental reservation (*restrictio* or *reservatio mentalis*). If a confessor, for instance, were asked to break the seal of confession by the Inquisition in its prosecution of one whose orthodoxy was in question, he could equivocally swear an oath of ignorance, while mentally reserving that he had heard an incriminating confession as God and not as a man. Similarly an adulterous wife could deny her adultery to her husband by swearing: 'I did not commit the offense' while reserving 'on such and such a day.'

It will be seen from the above examples that moral probabilism was not always moral nor even always a system concerned for lawful action, but an offshoot of theology that became a method of mind. It spawned a new vocabulary and established a series of new moral presuppositions. Its omnipresence is reflected in the *comedia* in diluted form, its rhetoric employed in dialogue and the decision-making capacity of the king turned into an opportunity for reaching ingenious and benign resolutions of the conflicts raised by the drama. As we have said, the Counter Reformation theater sought to find a way out of a labyrinth with no exit. These manifestations of probabilism in the *comedia* express in literature the preparedness of a tortured age to settle for a less-than-ideal, middle ground.

Philosophic Skepticism and the Criteria of Knowledge

No historian of ideas would deny that in the Renaissance twilight

---

35. The authenticity of *La mujer por fuerza* has been challenged, mostly because it appears in the enigmatic and controversial *Segunda parte* and because of textual corruptions. The play, however, bears innumerable Tirsian fingerprints (see Chapter III) and Dr. Premraj Halkhoree adds a discussion of the play in an appendix to his study of Tirso, in the belief that the Mercedarian may certainly have participated in its composition. See his doctoral thesis, "Social and Literary Satire in the Comedies of Tirso de Molina," (Edinburgh University, 1969), Appendix A. At all events, the question of authorship does not invalidate the point in question.

Europe witnessed a rebirth of philosophic skepticism that endured throughout the next century and even into the eighteenth. For lack of statements to the contrary, Spain is generally regarded as having remained unaffected by any skeptical crisis during the Counter Reformation, when in fact the presence of skepticism, as a purely *philosophical* current, can easily be demonstrated. The thinkers termed 'critical philosophers' by Marcial Solana[36] such as Gómez Pereira, Francisco Sánchez of Toulouse, Miguel Sabuco, Pedro de Valencia, Francisco Sánchez "el Brocense" were in reality those who articulated the skeptical ideas that became widely diffused during the seventeenth century, as examples from popular poetry and the theater will show. Since no account of skepticism in Spain exists to my knowledge, at least in relation to the drama, a brief review of its progress will be given here with an explanation of its background importance for the *comedia*. The fullest working out of their interdependence is reserved for the chapter on the Baroque.

Philosophic skepticism cannot be described as a system of thought; rather it is a critical attitude of mind which employs certain dialectic forms of inquiry to question and challenge the systematic statements of dogmatic philosophies. In this sense it is parasitical, but salutary as a corrective to extreme claims to certainty. By challenging dogmatic authority, the skeptic places the actual criteria of knowledge under the microscope, and may come to cast doubt on the evidence of the senses as a source of truth. The same methodical doubt with regard to the senses may be extended to a moral and logical skepticism; indeed, by its own negative thoroughgoingness, its exponents contend that skepticism can like a purge sweep away all positive notions including itself.[37] The stimulus to the skeptical revival in Spain was provided by the stormy controversies of the Reformation and the Reformers' challenge to the traditional criteria of religious authority, including that of the Pope, the

---

36. See Marcial Solana, *Historia de la filosofía española, época del renacimiento, siglo XVI,* 3 vols. (Madrid, 1941), vol. I, pp. 5-8. This is probably the most thorough history of Spanish philosophy of the Golden Age, but its direct summary format detracts somewhat from its usefulness.

37. Although under Pyrrho and Timon skepticism was a separate school, on Timon's death (235 B.C.), skepticism was absorbed by the Academy (founded by Plato) which preserved a skeptic bias for nearly two hundred years (e.g. Carneades c. 213-128 B.C., Clitomachus); this gave rise to the rather odd equivalence of 'Academic' and 'skeptic.' The works of Lucian and Sextus Empiricus of the second century A.D. belong to a later skeptical tradition.

Councils and even the Scriptures. What the Word of God actually *said* became a major problem of scholars, and all Europe expended immense effort on the editing, translating and printing of new, more exact versions of the Bible. In Spain, however, the mood of radical rethinking was always confined to the problem of knowledge; never developed into a weapon against the Christian, or more specifically, the Catholic faith. Finally, the printing in 1562 of the works of Sextus Empiricus, the skeptical philosopher of the second century A.D., made widely available the most thorough exposition of Ancient skepticism that has come down to us. As the skeptical crisis in the Counter Reformation deepened and lack of philosophical certainty increased, the nagging thought that life in general was just an illusory spectacle, found in the theater (itself an illusory spectacle by definition) the ideal vehicle for an artistic expression of the epistemological uncertainties of the age.

The first important Spanish work to challenge a dogmatic ideological position was the *Antonia Margarita* of Gómez Pereira (Medina del Campo, 1554),[38] a curious and controversial book which attempted to prove that animals differ from man by being insensible and that their movements are automatic and involuntary, doctrines violently combatted and mocked in Spain. But while his attacks on the Scholastico-Aristotelian account of sensation, the rational soul and movement in men and animals, and Pereira's marked inclination towards nominalism have considerable pre-Cartesian historical interest, his most far-reaching statements are to be found in the book's prologue. There Pereira states that he had begun to doubt many doctrines held by physicians and philosophers to be indisputably true, and found upon subsequent experiment that they were indeed false. He also states that he would not subject his own judgment to any other authority (except in matters concerning religion), because in speculative philosophy only reason must determine individual assent. Solana has observed of the author's unusual attitude towards authority that: "... sobre todo, Gómez Pereira es eminentemente crítico: nada admite en Filosofía fundándose en la autoridad ajena, sino que quiere comprobarlo todo con el raciocinio y con la observación y la experiencia; no dudando en ponerse

---

38. The work's full title was *Antoniana Margarita, opus nempe physicis, medicis, ac theologis non minus utile, quam necessarium* (Medina del Campo, 1554). In point of fact, the colophon bears the date 1555 indicating that it appeared a year after the date on the title page. The strange title is derived from the names of Pereira's parents, Antonio and Margarita.

frente a la totalidad de los filśofos de su época y combatir doctrinas unánimemente aceptados..." (*Historia...*, vol. 1, p. 262). This bold, skeptical independence of judgment and the precocious ontological note struck in Pereira's syllogistic proof of personal existence ("I know that I know something, and whatever knows is, therefore I am")[39] led Menéndez y Pelayo in his *La ciencia española* to the apt observation that Gómez Pereira was "cartesiano antes que Descartes."[40] Indeed, it has long been recognized that Pereira is only one of many Spanish philosophers to whom the founder of modern philosophy owes a debt.[41]

The sixteenth century's most technical and thoroughgoing statement of philosophic skepticism was written by an Iberian refugee, Francisco Sánchez, by coincidence a distant cousin of the French skeptic Michel de Montaigne. This work is the *Quod nihil scitur,* published in Lyons in 1581, the year after the first edition of Montaigne's *Essais.* Born around 1550 in either Braga, Portugal or more probably Tuy in Galicia of *converso* parentage, Sánchez taught philosophy and medicine for most of his life in Toulouse. An original thinker, he anticipated Pierre Bayle's long essay *Pensées sur la comète* in his *Carmen de Cometa* by over a hundred years, a critical examination in verse of the astrological interpretations of the comet of 1577.[42]

Sánchez's great work, the *Quod nihil scitur* attempted a systematic

---

39. The original Latin runs as follows: "Nosco me aliquid noscere, et quidquid noscit est, ergo ego sum" (Solana, vol. I, p. 267).

40. See Marcelino Menéndez y Pelayo, *La ciencia española,* 3 vols. (Santander: Ed. Nacional, 1953), vol. I, p. 13.

41. See especially Eloy Bullón y Fernández, *Los precursores españoles de Bacon y Descartes* (Salamanca, 1905).

42. It has been claimed that F. Sánchez wrote a treatise on scientific method. Richard H. Popkin (see n. 45, below) maintains that his *Método universal de las ciencias,* if it ever existed, would have been the earliest piece of writing on the subject in modern times. It is difficult to gauge the degree of influence exercised by the *Quod nihil scitur,* inside or outside Spain. But Solana observes of its orginality and intrinsic importance: "Es, pues, el *Quod nihil scitur* verdadera panoplia del escepticismo en las postrimerías de la décimasexta centuria; y ésta es una de las mayores novedades que presenta la labor filosófica de Sánchez. Aunque no de tanta relieve como el escepticismo, tiene la doctrina de Sánchez otra nota muy personal y caracteristica, también acentuadísima: el espíritu crítico con que juzga los trabajos y doctrinas de los filósofos anteriores, incluso de los grandes maestros; y la proclamación de independencia de criterio de libertad filosófica, frente a toda autoridad dogmática puramente humana." See his *Historia...* vol. I, p. 403.

analysis of Aristotelian epistemology. Sánchez both denied the possibility of knowing anything for sure, and then advanced a sort of constructive skepticism as a way of answering questions through patient and careful empirical research. He announces in the first paragraph, glossing Socrates' famous dictum, that he does not even know if he knows nothing. The hostile exposition of Aristotle that now follows is really an expression of Sánchez's own views, and in his treatment of terms and definitions, he displays a thoroughgoing nominalism. A plurality of names for the same thing, he argues, are either all identical in meaning, in which case they are superfluous and do not explain the object, or else they mean something different, hence the names are not the names of the object. This nominalism is then applied to the Aristotelian view that science is certain knowledge from true definitions. These latter says Sánchez echoing Timon, we do not possess in the first place; secondly the syllogism provides no new knowledge. A demonstration by syllogism is only a form of circular reasoning, since the conclusion to be proved is part of the evidence for the premises. Next, formally speaking, anything can be proven syllogistically if one starts with the right premises. The demonstration's construction is no proof that the conclusion is actually true. A further element of Aristotelian science, the true knowledge of things in terms of their causes, is viewed by Sánchez as an unattainable goal. This would require the infinite erudition of the cause of the cause, the cause of the cause of the cause and so on.

Sánchez, in a letter addressed to the astronomer, mathematician and editor of Euclid named Christopher Clavius or Christoph Klau[43] (around 1574-75), attacked also the Platonic theory of knowledge. We cannot know through mathematics, he asserted, since the objects studied by mathematics are not real, natural ones, but ideal or impossible ones such as points or lines. Mathematical relations explain nothing about the causes of anything in experience, unless we know independently a) the nature of the experienced object, b) that it has certain mathematical properties, and c) that the principles of mathematics are, in fact, true. Hence this study is only a conjectural or hypothetical, mental game.

Returning to a more positive tack in his *Quod nihil scitur,* Sánchez

---

43. Christoph Klau was a German Jesuit and, in addition to his studies in mathematics and astronomy, he contributed to the Gregorian calendar and gave his Latinized name, Clavius, to a lunar crater that he discovered.

says that true science is the perfect knowledge of a thing ("scientia est rei perfecta cognitio"), the immediate intuitive understanding of all the real qualities of an object. Menéndez y Pelayo expresses Sánchez's conception of the cognitive process in the following terms: ". . . lo que piensa es que en el problema del conocimiento hay que distinguir tres términos: la cosa que ha de ser conocida (*res scienda*), el ente que conoce (*ens cognoscens*) y el conocimiento mismo (*cognitio ipsa*)."[44] Generalizations beyond this have no certitude, insists Sánchez, they involve merely concepts, abstractions or fictions. But such perfect knowledge is only attained by God, and since objects are interrelated, interconnected and unlimited in number, no complete knowledge is attainable by human beings; nor do objects ever achieve a final, knowable form. The second obstacle is the unreliability of our own senses; thus we perceive only surface characteristics, not the true nature of objects. Again in Menéndez y Pelayo's words: "Juzgamos de las cosas por sus simulacros; esto es, por meras representaciones de accidentes que no tocan a la esencia, ni nos dan razón de ella" (loc. cit. at p. xlv). Popkin[45] observes of this step in Sánchez's argument that the traditional skeptical evidence plus Sánchez's medical studies had provided him with much extra detail about the imperfections and limitations of human nature.

Sánchez's conclusion is that the only genuine scientific knowledge cannot be attained by man at all: a sweeping negative conclusion that goes beyond even Montaigne. Sánchez has attempted to state what genuine knowledge *would* be and then show why it is beyond reach. He does, however, advocate a procedure to deal constructively with experience through patient, careful empirical research, as well as cautious judgment and evaluation of data, a conclusion concretized by Menéndez Pelayo in the lapidary formula: ". . . guerra al silogismo, paso a la inducción" (p. xlviii). This will provide a source for the best information *available,* really the modern view that having abandoned

---

44. The references in this section are to the Introduction by M. Menéndez y Pelayo to the Spanish translation of Sánchez's work *Que nada se sabe* (Buenos Aires, 1924). There is a more accessible reprint of this edition in Espasa-Calpe's Austral collection (Madrid, 1972).

45. See the articles of Richard H. Popkin "Skepticism" and "Sánchez, Francisco" in *The Encyclopedia of Philosophy,* vol. VII (New York: Macmillan, 1967). See also his excellent general study *History of Skepticism from Erasmus to Descartes* (Assen, Holland: Van Gorcum, 1960). I am heavily indebted throughout this section to Popkin's lucid expositions of Sánchez's treatise.

the search for absolute certainty about the true nature of things, science is the only profitable study. The striking originality of this is Sánchez's suggestion that a probabilistic empirical study of experience could replace the hopeless quest for certainty, though not actually substitute for it. A probabilistic solution such as this in the field of epistemology clearly matches the contemporary espousal in Spain of probabilism in the field of moral theology.

Throughout the *Essais,* Montaigne had turned the traditional arguments about the imperfection of the senses into a veritable crisis of subject and its perception of the object, and forcefully dramatized the deceiving power of the imagination. Theories and arguments similar to Montaigne's appeared almost simultaneously in Spain in the 1580 s. Writing under the pseudonym Oliva Sabuco de Nantes Barrera, one Miguel Sabuco published his *Nueva filosofía de la naturaleza del hombre* in Madrid in 1587 (second impression 1588). Really a physician interested in improving the lot of mankind, Sabuco combines in his rambling treatise a marriage of natural philosophy, medicine and moral philosophy — enthusiasms shared by Sánchez of Toulouse and frequently found side by side in the sixteenth century. Cautioning that emotional ills can kill man as surely as physical ones, Sabuco is led in his early pages to consider the effect of *non-existent* ills on the system that are held to be real in the imagination.

Echoing Montaigne, he states that: "... el enojo falso o imaginado, también mata como el verdadero" (p. 19, r.). Pyramus, he recalls, seeing Thisbe's bloodied mantle at Ninus' tomb, erroneously imagined his beloved was dead and stabbed himself to death; in the same way, violent fear of death in pregnant women can cause them actually to miscarry such that: "... con sola la imaginación el miedo las mata" (p. 21, v.). Discoursing on the power of the imagination and how this may be observed in animals, Sabuco turns to errors of perception and the problem of truth in general. He writes: "La imaginación sensitiva engaña también el hombre, como algunos animales, ora sea en vigilia, ora sea en el sueño, [y] obra aquello mismo que la verdad" (p. 82, v.). Ostriches, when startled by fear at the approach of an enemy, plunge their heads into sand thinking thus that an unseen danger is a nonexistent one. The author notes: "Assi el hombre lo q[ue] tiene en su imaginación (ora sea en vigilia, ora sea en sueño) aquello es para él, en tanto que si se sueñan, y piensan dichosos y felices, obra en ellos, *como si fuera verdad*" (p. 83, r. My italics). Thus Sabuco comes via his medical experience to the same conclusion as Montaigne: that man's emotions and imagination can deform the objective world and make truth contingent upon subjective perception.

Shortly after Sabuco's treatise appeared the most complete exposition of skeptical doctrines to be published by a Spaniard; this was the *Academica* of Pedro de Valencia (Antwerp, 1596) written in Latin.[46] Valencia's work offers an excellent example of the use of Pyrrhonian conclusions to *defend* Catholic Christianity, since in his survey of Ancient skepticism, Valencia argues that if the Greek philosophers had not found truth, then one must turn from the philosophers to God and to Jesus as the only sage. This conclusion, it must be admitted, is limited to the final paragraph only, and the interest of the work lies rather in its highly competent and thorough exposition of the skeptical doctrines, and its concentration on the growing problem of the power of the imagination to deceive man. It is only a small step from Valencia's treatise to the author-invented confusions and mistaken perceptions that harass the protagonists of Spain's Baroque theater.

Valencia first shows that the skeptical maxim 'every contention is equal to any other' undermines our understanding and even our chances of probable certainty. After his treatment of Carneades, the Spanish philosopher demonstrates that man was given no skill by which he might discern truth from falsehood and hence form valid judgments. Similarly he says, any subject perceiving phantasms is unable to say of what they are images, how they are absorbed, whether they are true or false, or whether harbingers of truth or lies. Valencia suggests an anecdotal example of his own in this regard. Consider the various busts of Julius Caesar, he says, a man whom I have never seen. To gain knowledge of this man, I examine many representations, but not even the Stoics will say that I have known or understood his true face. Even if I choose one, it will be the one that *pleases* me most that I shall praise as the most probably true effigy.

Valencia now broaches the all-important subject of the representation of reality. Some appearances are true, he states, others are false; that is to say some appearances correctly represent the object from which they are emitted; others do not reflect a true image of the object (". . . aliae rem, a qua sunt immissae, recte repraesentant. Alias veram

---

46. This work's full title was *Academica, sive de iudicio erga verum ex ipsis primis fontibus* (Antwerp, 1596). It may also be read in the collection edited by F. Cerda y Rico, *Clarorum Hispanorum opuscula selecta* (Madrid, 1781), the edition quoted here.

rei imaginem non reddunt" p. 204). Invoking Epicurus (via Laetius), Valencia repeats the Ancient philosopher's claim that even apparent objects that madman and sleepers see must be real, since they are moved by them, and what in truth *is* not, does not move. Further pursuing the question of fidelity of perception and the stability of the object perceived, Valencia distinguishes a third order of self-delusion that can arise through erroneous opinion. Taking the skeptics' example of a tower which seen from a distance appears round and small and proves on closer examination to be square and large, Valencia argues that of course, while a deformed image of the tower reached us, the image which the tower offered to the mind did not in fact lie, but the senses were thrown into confusion by an illusion (*specie*). Again, if someone exhausted from a long and tiring journey and with his mental impression of it rapidly fading, considers the same tower of the same shape not to be solid, he is misled by opinion and not by the senses. Likewise another, if through aural perception he believes that a powerful voice borne towards him from a great distance is really a weak one, it is he who is in error, not his senses. For the hearing registered it as it was conveyed to the ear and represented it faithfully (pp. 246-247). The treatise ends on the note of Christian fideism already described above.

In 1612, Francisco Sánchez "el Brocense" (not a relative of the *converso* philosopher) published his translation of Epictetus,[47] where the views we have been examining are squarely and unequivocally applied to the theater and the theater of life. After his versions of each original chapter from the Greek, Sánchez added his own commentaries to fill out the pagan philosopher's meaning. Though the work mainly concerns moral philosophy and the notions of tolerance and continence, there are moments when the Spanish author brings the skeptical conclusions about the false representation of reality which life offers us, a step closer to the widely held idea in the seventeenth century that all life differs little from the false reality represented on a

---

47. In his Prologue to the *Epicteto* (Madrid, 1612), El Brocense claims for his translation of a pagan philosopher that Epictetus' moral teaching was analogous in essence to that in the Christian Testaments. He writes: "Nuestro Epicteto más sigue a los Stoycos y conforma mucho con las sagradas letras, y tanto que si de su doctrina sólo se quitasse el hablar de los dioses en plural se parece al Ecclesiastes de Salomón, y las Epístolas de S. Pablo, y de los otros Apóstoles." I have expanded Sánchez's words where necessary and modernized the diacritics.

human stage. Sánchez translates chapter xix (p. 38, v.) as follows: " 'La vida es una comedia, y Dios el que da los personajes y los dichos.' No se te olvide que toda la vida del hombre es una representación, si el Señor de la representación quiere darte el dicho breve o largo, tú assi lo representa. Si manda q[ue] representes un mendigo, hazlo co[n] destreza, y assi un coxo, un príncipe, y un particular. Porq[ue] a ti solame[n]te toca hazer bien tu personage, y de otro es el escogerlo y repartirlo." In his Annotation to this chapter, Sánchez comments repeating the topos *scena est omnis vita,* that what is represented in stage comedy may appear, but must not *be,* a true reality. He writes: "Puédese también aplicar este capítulo a lo passado, como dezir que aunque llores en la representación, que no sea de veras, y aunque representes un muerto que no te mueras, ni te aflijas de veras, sino fingido" (p. 39, r.). No reader can fail to be struck by the similarity of these ideas to the action of Calderón's *El gran teatro del mundo* and the crucial ambiguities of the shifting term *representación.*

It is easy to see in these popularizing works how skeptical doctrines could be disseminated and give fuel to the intellectual uncertainties of the age. The objection may be raised that the cost of such books, their availability, the ordinary man's ignorance of Latin or even lack of literacy in Spanish provided an effective check to the spread of speculative ideas; the evidence of popular poetry in the period and recurrent themes in the *comedia,* however, would seem to invalidate such a contention. The celebrated sonnet by one of the Argensola brothers, "Yo os quiero confesar, don Juan, primero...", talks of the superior facial beauty of Elvira's painted features to that of a real face. The poet then draws the comparison with the illusions of Nature herself:

> Mas, ¿qué mucho que yo perdido ande
> por un engaño tal, pues que sabemos
> que nos engaña así Naturaleza?
> Porque ese cielo azul que todos vemos
> ni es cielo ni es azul: ¡Lástima grande
> que no sea verdad tanta belleza! [48]

---

48. By one of the Argensola brothers and anthologized by Elias L. Rivers in *Renaissance and Baroque Poetry of Spain* (New York: Scribner's, 1966), p. 153. There was a posthumous edition of their works in 1634, but the sonnet was obviously written long before, as its diffusion shows. In 1596, the year of Valencia's *Academica,* Lupercio was thirty-seven years old, Bartolomé was thirty-four.

The false appearance of the blue sky rapidly became a topos of Spanish literature and it reappears often in Calderón. In his *Saber del mal y del bien* (1628), the dramatist precedes his reminiscence of Argensola with a passage of epistemological skepticism of the type that we have been discussing. Don Alvaro says in Act III:

> ....adviertas,
> que tal vez los ojos nuestros
> se engañan, y representan
> tan diferentes objetos
> de lo que miran, que dejan
> burlada el alma. ¿Qué más
> razón, más verdad, más prueba,
> que el cielo azul que miramos?
> ¿Habrá alguno, que no crea
> vulgarmente que es zafiro,
> que hermosos rayos ostenta?
> Pues *ni es cielo ni es azul.*[49]

Concerning the subject of skepticism in the theater, a word on Calderón's *La vida es sueño* seems appropriate. The title itself is, of course, a skeptical proposition eventually refuted by the playwright. In his profound analysis of the problem, however, before the play's climax, Calderón puts the following words in the mouth of the still doubting Segismundo:

> Ya
> otra vez vi aquesto mesmo
> tan clara y distintamente
> como ahora lo estoy viendo,
> y fue sueño.[50]

The phrase "tan clara y distintamente" in such a context cannot but remind one of the Cartesian criterion for self-evident truth, his "idées claires et distinctes" in the first step of his method.[51] There is no

---

49. Quoted from *Obras de D. Pedro Calderón de la Barca, BAE*, vol. VII, p. 34a. Such skeptical arguments about color are termed in modern philosophy the 'argument from illusion.' Since things appear different to the same observer in different circumstances, color cannot be said to 'inhere.' Hence, if P is veridical or illusory, we cannot say what colors things are, only what they look.

50. See *La vida es sueño,* ed. Albert E. Sloman (Manchester: Manchester Univ. Press, 1961), p. 70, ll. 2348-52.

51. In the phrasing of the first principle in his Method, Descartes uses the adverbial forms of the adjectives of present interest, as does Calderón. He states: "Le premier était de ne recevoir jamais aucune chose pour vraie que je ne la connusse

evidence that the two writers knew each other's work, but both unquestionably knew the *Disputationes metaphysicae* (1597) of Francisco Suárez S.J.; Descartes by his own admission, and Calderón because his early training had been with the Society of Jesus at the Colegio Imperial in Madrid, and the *Disputationes* became a standard text in both Catholic and Protestant universities for nearly two centuries. Suárez's metaphysical edifice, really a synthesis of theology and speculative philosophy, does not ultimately doubt that there were indeed rational grounds for supposing degrees of certainty and knowledge. Descartes in the *Discours sur la méthode* (1637) and Calderón in *La vida es sueño* (1635) also reviewed the skeptical doubts of their contemporaries in order to reach positive conclusions. The act of cogitation itself for the Frenchman and the transcendent value of good works for the Spaniard seemed to ensure man against despairing of the real existence of the external world altogether.

Further Applications to the *comedia*

In outlining some intellectual problems of the Counter Reformation, reference has already been made to their expression in specific plays and the claim stated that the explosion of play-writing in Spain (indeed all Europe) was a response to the spiritual, moral and intellectual confusion of a world in violent change. The revolt of certain individuals against the medieval tradition (e.g. Luther, Henry VIII, Copernicus) initiated what may be termed a protracted antinomian conflict between the theocentric, static, finite, and well-ordered world which medieval Christianity presupposed, and a modern, evolving anthropocentric order. The myriad predicaments subsumed in such a conflict engendered an extraordinary resurgence of the European theater, and seventeenth-century drama may be viewed as frustrated partial syntheses in this evolution. Nowhere was this truer than in Spain, where the sheer volume of dramatic production easily surpassed that of the other seventeenth-century national dramas, whether English, French, Dutch, or German. Despite opposition, the theater was never sup-

---

évidemment être telle; c'est-à-dire d'éviter soigneusement la précipitation et la prévention; et de ne comprendre rien de plus en mes jugements que ce qui se présenterait *si clairement et si distinctement à mon esprit* que je n'eusse aucune occasion de le mettre en doute." See Descartes, *Oeuvres et Lettres,* ed. André Bridoux (Paris: Gallimard, 1953), p. 137. My italics.

pressed and the abundance of writing and unfailing popularity of the *corrales* reflect a deeper significance for the theater in Spanish national life than has hitherto been suspected.

The Spanish drama contained the basic antagonisms of the Counter Reformation itself, i.e. Renaissance liberation in conflict with a medievalizing reaction; the *comedia* was a theater that restated medieval values, but explored the scope of human freedom without being able to help itself. In the context of this broad phenomenon, we must also remember that Spain was a country intellectually isolated by the Inquisition, a stiff censorship and a ban on the importation of foreign books; she was politically muted by quasi-dictatorial *privados,* tense also about the impure blood in the converted populations and beginning to grow alarmed at the evidence of her incipient decline. The popular stage therefore was the only public debating-chamber left for the representation and reinforcement of national myths, for the subtle probing of mass concern about personal worth and honor, the true road to salvation, the legality by which a king governed his people, the destructiveness of uncurbed sexuality, ethical doubts and confusions of every complexion, while the very medium itself conveyed doubt about the reliability of the senses. Of course the plays were entertainment, comedies of diversion, but the mainspring of their popularity and their continuing sublimity lies in the success with which the *comedia* provided an insecure populace with the homeopathic balm of relief from real confusion by synthetic confusion; of private agonies acted out in public, the exploration of every aspect of life through the one medium that most resembled it – the drama.

If official and semi-official opposition to the theater in the seventeenth century (which was successful in the Puritan suppression of 1639 in England) had a partial success in Spain, this merely confirms the gravity of the issues that the *comedia* discussed. In no other way can the implacable hostility of theologians, moralists and contemporary churchmen be explained. So far, two main explanations for this hostility have been offered: the arguments on grounds of the plays' 'immorality' and the complaints that they did not observe the rules of art. There is ample documentation of the neo-Classicists' quarrels with the exponents of the *comedia* and these can easily be consulted.[52] The

---

52. The curious reader may be directed to the following brief selections from the enormous bibliography on this subject: H. J. Chaytor, *Dramatic Theory in Spain* (Cambridge, 1925), esp. pp. 57-63; E. Cotarelo y Mori, *Bibliografía de las*

charge that the *comedia,* particularly by the 1620 s, had become immoral and obscene also had some justice in it. Miss Margaret Wilson, in her recent study, declares: "Declining moral standards in the 1620 s caused concern; the theater was again blamed; and as the Aristotelians were silenced, the moralists became more vocal . . . few readers in any age could fail to find distasteful such plays as Guillén de Castro's *Los mal casados de Valencia,* in which four out of the five main characters are adulterous in fact or in intent . . . ."[53]

These charges supposedly applied not only to the immorality of the plays as such, but also to the alleged licentiousness of the actresses and actors and their sexual promiscuity.[54] A further argument set forth by Bertrand Russell and others as an explanation of hostility to the stage, points to the view of art adumbrated by Plato, a philosopher widely read in the Renaissance, in the seventh book of the *Republic.* There Plato attacks the fictions of the poets as reprehensible delusions, defor-

---

controversias sobre la licitud del teatro en España (Madrid, 1904); J. de Entreambasaguas, "Una guerra literaria del Siglo de Oro. Lope de Vega y los preceptistas aristotélicos," in *Estudios sobre Lope de Vega,* Vols. I and II (Madrid, 1946 and 1947); M. Menéndez y Pelayo, *Historia de las ideas estéticas en España* (Madrid, 1890-1912), cap. x; Duncan W. Moir, "The classical tradition in Spanish dramatic theory and practice in the seventeenth century," in *Classical Drama and its Influence. Essays presented to H. D. F. Kitto* (London, 1965) and Moir's edition of Francisco Bances Candamo's *Theatro de los Theatros* (London: Tamesis, 1970); Margarete Newels, *Die dramatischen Gattungen des Siglo de Oro* (Wiesbaden, 1959); Luis C. Pérez and F. Sánchez Escribano, *Afirmaciones de Lope de Vega sobre preceptiva dramática* (Madrid, 1961); M. Romera-Navarro, *La preceptiva dramática de Lope de Vega* (Madrid, 1935), "Lope de Vega y las unidades dramáticas," *HR,* 3. (1935), 190-201, "Querellas y rivalidades en las academias del siglo XVII," *HR,* 9 (1941), 494-99; Sánchez Escribano and A. Porqueras Mayo, *Preceptiva dramática española,* 2nd ed. rev. (Madrid: Gredos, 1972); Sanford Shepard, *El Pinciano y las teorías literarias del Siglo de Oro* (Madrid, 1962); A. Villanova, "Preceptistas españolas de los siglos XVI y XVII," in *Historia general de las literaturas hispánicas,* vol. III (Barcelona, 1953); W. Margaret Wilson, *Spanish Drama of the Golden Age* (Oxford: Pergamon, 1969), esp. pp. 24-37, "The Controversy."

53. See her *Spanish Drama . . .* p. 36.

54. Cotarelo's *Bibliografía . . .* gives abundant extracts which condemn the 'obscenity' and supposed promiscuity of the actors and actresses in the Spanish theater. The use of dances between the play's acts was considered particularly licentious, the *chacona* for example. Some of the clerical attacks are so lurid and explicit, however, that it may be doubted whether they are any more edifying than the alleged abuses under discussion.

mations of a reality itself illusory, which distract us from the perception of the true essence of things, the Platonic world of Ideas.

All these explanations carry some weight, but examined separately or even together, they hardly explain the persistent, almost paranoid acerbity of the attacks on the stage and a truer answer is to be found in the fact that the Spanish dramatists at worst were maintaining a free and daring dialogue with the public on issues that were potentially dangerous (as heresy, as a political threat or socially subversive), or at best choosing to dramatize issues that theologians could well deem outside the playwrights' legitimate province and competence to handle.[55] By this reckoning, the clerical attacks on sexual license may simply have concealed a deeper opposition: the fear that grave theological issues could be bandied about in a vulgarized form in the *corrales* and stimulate controversy among the illiterate.

The Guerra controversy of 1682[56] and the *Theatro de los theatros* written in reply to P. Camargo by Bances Candamo (1689-93) lend further support to this notion. Fr. Manuel Guerra defended Calderón's theater in an approbation to the *Verdadera quinta parte* on *theological* grounds and provoked a colossal assault on himself by the Jesuits P. Augustín de Herrera, P. Pedro Fomperosa and others. Bances Candamo in turn offers several fascinating insights into the history of clerical opposition and hints that the death of the controversy was only the

---

55. As regards the playwrights' theological competence or the lack of it, it should be noted that several trained theologians and playwrights such as Mira de Amescua, Tirso, Tirso's correligionist Fr. Alonso Remón and many others had been in orders since early youth. The great Calderón, at the height of his career, tangled with the Inquisition in 1662 over the orthodoxy of his *auto, Las pruebas del segundo Adán* and won! The Holy Office prohibited the performance of the work because, they maintained, in the play's certification of the *limpieza de sangre* of the second Adam (i.e. Christ), only the purity of the paternal line had been placed beyond doubt not the maternal, which Calderón based on the immaculate conception of Mary. The Inquisition disagreed with him about this thesis and rejected the work even after modifications had been added. Calderón, however, was within the orthodoxy of Pontifical doctrine. See Jose I. Tejedor, *Calderón de la Barca* (Madrid: C. B. E., 1967), pp. 44-46.

56. The Guerra controversy urgently requires a substantial monographic treatment. See, however, the basic *Bibliografía*... of Cotarelo, Edward M. Wilson, "Las 'Dudas curiosas' a la aprobación del Maestro Fray Manuel de Guerra y Ribera," *Estudios escénicos,* 6. (1960), 47-63, and my own thesis "Two hundred years of Calderonian criticism, 1681-1881," (Harvard, 1970), where the issue is treated in Chapter I.

natural result of the death of the drama. He writes: "La ocasión, porque, después de hauer escrito tantas y tan graues plumas [sobre] esta materia sin añadir a ella cosa notable, la emprende por un grandíssimo trauajo en la decrépita edad de esta miserable arte, quando ya la comedia va por sí misma espirando y acabándose naturalmente...."[57]

In a provocative passage elsewhere, Bances claims that theologians were not qualified to offer opinions on the theater, thus putting the argument induced above by me on its head: that playwrights were not qualified to offer opinions in theology. Bances states: "Cosa es mui vulgar que la jurisprudencia y la theología, en las materias que no caen debajo de sus preceptos y noticias, se resignan totalmente al parecer y declaración de los profesores de aquella facultad o arte *circum quam versatur*, porque fuera mui improprio que declararse el Jurisconsulto la essencia de una herida, lo caduco de una casa, ni otras materialidades que *sub se non cadunt*..." (*op. cit.* at. p. 4).

Of the three main topics chosen for discussion in this chapter, the controversy on grace, probabilism and skepticism, two directly concerned theology and one concerned philosophy, although the skeptics in Spain kept their doubts short of religious orthodoxy. All three subjects come up, assuming various guises, in scores of Spanish plays, and by way of conclusion, I should like to list a selection of familiar *comedias* whose themes fall partly or wholly into our three categories.

Grace

The host of plays that deal with some aspect of grace (plays about *santos y bandoleros*, redeemed sinners, diabolic pacts, etc.) all have one thing in common: they unfailingly present the case of spectacular wrong-doers (male or female and sometimes both) who against the apparent odds die a death of contrition or martyrdom and go to glory. These plays reacted, whatever their particular emphasis, against the pessimistic determinism of the Protestants and especially the idea that *any* man could be denied the chance of salvation. If the dramatists occasionally overdid it and portrayed real fiends who nevertheless win salvation, their optimistic zeal must be added to the natural attractiveness of wickedness to both author and public alike. Such is the case of Lope's Leonido in *La fianza satisfecha* and Calderón's Ludovico Enio in *El purgatorio de San Patricio*.

Other plays such as Mira de Amescua's *El esclavo del demonio* and

---

57. See Moir's edition of the *Theatro de los theatros*, p. 5.

Calderón's *El mágico prodigioso* dramatize situations where the hero has, of his free will, consigned his soul to the Devil in a satanic pact. The *dénouements* of these plays illustrate that God's mercy is infinite and that the pacts may be providentially rendered powerless. Calderón's early play *La devoción de la cruz* has some of the qualities of a martyr drama and illustrates the miraculous, talismanic power of the Cross in rescuing the souls of Eusebio and Julia for the supreme reward.

As we have seen, Tirso gives the problem deep thought in some thirteen plays and — the most severe of the Spanish dramatists — consigns a personáge to hell in three of them (*El condenado por desconfiado, El burlador de Sevilla, El mayor desengaño*). These condemnations, however, only serve to emphasize the true path to salvation. In his philosophical *summa, La vida es sueño,* Calderón treats the problem of free will (" ¡Y yo, con más albedrio, / tengo menos libertad! " I, ii) and the violent hero's salvation to divine glory ("¿quién, por vanagloria humana, / pierde una divina gloria? " III, x). There are numerous Segismundo-like characters in Calderón's theater after 1635 and a thematic catalogue of the *comedia* would furnish many more.

Probabilism

Probabilism, being a mass of opinions *ad casum,* is a diffuse topic by its very nature. Situations where the moral options are deliberately made dubious and indifferently probable have been mentioned: Lope's *Fuenteovejuna* and *Peribáñez* and the Duke's speech of self-justification in his *El castigo sin venganza* provide examples. Several plays of Tirso have been cited: *Antona García, Amar por razón de estado, La vida y muerte de Herodes, La fingida Arcadia, La mujer por fuerza,* etc. Calderón, conceivably the greatest probabilist among all the Spanish dramatists, presents situations that appear to justify uncastigated uxoricide in *El médico de su honra, A secreto agravio, secreta venganza,* and *El pintor de su deshonra.* The various probabilistic doctrines defended in *Luis Pérez, el gallego* have been mentioned above. Calderón's complex portrayal of behavior here, and the implied canonical justifications of the protagonists' claims to be acting in the right, do not necessarily represent his own position, even if he had one. The utility of probabilism lay in the latitude of the canonical authority (even if only that of a single theologian) by which a character could invoke probable grounds for unusual, hence potentially dramatic courses of action. Moreover, the heavily problematic nature of the dilemmas Lope, Tirso and Calderón sometimes sought to portray frequently drove them to a probabilistic compromise as the only possible basis for action.

Skepticism

Skepticism expresses itself in the *comedia* in two ways: by the choice of situations where the evidence of the senses is placed in epistemological doubt, and the ubiquitous implication of the Spanish drama that the difference between the reality portrayed on stage and the reality of life itself was merely one of degree. Lope's *Lo fingido verdadero*, a play on the life of the Roman actor San Ginés, falls in this latter category, as do all the dramas containing plays-within-plays. The creation of persons who exist in two personae or disguises and thus cause untold confusion, appear in countless plays such as Tirso's *Don Gil* and *La mujer por fuerza* and as goblins or spirits in Calderón's *La dama duende* and *El galán fantasma*. The ruse of a passage, trapdoor or secret door enabling a character to appear in two places at once is exploited in Tirso's *Por el sótano y el torno, Los balcones de Madrid. En Madrid y en una casa* and in Calderón's *Casa con dos puertas*, etc. Calderón, perhaps the most persistent and unnerving of the skeptical dramatists, reduces the objectivity of the external world to a matter of subjective perception in *La vida es sueño, En esta vida, todo es verdad y todo mentira* and *Gustos y disgustos no son más que imaginación.*

From contemporary remarks, Spaniards had the reputation of being histrionic in life and this gave new skeptical force to the old *theatrum mundi* cliché.[58] Hence there was almost no difference between the stage and the street; men wore actor's clothes in life. The neo-Classical school said art was a mirror of life and yet Plato and the skeptics said that even life was the representation of a higher reality: the "real"

---

58. See Jack Sage, "Texto y realización de 'La estatua de Prometeo' y otros dramas musicales de Calderón," in *Hacia Calderón. Coloquio anglo-germano, Exeter* (Berlin and New York: Gruyter, 1969), 37-52, where he develops the theory of a vehement style of representation particularly adapted to the Spanish temperament. He writes: "Había en la España de la época de Calderón varios modos de representar en el *corral* y en el palacio, figurando entre ellos en primer plano el burlesco y en segundo plano el más refinado, melancólico o sentimental. Sobre todo, *había un estilo de representar hablando o cantando que podría denominarse nacional, estilo que se caracterizaba de un dramatismo vehemente,* apoyado en la exteriorización de vivos afectos interiores. Los comediantes solicitaban la "admiración" afectiva más que cerebral" (p. 43. My italics). This point is made by Emilio Orozco Díaz at considerable length in his *El teatro y la teatralidad del barroco* (Barcelona: Planeta,

truth, the transcendent entities behind an imperfect, even unknowable world. Hence, if life was a theater and the theater was an illusion, was life an illusion? Could the stage and the street be indifferently transposed? The increasingly histrionic behavior of European courts in the seventeenth century suggest that contemporaries tended to answer those questions positively.[59]

According to Kerr,[60] comedy is pessimistic, because it shows what man cannot do; tragedy is optimistic because it explores the possibilities of human freedom. Since in the Spanish drama, the comic vein prevailed over the tragic, we might be justified in supposing that the pessimism thereby implied fitted logically with the pessimistic tones of the Counter Reformation. The small number of undiluted tragedies in the *comedia* indicates how gingerly the possibilities of human freedom were, explored. But the exponents of the *comedia nueva* constantly claimed that their art was hybrid by definition, and if we are to isolate a single, unifying characteristic of all directions of Spanish thought described in this chapter, it is the paradoxical one with which we started: the constant desire of Spanish thinkers, especially the Jesuits, to defend man's right to scrutinize his world as he thought he saw it and act freely within it; and to accomodate these human freedoms to the exigencies of religious orthodoxy. The theater, as the most unfettered and dynamic of all public institutions, became the living incarnation of that desire. It is to an examination of Tirso's personal view of this theater's status, its theoretical bases for legitimacy and its singularly Spanish system of preceptive that we must now turn.

1969); he writes (p. 109): "Esa teatralización de la vida [...] alcanza [...] incluso a las más corrientes formas del individual vivir cotidiano, al ser y comportarse del hombre. Se prodigan entonces actitudes y gestos en graves circunstancias, que acusan obedecer al sentido de representar un papel que no es el que espontáneamente se vive, sino el adaptado a una escena de vida concebida como un gran teatro en el que nos contemplamos unos a otros."

59. Orozco observes in this regard (p. 89) that: "... se vive en las cortes europeas una vida de fiestas suntuosas, en las que la realidad y la ficción dramática se confunden e incluso se superponen. Los mismos monarcas y nobles intervienen en ellas y hasta aceptan presentarse en la fiesta de corte como un personaje de ballet o de comedia..."

60. See Walter Kerr, *Tragedy and Comedy* (New York: Simon and Schuster, 1967). Quoted by Halkhoree, "Social and Literary Satire..." p. 29.

II

TIRSO'S THEORY OF DRAMA

> "Gusano es su autor de seda: de su misma sustancia ha labrado [...] cuatrocientas y más Comedias. . . ."
> Dedication of the *Tercera parte*.

Although Tirso never wrote a comprehensive treatise on poetics or the theory of the drama comparable to Lope's *Arte nuevo de hacer comedias* (1609), there exists a surprisingly large number of passages in his plays and prose works which, taken together, form a cohesive and fairly detailed commentary on his art. The sources from which Tirso's theory of the drama may be reconstructed are the following: several dialogues in *Los cigarrales de Toledo* (1624) notably the debates after each of the three intercalated plays (*Cigarrales* I, IV and V); the Dedication and other stray remarks found in *Deleitar aprovechando* (1635) and the Dedication of the *Quinta parte* (1636); passages in Act II, xiv of *El vergonzoso en palacio* (probably revised 1621); many scenes in *La fingida Arcadia* (1621) and sundry passages attacking Gongoristic diction in *Celos con celos se curan, Amar por arte mayor, Amor y celos hacen discretos* and *La celosa de sí misma*. It will be seen that the sum of these remarks is an eclectic *mélange* of traditional ideas, the revolutionary theories of the *comedia nueva* school, and occasional insights of striking originality. But though eclectic, Tirso's dramatic theory is affirmed with none of the hesitancy shown by his master Lope, and is everywhere consistent with Tirso's own dramatic practice.[1] Before

---

1. Lope's true attitude to his innovations in the theater has been a subject of critical controversy. Menéndez y Pelayo, in his *Historia de las ideas estéticas en España,* 2nd ed., III (Madrid, 1896), p. 433, called the *Arte nuevo* a "lamentable palinodia," while Menéndez Pidal, in his article "El arte nuevo y la nueva biografía," *RFE,* 22 (1935), p. 348, declared it to contain a new system of aesthetics. But all Lope's theoretical-critical manifestos contain contradictions and conflicting views. As an artist, he was an innovator and ignored the rules; as a humanist and a conservative eager for academic esteem, he could not easily reject the whole of Grecolatin authority, with its strong orthodox undertones, *a priori.*

embarking on an exposition of Tirso's statements on drama, however, a word on the literary debate that prompted them is essential. For while critical opposition to the Spanish *comedia* was nothing new in Lope's lifetime, the polemics and apologetics surrounding it reached a climax of unparalleled acrimony and intensity in the period 1616-1622. It should be noted that Tirso's remarks defending Lope (and thus, of course, himself) fall principally within the life of this debate.

Lope's *Arte nuevo,* seen by some as an answer to the strictures of the Canon of Toledo in *Don Quijote* (1605), I, 48, was reprinted in 1613 and his principal arguments (i.e. the criterion of contemporary popular taste, the legitimacy of a mixed genre as a truer reflection of life) were restated by Ricardo del Turia in his *Apologética de las comedias españolas* in 1616. Francisco Cascales replied attacking this position in his reactionary *Tablas poéticas* of 1617, while Suárez de Figueroa in his *El pasajero* (1617) heaped personal abuse on Lope's private conduct. An even more outrageous attack appeared in the *Spongia* (1617?) of Torres Rámila, no copies of which have survived. Lope's supporters replied with a compendium in Latin entitled *Expostulatio Spongiae* (1618), the most distinguished parts of which are by Francisco López de Aguilar and Sánchez de Moratalla. Hence, during Tirso's two-year absence in Santo Domingo, the literary world had been engaged in the most violent phase of a Spanish Quarrel of Ancients and Moderns centered on the drama,[2] and when Tirso returned to Madrid it was still at its height.

When we talk of Tirso's literary enemies, it is important not to group them together indiscriminately however. He drew hostile reaction from four distinct quarters. The opposition of clerics and moralists to his drama climaxed in a ban against Tirso by the Junta de Reformación in 1625. The publication of Góngora's *Polifemo* (1612) and his *Soledades* (1613-1617) sparked off a furious controversy on poetic style and language in which Tirso upheld the *habla llana* tradition and thus became a target of the *culteranistas.* In the third place, Tirso refers obsessively through his works to the envy and malice, real or imagined, excited in

---

2. Theodore S. Beardsley Jr.'s *Hispano-classical Translations Printed Between 1482 and 1699* (Pittsburgh: Duquesne Univ. Prsss, 1970), shows that Spanish translating activity of the Classics achieved a distinct peak in the period 1600-1624. These years virtually frame the life of the debate on the *comedia,* and perhaps a conservative intellectual reaction (?) may explain both classicizing tendencies.

rival authors by his own success.[3] Finally, the area of our present inquiry, Tirso defended the *comedia nueva* against the aesthetic condemnations of the neo-Aristotelian critics.

We have warned that Tirso's theories are eclectic and if they derive in part from older ideas, this should cause the reader no surprise. As to their reconstruction here, it would be possible simply to summarize Tirso's remarks in a convenient sequence with commentary, but this would certainly be a lengthy and repetitious process. Since his scheme derives from a set of theories of poetry well known in the history of poetics, a more succinct and pertinent approach is to develop Tirso's views as they follow or improve on Grecolatin or Renaissance prototypes. As to these, M. H. Abrams[4] distinguishes four main theoretical categories: the mimetic, the pragmatic, the expressive and the objective. The first two are directly relevant to Tirso, and the other two may be present in embryonic form. In addition, Tirso seems to have elaborated an aesthetic voluntarism, derived from a blend of Scholasticism and an awakening sense of the need for artistic freedom. Our exposé will be, then, a survey of Tirso's handling or restatement of familiar ideas, an analysis of his original contributions to literary theory, and a final section on what I have termed the "active participation" of the audience.

The Mimetic Theory

According to the mimetic or representational theory of poetry, the source or occasion of the poem is the universe; art reproduces aspects of the sensible world. When Doña Serafina says in *El vergonzoso en palacio*: "¿Quieres ver los epítetos/ que a la comedia he hallado? / De la vida es un traslado..." (II, xiv, 468), Tirso is echoing a critical tradition that goes back to Aristotle's *Poetics* and found its most famous formulation in the statement attributed to Cicero by Donatus:

---

3. The words of the seventh Castilian in *Antona García* have usually been regarded as autobiographical. The refugee from Madrid complains: "Pues véndese agora tanta/ envidia e ingenios diversos,/ que hay hombre que haciendo versos/ a los demás se adelanta;/ y aunque más fama le den/ es tal (la verdad os digo)/ que quita el habla a su amigo/ cada vez que escribe bien." (III, iii, 439).

4. I am indebted to Professor Abrams' distinguished studies on poetics, *The Mirror and the Lamp: Romantic Theory and the Critical Tradition* (New York: Oxford Univ. Press, 1953), and the article "Poetry, Theories of," in *Encyclopedia of Poetry and Poetics,* ed. Preminger et al. (Princeton: Princeton Univ. Press, 1965), pp. 639-49. All pages references are to Prof. Abrams' article.

"Comoediam esse Cicero ait imitationem vitae, speculum consuetudinis, imaginem veritatis."[5] Imitation is the Latin rendering of *mimesis* and reappears variously in the modern languages as "image," "reflection," "copy," "transfer," etc. To quote Abrams: "The focus of attention is thus on the relation between the imitable and the imitation, and the primary aesthetic criterion is 'truth to nature' " (loc. cit., p. 641).

This emphasis on "truth to nature" led Renaissance critics and proponents of the Spanish neo-Aristotelian school to formulate a rather narrow conception of mimesis as a literal copying, and, since according to Cicero the comedy was a mirror of custom, to insist on verisimilitude as the critique of actions and life portrayed on the stage. The stress on verisimilitude, furthermore, led Italian Renaissance critics to evolve the doctrine of the three Unities (esp. Castelvetro), extrapolating their conclusions from stray comments in the *Poetics*.[6] The importance of verisimilitude (about which Spanish playwrights and critics agreed) was, however, variously understood, and since both sides derived different conclusions from the same premise, this became one of their most interesting and fruitful points of contention.

In the *Arte nuevo,* Lope agreed with Robortelli that the playwright should: "Imitar las acciones de los hombres,/ Y pintar de aquel siglo las costumbres" (ll. 52-53). Later, however, arguing for the combination of comic and tragic elements in a single play, Lope proclaimed the wider principle: that art should imitate nature in all her compendious variety, since that is nature's true source of beauty and delight: "Que aquesta variedad deleyta mucho,/ Buen ejemplo nos da naturaleza/ Que por tal variedad tiene belleza" (*Arte nuevo,* ll. 178-80).

---

5. Lope updates these commonplaces in a memorable passage from Act I, i of his *Castigo sin venganza* (1631). The Duke is speaking: "¿Agora sabes, Ricardo,/ que es la comedia un espejo,/ en que el necio, el sabio, el viejo,/ el mozo, el fuerte, el gallardo,/ el rey, el gobernador,/ la doncella, la casada,/ siendo al ejemplo escuchada/ de la vida y del honor,/ retrata nuestras costumbres,/ o livianas o severas,/ mezclando burlas y veras,/ donaires y pesadumbres? " (ll. 214-25).

6. Aristotle says somewhat elliptically in the *Poetics* that tragedy endeavors to confine itself to one revolution of the sun – a statement construed by Italian critics such as Cintio and Robortelli to mean no play's action may exceed a twenty-four hour limit. The Unity of Place was a fiction deduced from the other two, and in some commentaries the Unity of Action actually became *subservient* to those of Place and Time. According to Spingarn, *Literary Criticism in the Renaissance* (New York, 1963): ". . . in fact, Castelvetro specifically says that the Unity of Action is not essential to the drama, but is merely made expedient by the requirements of Time and Place" (p. 62). This is a complete inversion of Aristotle.

Tirso, in his most famous defense of the *comedia* (*Cigarral primero*), puts in the mouth of a "presumido natural de Toledo" the standard charge that his *Vergonzoso en palacio* broke the bounds of literary propriety established by the Ancients. It violated all the Unities and stretched the Unity of Time by an unpardonable month and a half. Going then to the issue of verisimilitude, the speaker contends: "[...] pues aun en este término parece imposible pudiese disponerse una dama illustre y discreta a querer tan ciegamente a un pastor, hacerle su secretario, declararle por enigmas su voluntad y, últimamente, arriesgar su fama a la arrojada determinación de un hombre tan humilde que, en la opinión de ambos, el mayor blasón de su linaje eran unas abarcas, su solar una cabaña y sus vasallos un pobre hato de cabras y bueyes."

Don Alejo's famous rebuttal that follows is derived from the fundamental twin tenets of Lope's *Arte nuevo*: the need to delight the audience and the *comedia*'s conformity to modern taste and "laws" ("... las leyes de lo que ahora se usa ..." to quote Don Alejo). On the specific issue of verisimilitude, the speaker places a criterion of psychological probability over any rule avoiding mechanical infraction of the Unities. For, he says, if the Greeks prescribed that a comedy should represent actions that could morally only take place in twenty-four hours, how can a lover fall in love, woo his lady, court her and marry her between the morning and evening of a single day? How can the dramatist portray jealousy, despair, hope and the other emotions of love, without which the depiction of passion is nothing? Or how can a lover give proof of his constancy in one day? Through his spokesman, Tirso affirms that such affronts to the audience's credulity throw up much graver obstacles to verisimilitude and psychological acceptance than the fact that an action should run into several days. Just as an historical narrative reduces widely-spaced events to the time necessary for their relation, so the *comedia* must imitate the natural depiction of lovers' actions and give the illusion of a time-span consonant with a genuinely perfect action, even if the play lasts only two hours in real life.

This capital point in Tirso's defense, the condensation of multiple events into an albeit illusory framework that can contain them in accord with inner logic and psychological probability, leads him to invoke the parallel of painting. The canvas, by the use of perspective and receding impressions of distance, *persuades* the senses to accept its visual significance. If this license is admitted in one artistic medium, how much more easily will poetry achieve such illusory effect through its articulate verbality. The use of the word 'persuade' is noteworthy here, since Tirso thereby indicates his consciousness that art is always an illusion which secures the "willing suspension of disbelief" (Coleridge) of the beholder. In this manner, Tirso surpasses the literal-mindedness of the neo-Aristotelian critics and their insistence on mechanical implementation of the mimetic theory.

In this same passage dealing with verisimilitude, the following definition of the *comedia* is tossed out carelessly in a parenthesis: "... que es una imagen y representación de su argumento...." Though unobtrusive, this is a claim of considerable originality. In the debate on imitation, it had been maintained *ad nauseam* by both sides that the comedy was an imitation of life. Tirso, including a new factor in the equation, states that it is an image or representation of its own argument. In a very practical sense, of course, the play seen on the stage is always the visible representation of an action set down in a script. By the same token, a symphony 'exists' aurally as it is performed and 'potentially' in any edition of the score. A painting on the other hand, is the unique expression of its own conception, since the plastic arts do not necessitate a time-dimension. Tirso correctly states that the play we see on stage is not an image of life at all, but merely of itself; the active representation of a passive artifact of the imagination.[7]

The philosophical and theoretical implications of such a claim, as I have said, are considerable. According to Tirso, between the art and life equation, a new factor must be interposed: the argument or plot, the tale of the dramatist derived from his own experience of life and nature. The play then exists in a dual capacity; once as we see it in real life before our eyes, and again as it is a representation of its creator's inner vision. It is easy to spin paradoxes of self-reference out of this duality, and when Tirso introduces play-within-play into an action, he is tacitly indulging in this game. This not only makes the Baroque theater an ideal model for a skeptical view of experience, it also gives the clue to Tirso's most typical manner of dramatic procedure: in that

---

7. This odd double vision is sometimes extended by Tirso to people. Naboth in *La mujer que manda en casa*, surveying the supposedly sleeping Jezabal, sees her as both herself and an image of herself simultaneously. He soliloquizes: "La cama Real, los vestidos/ reverencian bien nacidos,/ el sello Real, el retrato,/ en su original su copia/ goza la Reina esculpida/ pues mientras está dormida/ es la imagen de si propria" (I, viii, 592).

he liberates the behavior of the protagonist towards his fellow characters.

For raising the intermediary status of the play proper (i.e. its argument in written form) to an order of reality between the natural world from which it derives and — *mutatis mutandis* — to which it later actively addresses itself, has the effect of keeping the play always in an illusory realm. Tirso uses this design to promote his protagonist (customarily a woman) to an unusually privileged position with respect to the remaining *dramatis personae,* who become collective dupes or victims in a metatheatrical situation. Since the dramatic universe never ceases to be a theater, a representation of its action, the protagonist can slip in and out of a multitude of roles, assumed identities and effortlessly spun fictions, in order to control the actions of the rest.

The ultimate consequence of such a design is to maintain a subtle but strong chain of conspirational intimacy between author, protagonist and audience. Hence, notably in the *comedias de enredo,* one of Tirso's distinctive trademarks as a dramatist is his systematic exploitation of the subsidiary illusion as a method of plot generation and his promotion of the protagonist to the role of co-creator of the plot with him. This complementary practice of illusion and deceit by the protagonist is so much a Tirsian ploy, in fact, that the whole of Chapter III is devoted to exploring it in detail.

The Hybrid Drama of the Moderns

The enlarged understanding of imitation and verisimilitude propounded by Lope and his school must inevitably have raised, and still does raise, a range of new theoretical questions regarding the hybrid *tragicomedia.* It is clear from his defense of the *comedia* in the *Cigarrales de Toledo* that Tirso regarded the new form not as a mixture or juxtaposition of the comic and tragic genres so much as an intimate blending or grafting of the two. The new *comedia* selected all that was best of comedy and tragedy and transformed them into a separate species of drama.

Tirso reaches this conclusion quite explicitly through what is really an early theory of progress. While conceding the respect due to the Greeks in having invented the drama, Tirso's spokesman, Don Alejo, argues that succeeding generations may improve upon ancient prototypes. The progress made in the manufacture of musical instruments is cited as an example. Tirso then extends his argument to the realm of nature which, he states, cannot normally vary in the regeneration of its species: the pear-tree will always produce pears, the oak-tree its acorns etc. Certain varieties, however, are descended from a parent type (the various species of vegetable and fruit marrows, for example) and man, by his skill, can stimulate a similar process artifically. The *durazno*, when grafted onto the quince, produces a distinct new fruit, the peach, which combines the best characteristics of both. If, in the 'artificial' realm of human invention, man is free to impose changes on his own artifacts, and in the natural realm he can also effect changes, why should he not then have the right to vary the norms of the drama? Why cannot he graft the comic onto the tragic and create an agreeable hybrid that combines the best of each genre? Señorita Juana de José Prades, commenting on this aspect of the *comedia*'s undoubted originality, writes: "Lo que sí es novedad, en cambio, es la mezcla 'sui generis' de elementos trágicos y cómicos propria de los dramaturgos españoles de la Comedia nueva."[8]

Tirso's fullest statement on this variety in the *comedia* is to be found in *El vergonzoso en palacio* (II, xiv). Doña Serafina is speaking:

> ¿Qué fiesta o juego se halla
> que no le ofrezcan los versos?
> En la comedia los ojos
> ¿no se deleitan y ven
> mil cosas que hacen que estén
> olvidados sus enojos?
> La música ¿no recrea
> el oído, y el discreto
> no gusta allí del conceto
> y la traza que desea?
> Para el alegre, ¿no hay risa?
> Para el triste, ¿no hay tristeza?
> ¿Para el agudo agudeza?
> Allí el necio, ¿no se avisa?
> El ignorante, ¿no sabe?

---

8. See *Arte nuevo de hacer comedias*, ed. and preliminary study by Juana de José Prades (Madrid: CSIC, 1971), p. 122. One might add that apart from rearguard action by the French, European drama since the seventeenth century has remained a hybrid genre, indifferent to exclusive categories. As Ezra Pound well observes in his *Spirit of Romance*: ". . . he [Lope] gave Spain her dramatic literature and from Spain Europe derived her modern theatre." Quoted from Luis C. Pérez and F. Sánchez Escribano, *Afirmaciones de Lope de Vega sobre preceptiva dramática* (Madrid: CSIC, 1961), p. 7.

> ¿No hay guerra para el valiente,
> consejos para el prudente,
> y autoridad para el grave?
> Moros hay si quieres moros;
> si apetecen tus deseos
> torneos, te hacen torneos;
> si toros, correrán toros.
> ¿Quieres ver los epítetos
> que a la comedia he hallado?
> De la vida es un traslado
> sustento de los discretos
> dama del entendimiento,
> de los sentidos banquete,
> de los gustos ramillete,
> esfera del pensamiento,
> olvido de los agravios,
> manjar de diversos precios,
> que mata de hambre a los necios
> y satisface a los sabios.
> Mira lo que quieres ser
> de aquestos dos bandos.
> (II, xiv, 467-68)

The whole burden of this passage is to the effect that the *comedia* contains everything there is in life or that one could ever wish to see. The following propositions are suggested by Tirso:

a) The new *comedia* recognizes no limits in genre or matter.

b) All things: Moors, tournaments, bulls, *a piacere,* may be suggested by its verses.

c) Laughter and sadness go hand in hand.

d) It contains serious elements, moral counsel and authority for prudent persons.

e) It contains tragic elements.

f) The *comedia* is a transfer (*traslado*) of life.

g) The pleasures and mental subtlety of the *comedia* enchant both the senses and the intellect, making the audience participate in a kind of banquet.

Some of these propositions receive comment elsewhere in this chapter, but in our present context, Tirso's claim for the *comedia nueva*'s compendious variety lead, it seems me, to two important conclusions: that an untrammeled genre may depict *complexity* as well as variety; and that if comic elements are allowed in a serious play (one of the most frequent neo-Aristotelian complaints), then serious moments may be allowed in a comic play. As to the first point, pure tragedy or pure comedy obviously do not genuinely do justice to the complexity of life Life is never either/or, it is both. Tirso, in common with his contemporaries, had little patience with formal restrictions on what sort of scene they might or might not write in a given play; they drew on the whole gamut of experience according to aesthetic need, or the exigencies of the play's theme. When, of course, Tirso claims that all things may be represented, he does not literally mean that a herd of bulls should be driven across the stage.[9] As he makes clear in *La fingida Arcadia* (III, iii), these spectacles address themselves to the inner eyes they are "fiestas o juegos que ofrecen los versos."

As to the second point, the grafting together of two dramatic strains, this presupposes *ex definitione* that if there can be comedy in tragedy, then the inverse corollary is true: that there can be tragedy in comedy. This is a proposition that many critics, even in the modern day, have been unwilling to concede. Because tragedy was not cultivated as an individual genre, goes the argument, Spanish playwrights produced no tragedy. The following assessment by Gicovate is fairly typical: "Yet it is well known that Spain has 'not excelled in the tragic genre generally.' It seems futile to try to revise the judgment of history; it has become so ingrained in our thinking that even by default the certainty of Spain's lack of tragedy makes for a comfortable picture of literary history . . . ."[10] Dr. Gicovate relents a little, however, and makes what is surely the main point. Referring to Tirso's remark about grafting comedy on tragedy, he writes: "Tirso's pronouncement may have still another interest for us: it seems to defend Tirso's own plays, certainly those of his that mixed to serious concerns and tragic outcomes the effervescence of humor [. . .] The strange thing is, however, that, while an analysis of Lope's attempts reveals only a temperament unqualified for tragedy, *many of the most famous of Tirso's works are tragic in outcome at least*" (p. 333. My emphasis).

---

9. Despite this, live animals do seem to have been used in performances of some Tirsian dramas. The opening of *La mujer que manda en casa* appears to make clear that Queen Jezabel entered the stage mounted on horseback, with live dogs running in the retinue. Tirso's stage direction reads: "Música de todos géneros, y por una parte suben al tablado (habiendo venido a caballo al son de un clarín), en hábito de caza, JEZABEL, RAQUEL, CRISELIA y cazadores con perros, ballestas y venablos" (I, i, 586). The dogs proleptically suggest the demise of the villainous heroine, and the image of dogs pervades the play.

10. See B. Gicovate, "Observations on the Dramatic Art of Tirso de Molina," *Hispania*, 43 (1960), 328-37, at p. 333. He is quoting Miss Ivy McClelland.

There is nothing "strange" here at all. Of course Tirso was defending his own plays, among them a number of deeply serious dramas that have an undoubtedly tragic outcome (e.g. *El burlador de Sevilla, La venganza de Tamar, La mujer que manda en casa, La vida y muerte de Herodes, El condenado por desconfiado* inasmuch as the play is Paulo's tragedy). In his study *Tragedy: Serious Drama in Relation to Aristotle's Poetics* (London: Hogarth, 1957), F. L. Lucas makes the valuable and timely observation that the ancient sense of the term 'tragedy' was precisely that of serious drama, and that the notions of a story with an unhappy close, or a drama with an unhappy close, are medieval and modern accretions respectively (p. 25).

We do not need to hazard guesses as to the existence of serious elements in seventeenth-century Spanish comedy; the practitioners of the art were wholly aware of this dimension themselves. Lope de Vega, towards the end of his *Arte nuevo*, makes just this claim in a string of Latin verses — whether from his own pen or another's is still unclear — that run as follows: "quae gravia in mediis occurrant lusibus et quae/ jucundis fuerint seria mixta jocis? " (ll. 381-82). P. José López de Toro[11] has rendered these lines into Spanish blank verse as follows: "en medio de sus chanzas qué cuestiones/ serias propone o entre alegres bromas/ qué asuntos trascendentes va mezclando." In the present writer's judgment, the construing of Lope's *gravia* and *seria* as "cuestiones serias" and "asuntos trascendentes" respectively, do not seem overtranslations.[12] This is doubtless what Lope meant to imply, and the same sentiment is echoed in Doña Serafina's words: "... esfera del pensamiento/ que [...] satisface a los sabios." The objection could be raised that the serious truth of human life is not fully synonymous with some modern conceptions of tragedy, and this must be conceded if nomenclature is not to be violated. But to recognize the existence of serious issues in the *comedia* is already an important and necessary step, and there is further contemporary evidence that obliges us to take that step.

---

11. The Spanish version of P. José López de Toro is cited from F. Sánchez Escribano and A. Porqueras Mayo, *Preceptiva dramática española*, 2nd ed. (Madrid: Gredos, 1972), p. 165, n.

12. This view of the implicit seriousness of the Spanish comedy is shared by Prof. Everett W. Hesse in his recent book *La comedia y sus intérpretes* (Madrid: Castalia, 1972). See especially pp. 81-98, "La comedia como tragedia" and pp. 105-09, "El sentido serio de la comedia."

In the preliminaries to the *Burlas veras, o reprensión moral* of 1645 by Quiñones Benavente, there appears a laudatory *décima* from the hand of D. Juan de Herrera Sotomayor which reads:

> A la humana condición
> más que deleitas enseñas;
> hasta las veras desdeñas
> con misteriosa elección;
> pues cosas del mundo son
> cuantas tu pluma retrata
> tantas sentencias dilata,
> y a la verdad te acomodas,
> que el que hace burlas de todas
> es el que mejor las trata.[13]

The thrust of this syntactically opaque poem is clear: the *entremeses* of Benavente, conventionally thought of as comic, contain more than humor, they have a profound lesson on the human condition to teach. Though in his work truth is apparently scorned, by a strangely appropriate choice of materials, Benavente does indeed deal with matters of the world, displaying abundant wisdom and "accomodating" himself to truth. Herrera Sotomayor goes as far as to make the bold and, for our purposes, highly pertinent claim that the playwright or author who makes fun of everything is the man who treats life's questions the best. The major implication here is that the comic vein, by its inversion of values, can go to the heart of serious matters more effectively, more pungently and more profoundly than a conventionally serious homily. Serious matters presented in a serious vein may risk being tedious or even offensive in their condemnation of human imperfection. Benavente's uncanny aplomb in this hybrid art is what we must understand by the phrase "con misteriosa elección."

Tragic Elements in the *comedia*

The modern unwillingness to read between the lines of the Spanish *comedia*, thus not perceiving its profundity and seriousness in travesty, if not outright tragic implications, has established a number of false assumptions that it will be convenient to dispose of here. Rebuttals of

---

13. Quoted from Quiñones Benavente, *Burlas veras, o represensión moral* ed. Don Cayetano Rosell (Madrid, 1872). Rosell's text was based on the 1645 edition of *Burlas veras*. I am deeply indebted to Jack Sage of King's College, London for drawing my attention to this significant and little known *décima*.

these false assumptions cannot readily be reconstructed out of theoretical statements by Tirso or his fellow dramatists, but they are implicit in the seventeenth-century world picture and the actual practice of the *comedia nueva*. Miss Margaret Wilson, for example, has recently rejected the possibility of Spanish tragedy using a perplexing logic. She writes: "It is frequently maintained that true tragedy [...] can only arise in a climate in which faith and skepticism are in equilibrium. If skepticism predominates, it is pointless to look for any meaning in the universe. If faith predominates, the answers are already known; drama can illustrate them, but it cannot lead the spectator into an apprehension of any truth not already revealed to him. Christian tragedy, on this showing is an impossibility."[14]

Obviously, Miss Wilson understands by skepticism a *religious* skepticism that is fundamentally atheistic, its common modern meaning. The skepticism that we have earlier discussed in this book reaches the point of Christian Pyrrhonism in the sixteenth century with Erasmus, and the atheism of the *libertins* in mid-seventeenth-century France. The point, however, is that with the proper terminological safeguards, Spain could indeed be viewed as passing through a period of faith threatened by religious skepticism, while philosophic skepticism had become well entrenched in Spain by Tirso's time. In the theater, it reaches its highest expression in the hands of Calderón, whose very playtitles – *Gustos y disgustos no son más que imaginación. En esta vida, todo es verdad y todo mentira, La vida es sueño* – indicate the nature of the Christian's battle with the unreliability of the senses, at least, as a test of truth.

Miss Wilson also remarks that: "It is tempting, and even legitimate, to judge Golden Age Tragedy according to our modern concepts, and by this standard it may sometimes be found wanting" (p. 203). She finds difficulties, therefore, in the alienating effect of moral judgments forced upon us by the *comedia,* the absence of personal catharsis, the absence of some clear anagnorisis or recognition of guilt by the guilty etc.... This simply will not do, however; to tax Spanish drama by a *pot-pourri* of "modern concepts" and Aristotelian tags, while utterly disregarding the contemporary intellectual background of Spain, and then to complain that "Christian tragedy [...] is an impossibility," lacks all rhyme and reason. As has long been recognized, the Spanish

---

14. See W. Margaret Wilson, *Spanish Drama of the Golden Age* (Oxford: Pergamon, 1969), pp. 202-03.

drama was a national theater written for the people. The behavior portrayed on the stage was therefore geared to social standards and social patterns. Since life and its problems were dramatized principally according to patterns of group thinking and social consensus, the treatment of the agony of a single individual could have little place in the *corrales*. If tragic experience were to be conveyed at all, it would have to be as a communal disaster, or as a disaster precipitated by a group. Such is, indeed the case, as Professor A. A. Parker's valuable studies have begun to show. Discussing tragedy in Calderón specifically, Parker has developed the theory that responsibility for misdeeds in the best plays is diffused subtlely among a plurality of characters.[15] The protagonist is punished, but not all the guilt belongs to him. One might add that in some plays, those dealing with uxoricide for example, the victim is almost entirely innocent and the burden of guilt lies subtly diffused among other characters who suffer hardly at all; hence the sense of outrage which the playwright seeks to generate.

Spanish playwrights have further been accused in our modern day of conformism and unwillingness to pursue a tragic theme to its ultimate conclusion. The theoretical reasons for "retraction" in Golden Age drama have been set out in our first chapter, but some particularized discussion at this point may help to clarify the issue further. For where a play develops a potentially tragic theme and resolves it happily at the last moment, it is not enough to say the tragic implications have been removed. Among the most celebrated of comedies, Rojas Zorrilla's *Del rey abajo ninguno* provides us with just such an example. In that play, the hero García is thrown into a terrible dilemma because the man he thinks to be the king has attempted to seduce his wife, Blanca. Should he exact the vengeance demanded by the honor code? Yet in doing so he would violate the sacred person of the king.[16] García attempts to resolve this impasse by the immolation of Blanca, but collapses in nervous convulsion before he can actually strike the blow. The dilemma is ultimately resolved when García discovers the true identity of the offender (known to the audience from the start) and murders him

---

15. See A. A. Parker, "Towards a Definition of Calderonian Tragedy," *BHS*, 39 (1962), 222-37.
16. Regicide was not merely a theoretical issue in the early seventeenth century. Henry IV of Navarre fell victim to Ravaillac's dagger in 1610, and in 1642, Charles I of England was "legally" beheaded by action of Parliament. An attempt to blow up both King James *and* his Parliament failed in 1605.

forthwith. No one, the king not excepted, shall escape the wrath of an offended husband.

But, we may ask, though everything is put to right when the curtain falls, what about the deeper issue? García has genuinely agonized over the legitimacy of murdering the king. Now suppose the king *had* been the offender (as the king is in *La estrella de Sevilla*), what then? During the play, the audience would inevitably have been reminded of the horror of regicide, and the more reflective could well have framed the question: 'if a monarch abuses his vassals' honor and the contract by which he holds power from them, can it be legitimate to kill him?' In view of the notoriety of P. Mariana S.J.'s *De rege* (1599), the doctrines of Machiavelli, and constant theoretical scrutiny of kingship, such reflections would be by no means far fetched. (Of the four great tragedies of Tirso's contemporary, Shakespeare, only *Othello* does not contain one or more regicides). Thus, in spite of the so-called conformism of Spanish dramatists, the revolutionary and the almost unthinkable may be presented by implication and tragic consequences, at a point beyond the play, can be followed through by those who seek them.

The Pragmatic Theory

The title of Tirso's second prose miscellany, *Deleitar aprovechando*, is a paraphrase of Horace's *utile dulci*.[17] According to this so-called pragmatic theory of poetry, the occasion of the poem is its audience; the poem aims to afford them delight and moral profit. As the theoretical basis of poetry, this notion had become commonplace by the late sixteenth century, and though the Lopean school consciously put delight before profit, the *comedia* abounds with the sententiousness that was the hallmark of almost all seventeenth-century writing.

Inseparable from the concept of poetry's pragmatic goal, is an emphasis on the poetic skills of native wit and craftsmanship as the

---

17. The lines where Horace gave most memorable expression to this principle run as follows:

> Aut prodesse volunt, aut delectare poetae
> . . . .
> Omne tulit punctum, qui miscuit utile dulci,
> Lectorem delectando, pariterque monendo.
> (*Ars Poetica*, ll. 333, 343-44)

means to this end.[18] On this relationship, M. H. Abrams has observed that: "We recognize pragmatic critics of poetry [...] by their tendency to regard a poem as a made object, a craftsmanlike product which (after due allowance for the play of natural talent, inspired moments, and felicities beyond the reach of art) is still, for the most part, deliberately designed to achieve foreknown ends [...]" (loc. cit., p. 642). In her prefatory *décima* to *Los cigarrales de Toledo,* Doña María de San Ambrosio singled out precisely the twin qualities of native wit (*ingenio*) and craftsmanship (*estudio*) as cause for praise of the author: "Sólo vuestro ingenio alcanza/ con el arte y la experiencia [...]/ délfico aliento de infusa [...]."

Towards the end of the Introduction to the same work, Tirso repeats this idea in a forceful allegory, by means of the famous water-tableau in which he himself figures as recipient of poetic laurels: "Tirso, que aunque humilde pastor de Manzanares, halló en la llaneza de Toledo mejor acogida que en su patria – tan apoderada de la envidia extranjera –, llegó en un pequeño barco, aunque curioso, hecho todo un jardín que hallara lugar entre los hibleos, y en medio dél una palma altísima, sobre cuyos últimos cogollos estaba una corona de laurel." Tirso (further identified by mention of the purple-bar insignia of the Mercedarians on his breast) climbs towards the laurel crown, borne aloft by two wings; on one is inscribed the device *Ingenio* and on the other *Estudio.* These wings bear him clear of the snakes of envy below and procure for Tirso: "... la gloriosa consecución de sus trabajos."

In the same work (*Cigarral primero*), during the post-mortem of his *Vergonzoso en palacio,* Tirso addresses himself to the specific issue of the didactic efficacy of that play, and by extension, to the pragmatic function of his work in general. This he achieves by introducing an unnamed devil's advocate into the debate on the *comedia,* in order to raise the question of the morality of his drama. The success of his *Vergonzoso* in delighting its audience was beyond doubt, but was the work indecent? The straw critic alleges that the play offered the very opposite of moral edification and brands the two sisters, Magdalena and Serafina as brazen, shameless creatures. The latter in particular is found

---

18. Both these terms are also Horatian:
> Natura fieret laudabile carmen, an arte,
> Quaestum est? Ego nec *studium* sine divite vena,
> Nec rude quid possit video *ingenium* ...
> (*Ars Poetica,* ll. 408-10. My emphasis.)

guilty of impropriety, ignorance and "una bajeza indigna de la más plebeya hermosura . . ." Don Alejo, as attorney for the defense, makes no direct rebuttal of this charge, but later, after the performance of *El celoso prudente* in the *Cigarral quinto*, triumphant claims are made for Tirso's morality and scrupulous compliance with the canons of good taste and pragmatic art.

Don Juan de Salcedo points to that play's warnings against jealousy and lying, its praise of prudence, constancy, keeping faith, paternal obligation, loyalty etc., and maintains that the severest prude could find nothing to blame therein. He proclaims that the modern Spanish theater is now cleansed of all indecency, delights as it teaches and teaches while giving pleasure. Don García agrees in a copybook expression of the pragmatic formula, replying that advice in disguise must be rendered palatable by art; the pill must be sugared. He concludes: "Ya las verdades que no se visten con metáforas ingeniosas y versos deleitables, dan en rostro y son dificultosas de digerir. Y aquí vienen tan bien guisadas, que el más delicado estómago las recibe, siguiéndose el provecho que no hiciera a venir sin adorno."

A more truly heartfelt Tirsian proclamation that art affords both pleasure *and* instruction is to be found in the actual Dedication of *Deleitar aprovechando*. Here Tirso states that of all five works thus far printed, *Deleitar* was his personal favorite, and that he had spent a year exclusively in its composition. Tirso explains he had a desire to write an edifying hagiographical work centering around three different saints, but had rejected the possibility of presenting such material in dramatic form. Tirso's five reasons for this decision are interesting as comments on the theater practices of his day, but illustrate even better his degree of disenchantment with the Madrid public and motives for writing a more consciously moralizing work.

In the first place he states that the contemporary theatergoers were unenthusiastic about sacred subjects; they were either filled with envy or ignorance (if indeed, adds Tirso in an embittered aside, there is any distinction between the two). Thirdly, the genuine piety of such works tended to be submerged under elaborate stage carpentry and painted scenery, and furthermore modern taste inclined towards plays replete with prodigious events and far-fetched miracles. This, Tirso adds, despite the strict injunctions of the Council of Trent against the fabrication of pseudo-miracles. Fifthly and lastly, the longest run a stage play in any category could expect to enjoy at Madrid was some two weeks and in the provinces some two or three days! Within three years, most of them were forgotten.

As far as the possibility of printed books was concerned, Tirso claims that hagiography in simple, narrative form was considered tedious; even the titles acted as a deterrent to the reader, and such books involved publishers in a financial loss. Novels and printed collections of comedies, however, sold by the dozen in a steady, secularized market. The solution he had hit on then was to sugar the pill, to write an improving miscellany that would be delightful without sacrificing due piety.[19] In a celebrated maxim, he continues, "Novelemos a lo santo, y entre lo marañoso y entretejido de lo raro de sus vidas fabriquemos estos tres panales que, lisonjeando al apetito enfermo, comunique confitado lo medecinal de sus ejemplos." The combination of the strange but true stories of saints' lives, clothed in the techniques of the popular novel, would prove irresistible and would rival the mere fictions of earlier writers (he cites Boccaccio, Giraldi Cintio, Bandello, Heliodorus, Fernán Méndez Pinto, the English Jesuit Barclay, the chivalresque, pastoral and picaresque novelists, Céspedes y Meneses' *El español Gerardo,* Cervantes' *Persiles* etc., etc.).

Despite Tirso's somewhat inflated hopes, *Deleitar aprovechando* was only reprinted once in the seventeenth century (1677) and once in the eighteenth (1765). Although the third panel of the triptych, *El bandolero,* has considerable charm and power, the novel form was not Tirso's forte, and undoubtedly the heavier didacticism here, combined with a rather involved and adorned style, detract from the narrative's flow. What the Dedication and Tirso's earlier remarks do illustrate, however, is the fact that he held to the pragmatic theory seriously, despite its unoriginality, and believed firmly that native talent and assiduous craftsmanship were indispensable prerequisites of fine writing.

Tirso's Aesthetic Voluntarism

So far we have discussed theories of writing that tend to minimize the role of the poet himself. The expressive theory (that poetry is an overflow of the poet's inner feelings) and the objective theory (that the

---

19. Tirso's metaphor describing the blending of the pleasant and the useful ["... a imitación de la abeja (que con su artificio y las flores de los romerales saca un *tercer mixto* que, saludable y dulce, ni es totalmente tomillo, ni romero, ni del todo degenera de sus virtudes y sustancia..."] is highly reminiscent of the formula describing the grafting of comedy on tragedy outlined above.

poem is its own created universe) transfer the emphasis to the individual writer and both theories have Renaissance precedents.[20] When we see these ideas foreshadowed in Tirso's writings, however, they seem to spring more from a protest for artistic freedom and an enquiry into the role of the imagination than anything else. I shall adduce two brief passages to support this claim and then outline what I have more broadly termed Tirso's aesthetic voluntarism.

In the Dedication to the *Tercera parte* (1634), the author, signing himself Francisco Lucas de Avila, writes the following of his uncle: "Gusano es su autor de seda: de su misma sustancia ha labrado la numerosa cantidad de telas con que cuatrocientas y más Comedias vistieron por veinte años a sus profesores, sin desnudar, corneja, ajenos asuntos ni disfrazar pensamientos adoptivos."[21] Two points are of great interest here: art as an expression of the poet's inner substance, and the premium set on originality; both features of the expressive theory, especially as developed by the Romantics.

The comparison of Tirso to a silkworm illustrates that the emphasis here is assuredly within; the poet spins out of himself. The Dionysiac associations of Tirso's pseudonym (i.e. Thyrsus = the wand of Bacchic revels), stressing poetic transport, as well as his scrutiny of intimate human reactions under stress fit well with a decided interest in the actual workings of the individual's creative faculties. The second claim that Tirso was no jackdaw (i.e. a literary thief) gives a theoretical basis to Tirso's practice of self-plagiarism, about which a considerable critical

---

20. The chief historical source for the expressive theory was Longinus' essay *On the Sublime*. Longinus' tract was published in the original Greek by Robortelli in 1554 and later in Latin, but its period of greatest influence may be dated from the middle of the seventeenth century. According to Theodore S. Beardsley Jr., op. cit. supra, no translation of Longinus appeared in Spain before 1699 and it is impossible to surmise whether the dramatists of the *comedia nueva* ever read the work. One of the earliest statements of the objective theory may be found in Sidney's *Defense of Poesy* (1583). A Spanish translation of this work was available in the early 1600's. In a letter dated Feb. 7th, 1974, Professor Edward C. Riley kindly informs me that an edition of the work is being prepared for the press by a British scholar. At the time of writing, Professor Riley was unable to recall the exact projected date of publication.

21. The question of the identity of the author in this instance has been impugned by Cotarelo, Blanca de los Ríos Lampérez and others. For the purposes of poetic theory, it is immaterial whether Lucas de Avila or his uncle actually penned the Dedication, since their intimacy was evidently very considerable.

literature has accumulated in recent years.[22] We may deduce from this distaste for borrowing, moreover, that if Tirso regarded the imitation of alien models with contempt, he therefore felt his own inner experience and nature to be the raw material of his drama.

The primacy of internal inspiration over external is also proclaimed in a passage that, on the most liberal reading, could be classed in the objective category. Refuting, as author and not in character, charges that his *Vergonzoso en palacio* contravened historicity, Tirso exclaims (*Cigarral primero*): " ¡Como si la licencia de Apolo se estrechase a la recolección histórica y no pudiese fabricar, sobre cimientos de personas verdaderas arquitecturas del ingenio fingidas! "

Here the dramatist claims that history only provides a basis for drama, over which the poet's imagination plays and which it works into a new fictional artifact. To be sure, this distinction owes a debt to Aristotle's division of history (life as it is or was) and poetry (life as it should be),[23] but against the standard Platonic charge that poets were liars, Renaissance apologists of poetry were driven to maintain that the poet actually transcended nature and created a new realm.[24] A good Tirsian example of this poetic license is his *La elección por la virtud*, where, by altering the chronological events of the life of Pope Sixtus V and adding a variety of miraculous occurences, Tirso heightens their dramatic effect. Guastavino Gallent has observed of this process: "Por todo lo expuesto comprobamos cómo Tirso toma el material histórico

---

22. On Tirso's self-plagiarism, see the following: G. E. Wade, "Tirso's Self-Plagiarism in Plot," *HR*, 4 (1936), 55-65; E. H. Templin, "Another Instance of Tirso's Self-Plagiarism," *HR*, 5 (1937), 176-80; André Nougué, "A propos de l'auto-imitation dans le théâtre de Tirso de Molina," *BH*, 64 (1962), 209-11.

23. Characteristically, this distinction was not lost on Lope de Vega who advised dramatists to give a story at least an appearance of probability and verisimilitude, but to recognize the special claims of poetry. In the *Jerusalén conquistada* he writes: "Que la historia, pinta las cosas hechas, y la Poesía como pudieran ser." Quoted by Pérez and Sánchez Escribano, op. cit. at p. 176. See also the study of A. A. Parker, "History and Poetry: the Coriolanus theme in Calderón," *Hispanic Studies in Honour of I. González Llubera* (Oxford, 1959), 211-24.

24. Sir Philip Sidney wrote in 1583: "Only the poet, disdaining to be tied to any such subjection, lifted up with the vigor of his own invention, doth grow, in effect, into another nature, in making things either better than nature bringeth forth, or, quite anew, forms such as never were in nature . . . ." From *The Defense of Poesy*, ed. Albert S. Cook (Boston, 1890), p. 7.

de que dispone [. . .] lo maneja con entera libertad poética y lo adapta a su propia visión dramática."[25]

But the notion of the poem as object depends on the *creative* capacity of the imagination as distinct from its purely mimetic one. Therefore what the imagination actually is and what role it plays in poetic creation is an important question. In a striking account of the creative process (*Vergonzoso*, II, xiii), it will be seen that Tirso moves away from the Aristotelian view of poetry as akin to knowledge (i.e. images from nature reproduced by the phantasy and abstracted by reason into ideas), and subordinates the imagination (or *sensus communis* in Scholastic terminology) and even the intellect, to the will. To this system I have given the name aesthetic voluntarism.

In the scene preceding Doña Serafina's oft-quoted panegyric of the *comedia* from Act II of *El vergonzoso,* her lover Don Antonio delivers an intriguing lecture on painting to his accomplice, himself an artist. His words constitute a highly elaborate praise of Serafina's beauty, conceived as a metaphor of spiritual painting of the beloved inside the lover's mind. Separated by so short a space from a deliberate defense of the *comedia,* however, the disquisition assumes unusual interest as an analysis of the creative process in general:

DON ANTONIO:	Pintores somos los dos;
	ya yo el retrato he copiado,
	que me enamora y abrasa.
PINTOR:	No entiendo ese pensamiento.
	(II, xiii, 466)

The explanation given by Don Antonio takes the form of a gloss on Aristotle's *Poetics,* hence as much an analysis of poetic creation as of creation in the fine arts. The full exposition runs as follows:

DON ANTONIO:	Naipe es el entendimiento,
	pues le llama tabla rasa
	a mil pinturas sujeto
	Aristóteles.
PINTOR:	Bien dices.
DON ANTONIO:	Los colores y matices
	son especies del objeto
	que los ojos que le miran
	al sentido común dan;

---

25. See Guillermo Guastavino Gallent, "Sobre 'La elección por la virtud' de Tirso," *RABM,* 27 (Jan.-June, 1965), 51-63, at p. 57.

	que es obrador donde están
	cosas que el ingenio admiran,
	tan solamente en bosquejo
	hasta con luz distinta
	las ilumina y pinta
	el entendimiento, espejo
	que a todas da claridad.
	Pintadas las pone en venta;
	y para esto las presenta
	a la reina voluntad,
	mujer de buen gusto y voto,
	que ama el bien perpetuamente,
	verdadero o aparente,
	como no sea bien ignoto;
	que lo que no es conocido
	nunca por ella es amado.
PINTOR:	Desa suerte lo ha enseñado
	el filósofo.
DON ANTONIO:	Traído
	de la pintura el caudal,
	todos los lienzos descoge,
	y entre ellos compra y escoge,
	una vez bien y otras mal:
	pónele el marco de amor,
	y como en verle se huelga,
	en la memoria le cuelga
	que es su camarín mayor.
	(II, xiii, 466-67)

This passage, complicated by metaphor within metaphor, seems to say the following: the understanding is a plain card (or *tabula rasa*) sensitive to a thousand paintings or images in nature. Colors and shades are the species (or outward accidental aspects) of an object which are transferred to the *sensus communis* through the eyes. This common sensory is a workshop which amazes the *ingenio* (the creational or subrational faculty of the artist) but only in an unshaped sketchform. Then comes understanding (the regulative function of mind) with a different sort of light which illuminates and paints these wondrous sense impressions, like a mirror shedding clarity on all of them.

Tirso now changes metaphor slightly, or rather adds a new one, by introducing the comparison of the sale of paintings. Once thus painted, the elucidated marvels are placed on sale. To achieve this, the understanding submits them to sovereign will (compared to a female buyer of good taste and discrimination) who perpetually loves the good (a pun on the word *bien* meaning both material 'goods' or articles, and the morally good), whether this good be true or apparent, just provided it is not an unknown good, since what is unknown is never loved by the will. Once the store of paintings is brought for appraisal, she spreads out the canvases and among them buys and chooses, well on one occasion, badly on others. She places the picture-frame of love around one canvas and since it is her pleasure to see it, hangs the framed picture in her memory which is her largest dressing-room (either in a theater or behind an altar for the dressing of images – another pun?). Don Antonio finishes by pirouetting brilliantly through the same sequence of metaphors and applying them to his love for Serafina.

Before attempting to apply the sense of this display to the creative process, it would be as well to elucidate some lines further. Tirso's analysis begins as a gloss on Aristotle's *Poetics* (while also being a metaphor about love), characteristically couched in Scholastic terminology. With the passage on the submission of mental artifacts to the will, however, Tirso's argument seems to spill over into the realm of Scholastic "faculty" psychology. The final remark about memory completes the stock medieval picture of the rational soul as being comprised of memory, reason and imagination.

According to St. Augustine, however, will was subordinate to reason and in this he was followed by St. Thomas, who gave the view the imprint of his authority. Beside the Thomist view, there existed since the thirteenth century a growing counterview called Scotism. By Tirso's time, the Scotistic school was flourishing in Spain, and was officially confirmed at the general chapter of the Franciscan Order held at Toledo in 1633. According to Duns Scotus and Ockham after him, it is the will and not the intellect that is the superior power in man, for man's ultimate end consists of love of, rather than in knowledge of God. This supremacy of the will or voluntarism was always associated with the Franciscans and is of a piece with that Order's mystical tendencies. Since the Mercedarians were closest to the Franciscans in their outlook, it is not surprising to see Tirso talking of *la reina voluntad* in the passage under discussion.

The lines: "... que ama el bien perpetuamente,/ verdadero o aparente,/ como no sea bien ignoto;/ que lo que no es conocido/ nunca por ella es amado," present greater difficulties, however; they seem to make an intellectual reservation about will's love of the good. In ethical voluntarism, it is what is desired that fixes men's actions, not human reason. In the attainment of a given desire, different appetitive demands are subordinated towards a given end according to prudence. The good depends therefore on the satisfaction of the will or appetite, and the bad on aversion. Tirso makes the reassurance that what is not known cannot be the object of either desire or aversion, and that the ultimate end of the will is the perpetual love of good (i.e. God).[26]

Having made this ethical reservation, Tirso can confidently assert that in the creative process the will is the final arbiter over the imagination and the intellect, and when she errs (i.e. when a work of art is flawed for any reason), this is essentially an aesthetic error and not an ethical or moral one. The will is the equivalent of artistic discrimination and the act of choosing in the ordination of the materials of a work of art. It must be stressed that it is the *individual* will of the artist that is implied here by Tirso. That is to say, the individual disposes his material according to inner, psychological criteria; he possesses an artistic freedom that is all but declared a principle of poetic liberty. This, with Tirso's stress on originality and the preference for spinning out of his own, inner substance, prefigures the expressive theories of the eighteenth century. Tirso's voluntarism is not limited to the aesthetic sphere by any means, as we shall see; it characterizes the ethical behavior of his protagonists and is reflected in Tirso's obsession with prudence and discretion, all matters taken up more fully in the following chapter.

Active Participation

Among the string of epithets which Serafina attaches to the *comedia* we found the following:

>Sustento de los discretos
>dama del entendimiento,
>de los sentidos banquete,
>de los gustos ramillete,
>esfera del pensamiento,

---

26. The painter's reply: "Desa suerte lo ha enseñado/ el filósofo . . ." indicates that the source of this doctrine is also Aristotle, since he was the only philosopher honored with this elliptical soubriquet. Aristotle distinguished between the irascible and the concupiscible will and in an even more elaborate analysis of the operations of the intellect and the will (*El amor médico*, III, v, 1005), Tirso repeats this distinction. In the same passage, Tirso reaffirms the supremacy and the nobility of the human will: "Formada la intelección,/ la voluntad, *que es quien rige/ todo el hombre, como reina,/ o la reprueba o elige* [. . .] La voluntad, que del alma/ es potencia noble y libre . . ." (my emphasis). See also the Duchess's questions to Don Pedro on the subject of creation, imagination and will in *Amor y celos hacen discretos*, II, iv, 1545.

>   olvido de los agravios,
>   manjar de diversos precios,
>   que mata de hambre a los necios
>   y satisface a los discretos.
>   (II,xiv, 468)

The play, then, addresses itself to the intellect and the senses in the most intimate way; indeed in the case of the *discretos,* those most finely adapted to appreciate its varied appeal, the play actually holds the spectator in a kind of forgetful trance and satisfies deeply all his inner needs. The image of a banquet in which the audience regale their non-material senses recurs elsewhere in Tirso. The foolish can only hope to leave this feast starving, for they cannot bring to the banquet the mental and gustatorial equipment which will allow them to participate actively in a two-way traffic of spiritual food.[27] This is not to say any more than is in the text, since Tirso carefully extends the metaphor of "sustento" in terms like "banquete," "manjar," "mata de hambre," "satisface" and so on.

I have termed this form of enjoyment "active participation," because Tirso clearly expected his audience to bring a great deal more than passive gazing to their appreciation of the events and dialogue on the stage. He makes it quite clear that only those who can follow the subtle thought, the fine conceits and strategems may derive the maximum benefit; the rest remain unsatisfied. In this sense, the Tirsian comedy also provides a dialogue between the stage action and the audience. If the playwright cannot count on a certain degree of active participation, active understanding, possession of factual knowledge, grasping of references, appreciation of poetic skills and verbal beauty, ear for meter changes, vivid capacity for imagining the scenes conjured up in the actors' words — then he cannot write the sort of play he would wish to. He must cater for the mob.

Tirso also intended the variety and spectacle he mentioned to be evoked in the mind's eye, not by gross or even subtle use of stage machinery, *tramoyas* and stunt effects. This point of view is elaborated in a passage from *La fingida Arcadia* which mercilessly satirizes playwrights and producers who settle for appeals to the material dimension of vision only. Pinzón is giving the *dramatis personae* a guided tour of a

---

27. There is a parallel here with León Hebreo's theory of love: that if one does not *know,* one cannot love and thus the ignorant are unable to share in that emotion.

poetic Hell and Purgatory. Above these sits Apollo himself atop Parnassus. Pinzón explains:

PINZON: Esa es la gloria de Apolo,
y aquel, el dios que las llaves
tiene del entendimiento
y premiar al docto sabe;
la corona es para quien,
escribiendo dulce y fácil,
sin hacerlo carpintero,
hundirle ni entramoyarle,
entretiene al auditorio
dos horas, sin que le gaste
más de un billete, dos cintas,
un vaso de agua o un guante,
ese se coronará.
ALEJANDRA: ¿Y los démas?
PINZON: Que se abrasen;
pues dándonos pan de palo
los ingenios matan de hambre.
(III, iii, 1423)

This is a most revelatory passage: props must be kept to a minimum, the excessive use of stage machinery, Tirso says, bludgeons the intellect, it does not entertain it. Again the image of spiritual food and hunger occurs, though this time (with his customary consistency), Tirso inverts its application. Normally the foolish spectator will 'starve' at a fine play; at a crude lavish spectacle, it is precisely the *discreto*, who will quit the *corral* starved of internal sustenance having been served merely "pan de palos." This accusation had already been developed at some length by Pinzón shortly before, where he specifies what tricks and abuses are exploited, how they insult the imagination and rain blows on its sensitivity:

PINZON: Pues estos venden
a todo representante
comedias falsas: con liga
de infinitos badulaques
han adulterado a Apolo
con tramoyas, maderajes
y bofetones, que es dios
y osan abofetearle,
y están corridas las Musas,
que las hacen ganapanes,
cargadas de tantas vigas,

> peñas, fuentes, torres, naves,
> que las tienen deslomadas,
> y así las mandan que pasen
> peñas y cargas eternas
> a sus culpas semejantes,
> y las atormenten sierpes,
> arpías, gritos, salvajes,
> que son los que en sus comedias
> introducen ignorantes,
> dando al ingenio de palos.[28]
> (III, iii, 1422)

Of the varieties of imaginative appeal the play could offer, word-painting was the most obvious. This view of active participation is shared by L. C. Pérez and Sánchez Escribano who write: "Dentro de este inmenso lienzo teatral, suele haber a veces pinturas en palabras, es decir, el poeta depende de la palabra para pintar. Esta es la segunda técnica pictórica que aparece en la obra del poeta. Es más dificil ver estas pinturas en palabras. *El público, para gozar de ellas, tiene que participar activamente, y no pasivamente como en el primer caso.* Ahora el cuadro dramático depende únicamente de la cultura y de la imaginación de cada uno. El papel de la imaginación es importantísimo en estos cuadros de palabras" (op. cit., p. 150. My italics).

The point about the active imagination and minimal use of stage-effects to hold the spectator must now be obvious. Tirso goes to great pains to explain his attitude. But what of the active participation of the spectator through his own culture? This, it seems to me, has not been understood nearly well enough by scholars of the *comedia*. In the first place the spectator would need a working acquintance with a skeletal outline of Spanish history and culture, such that in a very real way a considerable amount of the text lay in the head of the onlooker. It has been shown that *La prudencia en la mujer* was a caballistic parable, self-contained, but clearly directed at the Queen Regent and the teenage

---

28. A very similar feeling about *tramoyas* was expressed by Ben Jonson in England, as gorgeous masque supplanted subtle imaginative suggestion and the carpenter's skills of an Inigo Jones ousted those of genuine dramatic talent. As he says in the Prologue to *Every Man in his Humour* (1598-1616):
> He rather prays you will be pleased to see
> One such, today, as other plays should be;
> Where neither chorus wafts you o'er the seas,
> Nor creaking throne comes down the boys to please...

Quoted from *Selected Works,* ed. Harry Levin (New York, 1938), p. 560.

Philip IV. The audience would be required to extract a contemporary relevance from the saga of medieval history.[29] In another historical play, *El rey don Pedro en Madrid,* Tirso expected the audience to be familiar with Pedro's twin attributes of "justiciero" and "cruel": indeed these are developed and contrasted side by side in Tirso's exploitations of the paradoxical aspects of Pedro's character. What he does not dramatize in the play is Pedro's violent murder of a priest, an ominous act which haunts the king thereafter. The specter of the man of God appears terrifyingly to Pedro at critical junctures in both the first and last acts. But it sufficed to evoke this historical occurrence in the text; the informed members of the audience could be relied upon to take the point.

From the plays we possess, Tirso clearly expected his audience to know some Latin and Portuguese, enough at least to follow the action. The Latin is occasionally the farcical macaronic Latin of quack doctors (*La fingida Arcadia, El amor médico*) but sometimes serious, drawing on principles of Scholastic reasoning (cf. Lucrecia's letter in I, viii of *La fingida Arcadia*). Tirso expected his hearers to follow the subtle acrobatics of conceited images in their ingenious complications and extensions, his puns either blatant or recondite, his mythological references and so on. He would hope to get a mental pat on the back from a spectator who heard him change from one meter to another; not so much for the use of the maids-of-all-work, the *romance* and *redondilla,* but for the poetic finesse of introducing a *silva* or *lira* to suit a given moment or speech, the judicious use of the rare sonnet, the grandeur of a patriotic sentiment couched in *octavas reales,* the delicacy of a popular *letrilla,* the virtuosity of effortlessly handled *décimas.* He would be writing for the man who knew the Spanish poetic conventions and traditions perfectly and recognized glosses of the *romancero,* reminiscences from the Renaissance poets, echoes of his master Lope, parodies of the *culteranistas,* sentiments from the Latin Classics. He would hope that passages of sheer beauty would win applause for themselves alone.

That the culture of the audience lies like a contrapuntal ghost between the lines of the extant texts cannot be doubted. We should not therefore be surprised that the seventeenth-century dramatists —

---

29. See Ruth Lee Kennedy, " 'La prudencia en la mujer' and the Ambient that Brought it Forth," *PMLA,* 63 (1948), 1131-90.

Shakespeare, Vondel, Gryphius or Tirso — require elucidation by experts in foot-noted editions; the noteworthy circumstance is that even experts are at a loss to follow the thread in occasional passages which undoubtedly still stand as they were first set down. We have regrettably lost the secondary and tertiary connotations of words. Our sensitivities have also become bludgeoned by the realistic colorful spectacles of the cinema and television which perform all the work of imagination for us. Rhyme and rhythm in dialogue no longer matter; our function as spectators is an essentially passive one. To relive the *comedia,* we would need to relearn the culture and history of seventeenth-century Spain, cultivate their powers of imagination as we read, and relive the excited, active participation of a Spanish crowd following the subtle thread of logic that runs through the bull-fight.[30]

In reconstructing Tirso's theory of the drama, we have inevitably imposed an apparent order on these scattered remarks that they never possessed. They constitute a fragmented theory within a conveniently presented framework, and yet the organic care and intelligence with which Tirso chose to comment on his art cannot escape the reader. As stated at the outset, his theory is a surprising medley of critical commonplaces and remarkably forward-looking insights, which often go beyond a defense of Lope's innovations or even a narrow, self-interested justification of Tirso's own manner of composition. Goaded on by the steady assaults of the neo-Aristotelian critics, Tirso came close on occasion to formulating principles taken up some two or three generations later by Muratori, Addison, Bodmer and Breitinger, Sulzer, and the Romantics.

---

30. This point is touched on in the debate between Arnold Reichenberger and Eric Bentley on the limits of the *comedia*'s reach. See A. Reichenberger, "The Uniqueness of the Comedia," *HR,* 38 (1970), 163-73, and E. Bentley, "The Universality of the *Comedia,*" *HR,* 38 (1970), 147-62.

III

THE PERSONALITY OF THE TYPICAL TIRSIAN PROTAGONIST

> Yo no tengo por traiciones
> las industrias del ingenio,
> mayormente cuando amor
> ayuda al entendimiento.
>
> *La mujer por fuerza,* III, xvii.

In our three remaining chapters, we must study how Tirso's theory of the drama works in actual practice. One of the most striking features of Tirso's dramatic practice is the prominence which he gives to the central figure or protagonist in his plays. This figure, very frequently a woman, dominates the action and by his or her skilful manipulation actually determines its course. In this Tirso differs from Lope, in whose work the initiative is subtly distributed among five, six or seven personages, and also from Calderón, who tends to set up conflict situations where the initiative alternates between two, or at most three individuals. The dominant position of the Tirsian protagonist is important for two reasons. In the first place the 'one versus many' structure gives the basic clue to Tirso's principal method of constructing a play and generating plot; secondly the divisions set up within the main character, occasioned by his assuming differing roles within the play, reveal an 'inwardness' on which we can base a theory of personality. The two parts of this chapter, then, will seek to analyze and exemplify the Tirsian protagonist's behavior in ego versus situation conflicts and later move on to discuss deeper ego versus self conflicts. In the first part, we shall discuss trickery, disguise, the Tirsian conception of prudence and discretion, and the double plane of illusion within which the protagonist exists. In the second part, we shall discuss how 'part' and 'role' conflicts give rise to inward character, how inner disintegration falls short of schizophrenia by the power of the will, and how this will power results in an ethical voluntarism.

Ego Versus Situation

The claim that a Tirsian protagonist displayed a superb knowledge of human weakness and gullibility, and could use such skill psychologically to manipulate the rest of the characters in the play (thus maximizing his self-interest) was first set out by Professor Ion T. Agheana and myself in an article published in 1969.[1] In that article, a variety of situations were discussed where the notorious Don Juan used cunning, flattery and posturing to extricate himself from tight corners; lying, false oaths and simulated ardor to seduce his victims; deceitfulness even in the question of salvation. We concluded as follows:

> The preceding examples should suffice to indicate conclusively that Don Juan is the play's cleverest psychologist, precisely because he is ultrasensitive to other people's psychological makeup. He is dangerous because of his chameleon-like ability to adapt superbly to different people. He is a confidence trickster of genius, because one way or the other, he ultimately inspires trust. By the same token, he knows himself inside out as well, and displays only that side of his character to his victims that he knows they wish to see or *à la rigueur* creates a temporary persona. Everywhere, Don Juan is the manipulator or, in sociological terms, the situation initiator; until the statue provides him with *real* opposition, Don Juan literally runs rings around his elders, women of all ranks, the royal power and his peers; sometimes even his disenchanted valet (pp. 319-20).

In a broader consideration of the Tirsian canon, however, it becomes clear that the skills of trickery, situation initiation and manipulation, cunning exploitation of the less astute by the intelligent schemer, domination of the action by the protagonist etc., are by no means confined to *El burlador de Sevilla*. There is whole group of comedies which have a situation so basically similar and recurrent that it might be considered archetypal in Tirso. It is the mate-hunt situation with the sexual initiatives reversed. The heroine falls in love with or is seduced by the hero, who having promised her marriage then proceeds to abandon her. These events usually precede the play's opening. The heroine, faced with this overwhelming situation, instead of appealing to justice, her parent or guardian or the seducer's sense of chivalry, summons up her courage, disguises herself as a man and follows her lover (usually from the Spanish provinces to Madrid). In the capital, she entraps him in a web of successful machinations that exploit her double, triple or quadruple disguise identities and forces him to marry her. Her manipu-

---

1. See Ion T. Agheana and Henry Sullivan, "The Unholy Martyr: Don Juan's Misuse of Intelligence," *RF*, 81, no. 3 (1969), 311-25. The same article will be available in a German translation by Helga Hoock Quadrado, "Der unheilige Märtyrer: Don Juans Missbrauch der Intelligenz," in Brigitte Wittmann ed., *Don Juan: Darstellung und Deutung*, Wege der Forschung, vol. CLXXXII (Darmstadt: Wissenschaftliche Buchgesellschaft, 1975).

lation of the situation is what provides the business of the play, the suspense, the comedy and *enredo*, this last of often labyrinthine complexity. In the final dénouement, the heroine reveals the truth, wins her husband and reclaims her normal identity.

In her discussion of male disguise in this type of Tirsian *dama busca galán* comedy, Carmen Bravo-Villasante observed the following: "Los protagonistas de todas estas comedias no hacen alarde de su fuerza y valor, sólo se sirven de la astucia y el ingenio, cualidades indispensables para esta clase de trama."[2] Doña Carmen is claiming correctly, then, that the normal methods of imposing one's will (force, intimidation by the threat of force, bribery, open appeals to someone based on friendship and love) do not have much place in Tirso; the typical protagonist resorts to manipulative cunning. In *Don Gil de las calzas verdes,* the heroine Doña Juana, pursuing Don Martín, assumes one male disguise as Don Gil and a female disguise as Doña Elvira. In the climax of the play (III, x), her machinations multiply the Don Gils to four as Juan, Martín and Clara all don green hose for differing reasons. In *El amor médico,* Doña Jerónima disguises herself as a doctor to pursue an indifferent *galán* whom she loves. In the process, she creates a triple personality: her own, that of a doctor and that of 'his' supposed Portuguese sister. Doña Ana accomplishes a greater feat in *Bellaco sois, Gómez,* by taking *three* spurious roles apart from her own. She says in the final scene: "Vístesme a mí transformada/ en Greida, en Portocarrero/ en don Gómez y en doña Ana" (III, xxiii, 1405). In *La huerta de Juan Fernández,* the disguise ploy itself is reduplicated, since Doña Petronila disguised as a man pursues her own lover while Tomasa, a rustic girl also disguised as a man, enters the service of Doña Petronila to pursue an unfaithful soldier.

It will be seen, then, that the fundamental goal of the typical protagonist is to impose his (or more often her) will on one person or a group of persons in the attainment of a specific end. Now while a full discussion of the will in Tirso would be premature at this juncture, an analysis of the *method* by which the will is imposed is most pertinent. The method employed is clearly a form of intelligence, or to invoke Professor Agheana's term in his recent book,[3] "intelligence in action."

---

2. See Carmen Bravo-Villasante, *La mujer vestida de hombre en el teatro español* (Madrid, 1953) at p. 115.
3. See Ion T. Agheana, *The Situational Drama of Tirso de Molina* (New York: Plaza Mayor, 1972), at p. 44. Professor Agheana is quoting St. Thomas.

In his study, Professor Agheana analyzes *La mujer por fuerza,* a play similar to *Don Gil de las calzas verdes.* The former play anticipates *Don Gil* in the basic plot structure; Finea's pursuit of Federico to Naples disguised as a page Celio; her third (male) role as Alonso; the manipulation of Florela, Federico's fiancée, through the latter's jealous, changeable nature, and the dizzying coils of confusion she throws around the hapless Federico as the play progresses. Professor Agheana singles out this play because it illustrates so well the tendency of Tirsian protagonists to mold events to their own purpose. He writes of such figures:

> Most of them are not satisfied merely to take stock of reality and exploit the moment. They have long range plans which they pursue with intelligence and tenacity. They make conscious efforts to control reality, to engineer circumstances and psychological approaches which will force other characters to follow their precalculated design . . . . One of the best examples to be found in Tirso's theatre is Finea, the intrepid heroine of *La mujer por fuerza.* She singlehandedly manipulates the action and the rest of the play's characters until the very last scene when the king, traditional dispenser of justice, celebrates her intelligence and rewards her for it. Finea's actions are the result of a careful delineation and examination of motives and circumstances, processed by intelligence and guided by sensibility and intuition (p. 39).

But to talk of "intelligence [. . .] guided by sensibility and intuition" or "intelligence in action" involves us in problems of terminology, and Professor Agheana recognizes (p. 28) that we incur an anachronism in the application of the term "intelligence" to Tirso who never used it, at least not in Spanish.[4] We are certainly in the realm of manipulative intelligence, however, when we consider the flood of terms in Tirso's drama that express scheming actions and recur with an almost obsessive regularity: *industria, diligencia, sutileza, ingenio, enredo, engaño, embuste, cautela, ardid, traza, embeleco.* These with their adjectival derivatives, seem subsumed nevertheless under the wider mental refinements, commonly regarded as virtues, of *prudencia* and *discreción,* terms invoked by Tirso in every single act he wrote and key words of the entire Spanish Counter Reformation. By their very frequency, however, prudence and discretion admitted of an individual

---

4. See *The Situational Drama . . .*, especially p. 28, and the ensuing discussion. J. Corominas, *Diccionario crítico etimológico . . .* (Berne: Francke, 1954), vol. II, under "Inteligente" does give: "Inteligencia [...] 1499, H. Núñez y ya frecuente en el S. XVI; está en C. de las Casas y R. de Alarcón, pero no en Covarr[ubias]." Cervantes only used *inteligente* as a synonym of *entendido;* I have never found the noun in Tirso's dramas. In Shakespeare, 'intelligence' and 'intelligencer' meant 'covert information' and 'spy' respectively.

interpretation; they were for Tirso the equivalents of "intelligence in action" and precisely the qualities that distinguished his protagonists. While this writer would be the first to agree that counting words for their frequency, of itself, teaches us nothing about literature, terms of high frequency which have begun to 'spread' semantically by their constant use in this manner, can be very revealing about the fundamental preoccupations of a cultural moment and the perspective of an individual writer. No one can deny that *desengaño* in seventeenth-century Spain fell in such a category (so would 'wit,' 'enthusiasm' and 'sensibility' in eighteenth-century England and *réaliste* and *déterminer* in nineteenth-century France). What did the words to which we have drawn attention connote in Tirso's day?

Referring to the original list above, we find that Covarrubias in his *Tesoro de la lengua castellana* (1611) gives the following definition of *industria*: "Es la maña, diligencia y solercia con que alguno haze cualquier cosa con menos trabajo que otro. Hazer una cosa de industria, hazerla a sabiendas y a adrede, para que de allí suceda cosa que para otro sea a caso y para él de propósito; puede ser en buena y en mala parte." Of *cautela,* he writes that it is: "El engaño que uno haze a otro ingeniosamente, usando de términos ambiguos, y de palabras dudosas y equívocas." These meanings put us very much in the Tirsian world of machinations, deceit, imposture and manipulation. Covarrubias' suggestion that an *industria* is a form of energy-saving manoeuvre designed to profit the individual (and having a possibly pejorative sense), while appearing to be purely fortuitous to another, describes the behavior of the typical Tirsian protagonist fairly accurately. The term *cautela*, a deceit based on ambiguity and equivocal statements, could hardly be more *à propos*; indeed, one of Tirso's plays bears the title *Cautela contra cautela*. The interesting feature here, however, is the tinge of moral dubiousness that can apparently attach to these words and their suggestion of doubt or ambiguity.

This note is sounded more strongly by Covarrubias in his definitions of *discreción* and *prudencia.* He writes: "Discreción: La cosa dicha o hecha con buen seso ... Discernir: Vale vulgarmente distinguir una cosa de otra y hazer juyzio dellas; de aquí se dixo discreto, el hombre cuerdo y de buen seso, que sabe ponderar las cosas y dar a cada una su lugar .... Prudente: .... que pesa todas las cosas con mucho acuerdo." Quite evidently, the aspect that these qualities share is the ability to survey a multiplicity of alternatives of action, which may carry moral implications, and weight them according to some priority.

The definitions do not, however, insist on high morality as the final criterion of discretion and prudence; indeed my feeling is that Tirso as author wants us to forego judgments on single actions and let the *goal* or purpose carry the moral weight. In Tirsian usage, therefore, discretion and prudence are analytical gifts of mind, apparently close to synonymous, perhaps morally neutral as such, but sometimes less than moral in their effects.

Etymologically speaking, as indicated, discretion does in fact derive from the Latin *discernire,* meaning to distinguish one thing from another in a neutral sense. It subsequently acquired the ethical dimension of distinguishing good from bad, and eventually by the Golden Age, of the application of right reason to moral conduct. For Calderón, discretion was *the* virtue, the 'paravirtue' that tempered all others into a perfect balance, allowing no specific quality to degenerate into the defects of its excesses (e.g. fortitude into intransigence, justice into inclement rigor and so on). Calderón makes his view clear in his demonstration of Discretion's role in the *auto, No hay más fortuna que Dios,* discussed so admirably by A. A. Parker in his edition of that work.[5] Tirso, however, sometimes uses the word in a puzzling manner that suggests discretion can contain a measure of duplicity. In *La mujer por fuerza* (II, iv), the heroine enjoins Florela to secrecy in the following exchange:

> FINEA: Jura el secreto, si intentas
> saberlo.
> FLORELA: A fe de quien soy.
> FINEA: Si juras el ser mujer
> fue juramento *discreto*;
> que de no guardar secreto
> juró naciendo su ser.
> Mas si juras a quien eres
> yo me doy por confiado.
> FLORELA: Mucho, Celio, has afrentado
> el valor de las mujeres.
> (II, iv, 522. My italics).

The sense here is that if Florela swears by her womanhood to keep a secret, she is giving a specious oath, since women are supposedly notori-

---

5. Parker's remarks in his edition (Manchester: Manchester U.P., 1949, 2nd. ed., 1962) are in an appendix, "The Meaning of 'Discreción' in 'No hay más fortuna que Dios': The Medieval Background and Sixteenth- and Seventeenth Century Usage," at pp. 77-92. The piece has since been reprinted in *Calderón de la Barca,* ed. Hans Flasche in Wege der Forschung, vol. CLVIII (Darmstadt: Wissenschaftliche Buchgesellschaft, 1971), 218-34.

ously bad at keeping secrets; her oath is said to be "discreet" for this reason. The pejorative element in *discreto* has clearly not been lost on Florela, who tells the disguised Finea that 'he' has offended womankind. As Finea-Celio uses the term in this context, then, discretion comes close to Covarrubias' definition of *cautela*: "... usando de términos ambiguos y de palabras dudosas y equívocas."

Ambiguous oaths abound in Tirso — Don Juan Tenorio's promises of marriage sworn by the eyes of his beloved (i.e. not by her actual person) for example — and against the contemporary background of casuistical doctrines of equivocation and mental reservation, this is not surprising. Montaigne even talks of dissimulation being honored in the France of the late sixteenth century.[6] What saves Tirso's characters from moral turpitude is yet another casuistical doctrine: the direction of intention. Where Tirso's protagonists are obliged to lie or equivocate, they are either punished if reprobate (e.g. Don Juan) or absolved because the dubious means were undoubtedly employed towards a highly moral end. Though deceitful, both Juana in *Don Gil* and Finea merely require their lovers, in the name of love, to fulfill sworn commitments to the sacrament of marriage. Doña María de Molina employs ingenious and indirect methods in *La prudencia en la mujer* only to secure a political stability and the succession of the legitimate sovereign. What intrigues the reader is Tirso's occasional use of the terms *discreto/discreción* suggesting calculated ambiguity and duplicity.

Prudencia, as we have seen, is regarded by Covarrubias as a careful weighing of all factors in a sense akin to discretion. His article in the *Tesoro* goes on, however, to draw a comparison with the Roman deity Janus, always represented as having two faces, one looking back towards the old year, one looking forward to the new (hence the month January). For Covarrubias, the prudent ruler surveys both past and future events in his ideal government. Alciati's emblem book, says the lexicographer, paints the figure thus under the legend *prudentes* and he adds: "Imítenle, pues, quantos goviernan si quiera para que se vea que es más natural efecto de la prudencia que de la traición el tener un

---

6. In the *Essais* (1580), Montaigne frequently returns to the theme of truth and lie. The following extracts (in the English version of E. J. Trechman) are typical: "For with regard to this new-fangled virtue of hypocrisy and dissimulation which is now held in such great honour, I have a deadly hatred of it" (Essay XVII, p. 97). "Our truth nowadays is not what is but what we can persuade others to believe [...] dissimulation is among the most notorious qualities of this century" (Essay XVIII, p. 117). See *The Essays of Montaigne* (New York and London: Oxford U.P., 1948).

hombre dos caras." Covarrubias' remark is significant. Two-facedness (conventionally implying treachery in a man) is here promoted to a natural political virtue. This is not to praise duplicity as such, but to reduce its pejorative coloring to a point of parity with the prudence born of necessity: a juxtaposition that erodes the purely virtuous sense of prudence as much as certain Tirsian contexts do for discretion.

It is impossible at this juncture not to refer briefly to an extraordinary painting devoted to Prudence executed by Titian about 1565 or perhaps a little later. It portrays the Egyptian zoömorphic *tricipitium* surmounted by three human heads: a boy facing right, a mature man facing forwards and an ancient looking to the left, the whole beneath a Latin inscription. In his study *Problems in Titian,* Erwin Panofsky writes of the portrait: "The only 'emblematic' picture produced by Titian, it illustrates – or, rather, visually paraphrases – a maxim directly stated in an inscription. This inscription reads EX PRAETERITO/ PRAESENS PRUDENTER AGIT/ NI FUTURA[M?] ACTIONEM DETURPET ('[Instructed] by the past, the present acts prudently lest it spoil its future action')."[7] The picture for Panofsky "...glorifies Prudence as a wise employer of the Three Forms of Time: the present learns from the past and acts with due regard to the future. And these Three Forms of Time appear equated with the Three Ages of Man" (p. 103). As for Covarrubias, then, Titian's prudence requires an internal division of perspective serving long term action and, perhaps, the interim display of an enigmatic exterior.

Although prudence in Thomist thought has always been regarded as a cardinal virtue, Gracián, a near contemporary of Tirso carries the process of erosion a stage further. In Gracián's works, discretion and prudence are Machiavellian means of self-promotion and evasion. Discussing discretion in Gracián, Professor A. A. Parker characterizes the virtue as being for the Jesuit writer "... a self-sufficiency that denies all social responsibility by seeking security in the company of the elite."[8] Gracián's significantly subtitled treatise, the *Oráculo manual, o arte de prudencia,* is virtually a textbook on the judicious art of lying; the perfection he seeks almost as remote from any kind of religious inspiration as can be imagined. Gracián teaches a Jesuitical manipula-

---

7. See Erwin Panofsky, *Problems in Titian, Mostly Iconographic* (New York: New York U.P., 1969), p. 103. The painting is reproduced in his fig. 117.

8. See Parker's edition, loc. cit., p. 92.

tion of truth aimed only at the maximization of personal advantage.[9] Naturally, it is not my purpose to put Tirso on a par with Gracián. The comparison does, nevertheless, draw attention to the extent to which semantic erosion had set in with regard to these terms in Counter-Reformation Spain.[10] Their very elasticity and currency indicate that while prudence and discretion were always meant as accolades, their meaning varied according to the laudable or perverse conception of these virtues in the mind of him who bestowed the accolade. More generally, the universal agreement that the virtues involved making the 'best' choice among a multitude of options, speaks volumes for the chaos that reigned in moral sub-systems in the Spain of the period. Whereas the criteria and consequences by which prudence and discretion were to be estimated could vary, the actual need for such mental refinements was placed beyond dispute.

For Tirso in particular, discretion and prudence were arms with which to cross the no-man's-land between stupidity and destiny. In Serafina's panegyric of the *comedia,* we have read how the young woman reaches her peroration in a distinction between the stupid who starve at the play, and the wise who are satisfied. She hurls the final challenge at Juana thus: the *comedia* is a dish:

---

9. Gracián's apologists would doubtless find this assessment of the *Oráculo* unfair. Helmut Hatzfeld allows that the work is ". . . una prudente secularización de los principios de la sabiduría . . . ." in his *Estudios sobre el barroco* (Madrid: Gredos, 1964), p. 362. In *Gracián and Perfection* (Cambridge, Mass.: Harvard U.P., 1966), a broadly positive treatment of his subject, Professor Monroe Z. Hafter concedes: "The new emphasis in the *Oráculo manual* is on the friction between the pre-eminent man and the people who are represented as his enemies. . . . He is involved in an unceasing struggle to impose himself upon them. For this reason, Gracián breaks down the general techniques for achieving an impressive appearance into specific stratagems of defense and offense" (p. 151).

10. A strongly pejorative meaning for Prudence is to be found already in the *Enquiridión o Manual del caballero cristiano* of Erasmus, translated into Spanish in 1503/04: "Item prudencia llaman comúnmente a saber adquirir hazienda con gran diligencia y tener gran abilidad para trampearla, y después no sólo guardalla, sino doblalla y proveerse ombre para muchos días muy a su seguro. Y assí oymos a cada passo loar a otros muy en seso, y dizen luego: 'Aquel es un ombre diligente y granjero en estremo, sagaz y marcado, que no le engañará el diablo, muy ábil y para mucho y que se ha sabido muy bien valer'." See the edition of Dámaso Alonso (Madrid, 1932), p. 316. Quoted by Francisco Márquez Villanueva, *Espiritualidad y literatura en el siglo XVI* (Madrid and Barcelona: Alfaguara, 1968) at p. 97.

SERAFINA: ... que mata de hambre a los necios
y satisface a los sabios.
Mira lo que quieres ser
de aquestos dos bandos.
JUANA: Digo
que el de los discretos sigo
y que me holgara de ver
la farsa infinito.
(II, xiv, 468).

So the discreet for Tirso are here equated with the band of the *sabios,* but not by any means with all people. Elsewhere, he restricts the numbers of the discreet still further. In an intriguing and convincingly documented article, F. C. Halstead has argued that Tirso regarded the wise man as one capable of combatting any of multifarious natural inclinations imparted through divine, diabolic, or merely supernatural agency by means of an intelligent application of free will, a view consonant (as we have seen) with Tirso's ideas on grace.[11] Such scope for self-determination is not extended by Tirso, however, to kings who by reason of their proximity to the divine, astral sphere as earthly representatives of God, are powerless to dictate their own fates; nor indeed to ignorant, brutish mortals at the farther end of the scale, whose lack of human wisdom renders them prone to astral domination. But in the center of Tirso's scale may come those in possession of

11. See F. C. Halstead, "The Attitude of Tirso de Molina toward Astrology," *HR*, 9 (1941), 417-39. Halstead shows that, in Tirso, lovers even of differing class-backgrounds may be prone to astral determinism inasmuch as natural, physical attraction is attributable to the influence of heavenly bodies; but alone and unaided the stars are powerless. Similarly in the case of princes of royal blood, their semi-divine nature and closer union with the stars as God's intelligent agents leave them the prey of disorders in the heavens (e.g. the unpredictable intrusions of celestial rovers such as comets and meteors). Hence Tirso's unique view of astral influence as the cause of panic-stricken dynastic scrambles. Halstead writes: "One is not, then, astonished to find that just as the astral inclination might level the barriers of the rigid semi-caste system of the Golden Age, rendering spiritual intimacies and friendship possible, so might the intensity of astral inclination exaggerate all sentiment and emotion in the nobility, creating bitter enmities between blood kinsmen" (p. 437). An exactly similar distinction is made by Tirso in the case of friendship. True friendship, says Tirso via Don Manrique in *Cómo han de ser los amigos,* may only yield in the face of love or the impulse to rule. Even the powerful force of friendship becomes weakened, like that of human will, in the face of these two contingencies: "Mas ¡ay alma! ¿No reparas/ que a Armesinda me han de dar? / Gran premio, no hay que dudar;/ *porque si se ha de romper/ la amistad, sólo ha de ser/ por amor o por reinar"* (II, ii, 287. My italics).

sabiduría and intelligence, those capable of confronting the power of astral strength squarely with the freedom of the human will.

It can be seen, then, that the terms *discreto, prudente* and *sabio* are commonly near-synonyms in Tirso and it would not be an error in particular contexts to render any of *discreción, prudencia* or *sabiduría* as practical or "applied" intelligence in modern English. It is in the actual application of this intelligence that we encounter the semantic difficulties and ambiguities already discussed above. Nevertheless, armed with these capacities, the agile Tirsian protagonist forms his or her own destiny and achieves remarkable success in nullifying the forces of circumstance. Though Tirso attacked Molinism in his writings, one is bound to say that his protagonists behave as if they *were*, in fact, Molinists.

Thus far in our portrait of the typical Tirsian protagonist, we have found that he or she is usually a person cornered by circumstance, confronted with an overwhelming set of odds and willing to step adroitly in and out of a multitude of social and sexual identities in order to prevail against them. To this end, they draw on an extraordinary dynamism (often sexual in inspiration), remarkable will power and tenacity, and the gift of great practical intelligence; these forces of personality are directed towards the attainment of some goal. What makes them especially distinguished is the balance achieved between their irrational energies of love, desire, ambition or other drive, and the purely rational mastery and exploitation of such energies through self-imposed will, postponement of immediate self-gratification and a capacity for imposition of their will on others via manipulation. In terms of dramaturgy, this 'one versus many' situation provides the basic structure of a typical Tirsian comedy.

The goal towards which the protagonist's will is bent is not always sexually inspired however. In *La prudencia en la mujer*, Queen María seeks to impose a political will on her rebellious subjects through temporizing on the remarriage question, subtlely planned persuasion, the staging of striking emblematic tableaux, etc.[12] In *El condenado por*

---

12. See Ion T. Agheana, *The Situational Drama...*, pp. 48-50, for a good discussion of the psychological effectiveness of Queen María's shrewdly executed tableaux. This aspect of Tirso's dramatic art — the halting of the action to make the play freeze into an emblematic, four-dimensional metaphor of the play's meaning — requires much closer attention than it has received. There is a spectacular tableau in

desconfiado a satanic will is imposed, since the hero is started on his course toward damnation by the scheming interventions of the Devil (disguised as an equivocating Angel) permitted by God to test the vacillating constancy of Paulo's faith (I, iv). In *Los balcones de Madrid,* the manipulative initiative lies with the maid Leonor and the *gracioso* Coral, not with the rather ineffectual lovers. In *La fingida Arcadia,* the controlling agency in the action ceases to be a person at all.... It is a book — Lope's pastoral novel *La Arcadia* of 1598 — which captivates the imagination of the heroine, Lucrecia, and then gradually takes over the lives of all the *dramatis personae* in Tirso's play, thus creating a 'bogus Arcadia.'

The typical protagonist's unique position of standing in a 'one versus many' relationship with the rest of the *dramatis personae* leads us to consider two final techniques peculiar to Tirso's dramatic practice. While the typical protagonist is taking on the rest of the cast and outwitting them, he or she evidently stands in a 'one to one' relationship with the literary creator. As outlined in previous comments on Tirso's theory of the drama, there exists a conspiratorial triangle between author, protagonist and audience. The manipulator is carrying out Tirso's dramatic will in an illusory situation and is endowed with special intellectual gifts and privileges to allow the realization of a given goal. At the same time, the manipulator has in his or her possession from the start all the data and information to which we the audience have access. This conspiratorial privilege continues since the manipulator largely determines the play's action. The dupes are the rest of the cast. In a real sense, then, by operating in that order of reality closest to the poet's imagination with respect to the play as a whole, the protagonist is the accomplice of the dramatist in the generation of the action. This is quite Tirsian, and I know of no play where the dramatist suddenly thwarts his protagonist by the release of information known to himself, *qua* author, alone.

In the second place, the constant play-acting of the protagonist with respect to others inevitably diverts attention from the primary illusion

---

La república al revés (III, xiii); another in *La mujer que manda en casa* (III, vii). In *La vida y muerte de Herodes* (III, xv), the direction reads: "Descúbrese un portal de heno, romero y paja, lleno de copos de nieve, y en él, *la Adoración de los Reyes como se pinta"* (p. 1623. My emphasis). The theatrical implementation of *ut pictura poesis* in the *comedia* to make intelligible, moral commentaries on the action in progress has still to be studied.

(the play on the stage) to the secondary illusion (the machinations of the protagonist) and secures very effectively the willing suspension of disbelief of which Coleridge spoke. This Baroque sense of feigned depth and regressive illusion is in part what makes Tirso's work reach out and 'seize' the reader within the first few hundred lines in a manner only a handful of dramatists have managed with such repeated success. The two planes of illusion projected throughout a play also explain, it seems to me, the sense of Tirso's extraordinary definition of the *comedia* "... que es una imagen y representación de su argumento." Indeed it is in his hands: the argument or plot is worked out between the dramatist and protagonist, while the audience is constantly included in the conspiracy. The acting out of the plot is its physical representation on stage, the image on which we look, the illusion in which the 'many' are the butts of the joke.

As noted, it would be wrong to suggest that all Tirso's plays follow this pattern; they do not. What sets Tirso apart from his fellow dramatists is his *predilection* for this type of central figure and his predilection for the play built on intelligent manipulation. Regarding his theater *en bloc,* one cannot but be struck by the evident sense of ease and control over his material which Tirso displays when command of the action is firmly in the hands of his typical protagonist. When the initiative is divided or contested, or if initiators of the sort we have been describing are lacking, then the play is often scrappy, diffuse, lacking in tension and periodic climaxes. In *Cómo han de ser los amigos,* a play attractive enough in its theme, the only intriguer is Doña Violante, who drives a wedge between the friendship of Don Manrique and Gaston de Foix by her lie that the latter offered her marriage in gratitude for Violante's having saved his life. She hardly ever occupies the center of the action, however, and the whole play has a static, picturesque quality made up of noble sentiments, but lacking the fire and headlong *élan* of Tirso's better paced comedies and dramas.

Ego Versus Self

In our remarks so far, the Tirsian protagonist has been examined as a manipulator surrounded by a field of forces with which he deals by cunning and the assumption of differing identities; examined, that is, in terms of public and social action. The adoption of temporary identities, however, is not effected in Tirso's drama without a concomitant division of identity within. This internal division or splitting of personality is a hallmark of the Mercedarian's art, and, by careful definition and illustration, we may build upon it a Tirsian theory of personality.

In an outstanding article of 1945, Myron Peyton had already observed the Tirsian splitting process: "Lope created the *comedia* by setting up an opposition between life and a higher principle. His protagonists for the most part, are still spiritually integrated and psychologically sound. But in Tirso they are disintegrated. Man is not set against a higher principle but against the illusion, mockery, or emptiness of high human principles and noble emotions. Arching over the *persona,* or self, is the *personaje,* that is, the rôle which the individual plays or must play in his own peculiar situation."[13] Peyton would view Tirso as being Baroque because conflicting attitudes, the essence of all drama, are presented in Gabriel Téllez's theater not only as those between individuals and environment (i.e. ego versus situation) but also between the individual and himself (ego versus self).

Now terms describing personality are question-begging and vague at best. What do ego, self, persona, personality, part, role or personage really mean? Psychologists have attached strong, often polemic meanings to many of these terms, and it would be foolish to become further enmeshed in their hair-splitting. For the purpose of argument in this dramaturgical context, however, I would like to introduce a three-part distinction between part, role and character and also clarify the meaning I attach to ego.[14] Freud saw the ego as the psychic battleground where the instinctual desires of the id and the societal constraints of the superego syncretically forged the individual personality. Dramatically speaking, the individual onstage has an ego in the sense that he or she is seen functioning in social and stress situations that sufficiently counterfeit real life to make the application of parallel terms legitimate (whether a character can *really* have a 'personality' or a 'subconscience' is, for this reason, a critical dry well in my opinion). The ego, then, is the complete, socially functional individual in Tirsian drama.

By 'part,' I understand what a person simply is and cannot alter. Professor Everett W. Hesse has recently spelt out these characteristics in

---

13. See Myron Peyton, "Some baroque aspects of Tirso de Molina," *RR*, 36 (1945), 43-69.

14. For the elaboration of this distinction, I am deeply indebted to Professor William C. McCrary's remarks to me in conversation on April 27th, 1973 in Lexington, Ky.

detail under the aptly combined headings of physiology, sociology and psychology.[15] Thus Tirso's King Pedro is a king; he is male, he is Castilian, a man of specific age, proud, violent, likely to live and die a Christian etc. Tirso's Tisbea in *El burlador* is a fishergirl, poor, young, virgin, frigid.... By 'role,' I understand a temporary adoption of another persona, an assumed identity, an impersonation. Thus Don Juan Tenorio can play the role of the Marqués de la Mota (II, xiii); Pedro can assume the role of Acebedo, the 'intimate' of the king (I, viii); Doña Juana can act out the role of a man who never was, Don Gil de Albornoz. As we have seen, role-playing within the drama is a salient Tirsian fingerprint, but when the dramatist sets role against part and sends deep divisions into the individual's conscience, he gives the impression of having his hands on the genetic code. He achieves intimacy into 'character' through such fragmentation, and thus the debates between part and role produce an *interioridad* or inwardness which has struck all commentators on the Mercedarian's art. This, in a nutshell, is what I understand by ego versus self in Tirsian drama.

An outstanding example of the kind of torn individual under examination is Don Juan de Cardona in *Privar contra su gusto*. Here, the protagonist (I, v) saves his king, Fadrique of Naples, from a French assassination attempt as the latter is out hunting. The king, portrayed as a rather impulsive young man and prodigal with his political favors, offers Don Juan a *privanza* out of gratitude. Now the sad experiences of Juan's own father, once counsellor to the previous king of Naples, and the father's subsequent disgrace engineered by palace intrigue have soured the son against courtly life. He lives in rural tranquility with a sister, Leonor, and accepts the proffered post with the deepest reluctance becoming 'minister contrary to his inclination.'

Already committed, then, to a 'role' in life he finds unpalatable, Juan's tribulations increase as circumstance conspires against him. Earlier on the afternoon of the abortive *attentat,* the hero has spied a beauty bathing naked by a stream in the royal gardens. He cannot make out her face, but removes a garter from among her clothing as keepsake of his sudden passion for her. This object Don Juan inadvertently uses as a sling to support a wounded arm and when Isabela, the king's sister – the nude bather – sees the garter thus displayed, she deter-

---

15. See Everett W. Hesse, *La comedia y sus intérpretes* (Madrid: Castalia, 1972), pp. 34-35, the section "Las tres dimensiones de un personaje."

mines to punish him. The bewildered protagonist, his friends deserting him through Isabela's plotting, finds himself cornered, unable to pursue his legitimate love for her. He is perturbed by the king's sexual interest in his sister, concerned over his friend, Luis' mistrust, over a new assassination conspiracy and hence gradually immobilized in his 'role' as *privado*. He cannot live his 'part' of a man in love with the Infanta through their misunderstanding; he cannot uphold the honor of his comrade, Luis, in the 'part' of natural friend for the same reason; he cannot act his 'part' as brother protective of his sister's virtue out of deference to the sovereign; even his exertions in the 'part' of loyal subject are nullified by his diminishing credibility. The miserable hero thus decides to cut the Gordian knot, to split his personality and assume a new, more effective identity or 'role' – the *santo rebozado*.

Escaping from the strain of the *privado* role (II, xxv), the *santo* can continue to advise the king obliquely: to abandon his designs on Leonor's honor; to relieve Juan de Cardona (his other self) of the burden of favoritism; to elevate Luis de Moncada, the worthy friend, and marry him to his beloved Clavela. The *santo* also foils the gunpowder plot on the king's life. The degree to which the ego (Juan, a still socially functional individual but disguised) is pitted against the self (Juan in his full moral and psychic integrity) becomes heightened dramatically when Tirso makes Cardona protest to the king about the saintly figure's advice (thus lending credibility to the existence of his other self). This splitting assumes almost schizophrenic proportions when the same people who have condemned every action of the well-meaning protagonist in his public role, now applaud his exemplary preternatural wisdom in the assumed role. And yet, the protagonist is merely striving to realize the identical set of goals predicated by the play's opening scenes. Since the protagonist cannot transcend adverse circumstance by direct methods, he has assumed a new persona and by surpassing efforts of will, energy and prudence, overcome them. On throwing off his disguise, the hero's unfailing moral integrity is fully recognized, triple marriages are honorably concluded, the villains punished, Luis and Juan rewarded. Rehabilitated and reintegrated in himself, the protagonist can say at last: "El privado fuí por fuerza;/ mas ya lo seré con gusto,/ si os le ha dado esta comedia" (III, xvii, 1116).

So Juan de Cardona is a perfect example of what Peyton terms "the protagonist competing against himself" (p. 56); of one who represents an attempt "to flee out of an unsuccessful personality into a successful one, with the component parts being the same, and at the same time not the same, character ... a process of 'growing-out' or 'becoming' ... a projection of the dramatic Ego beyond identity" (p. 59). Such conflict, we repeat, creates 'character' in the truest sense of the word, an inwardness which can be experienced as the individual bares his conscience to us in soliloquy or acts out the fragmentation of his spirit in his many guises.

Ethical Voluntarism

We spoke earlier of Tirsian splitting as assuming almost schizophrenic proportions. The reservation is made advisedly. Though immense tension is created in Tirso's protagonists by their efforts to compete against circumstance in multiple roles within a single part, they do not actually suffer disintegration and descend into madness (though some come close). This is prevented because the decision to divide the personality has not been forced on the protagonist under pathological strain (as in clinical cases of the schizoid condition), but has been undertaken rather through a conscious act of the will. Hence, above the apparently disintegrated personality hovers the fundamental will power of the protagonist, holding all in check, maintaining superhuman control not only over the dramatic situation, but also over the splitting of the ego. Thus we find in any inferred Tirsian theory of personality the same emphasis on the will as was discovered in his aesthetic voluntarism with reference to artistic creation, in his religious views in the Scotist-Franciscan tradition and, almost certainly, in the poet's actions during his lifetime. To the pre-eminence of the will in judging cases of human interaction, the name ethical voluntarism has been given.

Richard Taylor has written that: "Voluntaristic theories of psychology represent men primarily as beings who will certain ends and whose reason and intelligence are subordinate to will."[16] On the subject of ethical voluntarism, he continues:

> It is obvious that the voluntarist conception of human nature contains implications of the highest importance for ethics. If ends or goals are entirely products of the will and the will is neither rational nor irrational, then ends themselves cannot be termed either rational or irrational and it becomes meaningless to ask whether this or that end is really good or bad independently of its being willed ... Wise behavior, on this conception, can be nothing other than prudence,

---

16. See the article "Voluntarism" in *The Encyclopedia of Philosophy* (New York: Macmillan, 1967), vol. VIII, p. 270.

that is, the selection of appropriate means to the attainment of whatever goals one happens to have (loc. cit., p. 271).

Taylor's use of the term prudence in this context is clearly much closer to the sense in which we earlier defined Tirsian *prudencia*, than it is to the cardinal virtue of tradition. Here, then, is the unifying clue to all facets of the personality of the typical Tirsian protagonist discussed so far: an end is willed, reason and intelligent scheming are subordinate to that willed end, prudence defines the methods to be used, ethics and morality become relative or irrelevant, and the power of will saves the divided personality from madness.

It is not my intention to lay at Tirso's door charges of Machiavellianism, Jesuitical 'holy cunning' (Fülöp-Miller)[17] or other forms of moral turpitude, though his contemporaries, some Romantic critics (Durán, Mesonero Romanos) and modern critics (Méndez Bejarano, Mario Penna)[18] have done so. I would concur with Peyton that Tirso entertained grave doubts as to the ability of the human character to maintain its essential integrity when confronted by the problems of life. In this Fray Gabriel Téllez was a skeptic and participated in the overall tendency of early seventeenth-century Spanish art to move away from the high ideals and noble emotions of the Renaissance, thence to question them, fault them and even mock them.[19] As in all things, Tirso de

---

17. René Fülöp-Miller uses the phrase of St. Francis Xavier in his *The Jesuits: A History of the Society of Jesus* (New York: Capricorn, 1963), p. 202. This is a translation of his *Macht und Geheimnis der Jesuiten* (Leipzig and Zurich: Grethlein, 1929).

18. On Tirso's diction and supposedly off-color humor, Mario Méndez Bejarano has written: "El lenguaje peca de obscenidad [! ! !], confundiéndose a menudo el chiste con la licencia. . . . el teatro de Tirso es modelo de gracia, no siempre fina, de costumbres y de facilidad en la versificación." Quoted from J. Sanz y Díaz, *Tirso de Molina* (Madrid: C.B.E., 1964), pp. 213-14. Mario Penna is taken to task for his protests about the alleged immorality of *Marta la piadosa* by Dr. Premraj Halkhoree in his thesis of frequent reference. The latter states: "It is Penna's failure to see the morally subtle ground on which the play moves which, quite understandably, makes him uncomfortable about its implications. Few, indeed, can read Tirso without experiencing unease." "Social and Literary Satire . . ." at p. 210.

19. See Diego Angulo Iñiguez, "La fábula de Vulcano, Venus y Marte," in *Archivo Español de Arte,* (April-Sept., 1960), 149-81, where the author draws together diverse material showing how the mythological deities held in reverence by the Renaissance were accorded an increasingly burlesque treatment from the late sixteenth century onwards. In his discussion of Velázquez's mythological paintings,

Molina was at bottom a frank and stubborn realist. He saw man as less than perfect, a victim of his impulses, unequal to the impossible demands of the superego fashioned by the Counter Reformation and lucky if he could transcend circumstance by being a little cleverer than his enemies. The failure of some Tirsian protagonists to maintain voluntaristic dominion of themselves and their circumstance (Amnon, Don Juan, Jezabel or Paulo) and their inability, by releasing forces they can no longer control, to stave off their own destruction, may even point the way to a definition of Tirsian tragedy. Our concern, however, has been with personality; not a conscious theory of personality perhaps, but such is the consistency with which Tirso demonstrated how his characters responded to the special stresses of their age, that their behavior virtually amounts to one by implication.

Angulo characterizes Vulcan as a dirty, ugly cuckold, Venus as a fat whore and Mars as a tired, flabby and moustachioed figure. His quotations from Juan de la Cueva expressing the older dramatist's disquiet at the growingly cavalier attitudes displayed towards the pagan gods, are of particular interest. As late as 1609, in his *Ejemplar poético,* Cueva could invoke the Grecolatin deities, especially Apollo, in the accents of sincerity revealed by the following:

¿Dejo de celebrar héroes famosos
en verso heroico, a Marte consagrado,
y en épicos, oráculos gloriosos?
Si en esto, como sabes, he gastado
mi alegre juventud, y en alabanza
de dioses cien mil himnos he cantado,
¿por qué permites sin hacer mudanza
que en tan infame abatimiento vea
de mis largos trabajos la esperanza . . .

Si no es justo, y tú debes amparallas,
como deidad suprema y retor suyo,
acude, ¡oh, sacro Apolo! , *a remediallas.*

See *Juan de la Cueva, CC,* 60 (Madrid: Espasa-Calpe, 1965), ed. Francisco A. de Icaza, at p. 129. My emphasis.

IV

THE BAROQUE IN TIRSIAN DRAMA

> Así deben de estar los que enloquecen
> como yo ahora, no creyendo nada,
> a quien varias imágenes se ofrecen,
> nubes de confusión, alma turbada.
>
> *La mujer por fuerza,* III, xii.

In considering Tirso's dramatic practice, the term Baroque has been employed on a number of occasions. The purpose of the present chapter is to analyze and develop this concept with respect to Tirso's theater inasmuch as the latter's overall aesthetic impact could articulate a contemporary world view. By this is meant an attempt to fix and exemplify those moments where Tirso's dramaturgy, apart from its self-sufficient meanings, shows philosophic skepticism at work in the *comedia* and actually conveys a sense of the early seventeenth century, or Baroque, in Spain. To this end, a preliminary discussion of the meaning and conceptual background of the term Baroque will be followed by a comparison of Velázquez's *Las hilanderas* (1657) and scenes from Tirso's *Vergonzoso en palacio* (rev. 1624). The theme of regressive illusion is pursued in an analysis of Act II of *El rey don Pedro en Madrid,* and rounded out by examining Tirso's interest in what André Nougué has termed the "aberration of the senses." A concluding section will attempt to place Tirso's Baroque theater within its ideo-historical context.

Definition of the Baroque

It is late in the day to take up cudgels for the term Baroque; it has been with us for a hundred years since Gurlitt and Wölfflin, and is here to stay.[1] The subject of one of the liveliest critical controversies of this

---

1. Cornelius Gurlitt, in his *Geschichte des Barockstils in Italien* (Stuttgart, 1887), already treated the Baroque without any pejorative association in the last century; Wölfflin's earliest essays date from the following year. See Helmut Hatzfeld, *Estudios sobre el barroco* (Madrid: Gredos, 1964), at pp. 13-14.

century,[2] its triumph in the nomenclature of music and art history is now complete, but remains a matter of some debate in that of literature. More problematically for Tirso, cold water has been thrown on the idea of applying the term Baroque to the Spanish *comedia* as recently as 1953.[3] I feel, however, that the word Baroque is felicitous in its dual etymology, meaningful in its application to Western music and painting and, given proper safeguards, illuminating when applied to Tirso's theater.

The very proper objections to literary application of the Baroque to drama might be summed up in the warning that a label can only be as useful as its meaning, and that this label should illuminate the literature in question, not force the literature into aprioristic categories filched from other disciplines illustrating the concept, perhaps, but at the risk

---

2. Hatzfeld devotes a comprehensive, updated chapter, "Uso y abuso del término 'barroco' en la historia literaria," to the question of the long history of the term (op. cit., 417-29). The word appears certainly to have been a crux formed from the Port. *pérola barroca,* meaning a misshapen pearl, and *baroco,* the name for the fourth mode of the second figure in the scholastic nomenclature of syllogisms. The two etymologies mutually reinforce the notions of 'strange,' 'bizarre' or 'extravagant.' See also Gilbert A. Highet, *The Classical Tradition* (Oxford: Oxford U.P., 1949), chapter XV, "A Note on the Baroque" and his notes to the chapter at p. 646.

3. Américo Castro was one of the first Spanish scholars to use the term Baroque in literature, actually in discussing Tirso de Molina. See his edition of *El vergonzoso* and *El burlador* (Madrid: *CC,* 2, 1932), his article, "Las complicaciones del arte barroco," in *Tierra Firme,* 1 (1935), 161-68, and his contribution to the *Hommage à Ernest Martinenche* (Paris, 1937), "El Don Juan de Tirso y de Molière como personajes barrocos," pp. 93-111. The best known attempt to apply Wölfflin's categories to the *comedia* was the work of D. H. Roaten and F. Sánchez Escribano, *Wölfflin's Principles in Spanish Drama 1500-1700* (New York: Hispanic Institute, 1952). Reviewing the book in his "Reflections on a new definition of 'Baroque' drama," *BHS,* 30 (1953), 142-51, Professor A. A. Parker correctly pointed out that the *comedia* had never been classical in the Renaissance period, and the contrast of Renaissance and Baroque as applied to the Spanish drama was meaningless. He summed up his own position saying: "But whatever the artistic coherence of the fully-developed *comedia* may be due to, it is obvious that its non-classical form is not a 'Baroque' feature, unless 'Baroque' is to be applied to the greater part of the sixteenth century.... The attempt to define the Spanish drama in terms of the plastic arts leaves us, I submit, exactly where we were, with the added disadvantage that 'Baroque' is made a more question-begging term than it was before" (p. 151). Needless to say, I do not share Professor Parker's pessimism about the term's utility, given proper safeguards and the non-contrastive approach being used here.

of disfiguring an author's meaning. In 1946, however, René Wellek[4] upheld the usefulness of the term Baroque in the following words: "It seems to me, it would be a very false nominalism to deny that such concepts as the baroque are *organs* of real historical knowledge, that in reality there are pervasive styles, or turning-points in history which we are able to discern and which such terms help us in distinguishing" (p. 86. Wellek's italics). The problem lies, as Wellek admits, in deciding whether Baroque applies to the world view — some have even said ideology[5] — of the period, to its style, or to both.

In the first chapter of this study, the chaotic state of spiritual life in Europe, with particular reference to Spain, was analyzed at some length. Writing on Tirso de Molina in 1945, Meyron Peyton saw the Baroque and the spiritual crisis of European man, I think correctly, as being one and the same.[6] Defining religion as man's feeling about his own destiny, Peyton regarded religion as splitting in different directions at the end of the sixteenth century. He argues (as I have also tried to show) that Renaissance man's view of himself as autonomous and able to rule himself, led to a weakening of the belief in a providential God. The Reformation, moreover, viewed human life and the soul's salvation as resting precisely on the autonomous behavior of man. Protestantism for Peyton thus represented a crossing of medieval transcendence and Renaissance immanence, attended by a greater confidence in salvation and correspondingly lesser anguish of soul. In southern Europe, however, the reassertion of the traditional Catholic doctrines of unbreakable ties binding man to a transcendent thought and will ushered in the Counter Reformation, thus precipitating a more crucial conflict in the individual's conscience. Peyton aptly compares this double conflict to the attempt of institutionalized Church and State to place a medieval church dome upon Renaissance liberation.

But if we are to regard the Baroque as an artistic response to this complex spiritual crisis, then it should not be restricted exclusively to

---

4. See René Wellek, "The Concept of Baroque in Literary Scholarship," *JAAC,* 5, no. 2 (Dec., 1946), 77-109. Wellek appended an exhaustive chronological bibliography of literary criticism using the term Baroque (pp. 97-103). There are other articles by W. Stechow and Roy Daniells in the same issue, the latter an examination of English Baroque in literature which is persuasively argued.

5. See Stephen Gilman, "An Introduction to the Ideology of the Baroque," *Symposium,* 29 (1946), 82-107.

6. This is the important article of frequent reference, "Some Baroque Aspects of Tirso de Molina," *RR,* 36 (1945), 43-69.

the art of southern Europe; a collective sensibility seems to have prevailed not only in the separate art forms of the seventeenth century, but in the several genres of literature, and this sensibility did not confine itself to one sector of Europe, to one country nor to one system of doctrinal adhesions. The period displayed general trends within which the supernatural became naturalized, the spiritual became material and sensual, eternity gave way to an urgent sense of time and the transitory, while the dimension of time itself sought a spatial realization. Expressing unrest and internal division, the different seventeenth-century art forms therefore shared many of the following in common: strained symmetry, reduplication and splitting, dynamic tension, large masses of energy and space in movement, delight in sheer spectacle, stunning grandiose effects and artful confusion. Synthesizing these intuitions about spiritual crisis and their expressive forms into a working definition applicable to literature, I have settled on the following two-part epitome for the Baroque: the artistic representation of an internal conflict caused by the irreconcilable claims of monolithic belief and irresistible doubt competing for the same metaphysical 'space'; the resultant work of art is forced to elaborate a form that can contain multiple, possibly antagonistic elements within the same aesthetic 'space.'

What is here understood by 'space?' Recently, Marshall McLuhan and Harley Parker have pursued the notion of space as a reality in poetry, and compared literary and pictorial examples systematically in the book *Through the Vanishing Point*.[7] In their preamble, the authors write that their "... manner of juxtaposing a poem with a painting is designed to illuminate the world of verbal space through an understanding of spaces *as they have been defined and explored through the plastic arts.* The verbal medium," they add, "is so completely environmental as to escape a perceptual study in terms of its plastic values. Everybody can talk, but few can paint. A dialogue between the different forms and qualities of the sister arts of poetry and painting needs no defense, but there has been little exercise of such dialogue..." (p. 1. My italics). Space is a psychoaesthetic reality in Tirsian poetic speech, apart from the more literal and obvious functions of dramatic space permitted by a stage and characters in motion. The successful

---

7. See Marshall McLuhan and Harley Parker, *Through the Vanishing Point. Space in Poetry and Painting* (New York, Evanston: Harper, 1969).

interplay of these and their necessary realization in dramatic time seem to me to partake of the essence of Tirsian dramaturgical Baroque. I am asking, then, that mental or metaphysical 'space' be admitted as a conceptual reality, as also the possibility of its translation into poetry and painting to occupy what I have termed aesthetic 'space.'

Miss Irene Rice Pereira, in her *Nature of Space. A Metaphysical and Aesthetic Inquiry* (New York, 1956), has persuasively argued that the notion of space is derived from the external world and internalized metaphysically as well as aesthetically. "Space," she writes, "is a phenomenon both in relation to the concrete, sensible world, and the ideal space of abstraction. Although man's first sensations of space begin with his apprehension of relative relationships of bodies in the space of his concrete practical life, space itself assumes dimensionality and, as a concept, remains absolute .... even if there were no longer visible relationships, the dimensionality of space would still be an inherent property of its [i.e. space's] nature, and it would still maintain its qualitative and quantitative character of extension and expansion, whether the space is occupied or unoccupied" (p. 46. My clarification). Contrasting Renaissance and Baroque perceptions of space, Miss Rice Pereira notes that in a three-dimensional world (Renaissance), the mind is able to form the image — or signal in her terminology — by which the inner and outer are merged to produce a simultaneous experience. In a four-dimensional world (Baroque), the mind has the capacity for dimensionality and extension in space through what she terms the symbol.

The new, fourth element here is what we call the dimension of time, for it fell to the seventeenth century, both in art and philosophy, to discover time as a reality.[8] The Baroque attempt to incorporate this newly appreciated dimension into art is, for our purposes, the heart of the matter. The Renaissance successfully added depth, or perspective, to breadth and height; the Baroque later sought to explore the relation-

---

8. Matter, space, time and motion and their interrelationships were characteristic preoccupations of seventeenth-century physicists, astronomers and philosophers; the monism of Spinoza, the *tourbillons* of Descartes, the observations of Galileo, Leibnitz's monads, the gravitational theories of Newton, all in some measure reflect the century's absorption in the nature of matter, its movement in space, relation to time etc. Dividing observable phenomena into *res extensa* and *res cogitans,* Descartes even conceived of the human mind as matter thinking and thereby existing through a sequential cogitation.

ship of time to these three static dimensions. Now, since motion is the measure of time and time the measure of motion, one method of incorporating time into the spatial arts is to procure the actual illusion of movement. This was achieved architecturally in various ways: *trompe l'oeil,* false recesses on plane façades, spiraled instead of fluted columns, dizzingly mounted church interiors — techniques later summed up by Goethe as 'frozen music' (*gefrorene Musik*). Thus space, essentially static, is made to imitate time by appearing to move through the insinuation of dynamic tendencies into stone, paint and other plastic materials. As William Fleming says: "Ceaseless activity and motion are also the chief characteristics of Baroque sculpture. There is an element of the eccentric and even at times of the grotesque. The Baroque caryatids, far from the serenity of their classical models, are satyrs and fauns in dizzy, ballet-like attitudes..."[9]

In the theater, the Baroque fascination with representing space and time in terms of each other was reciprocal. Hence time, the essential component of kinetic arts like music, dance and metrical poetry, was made to appear static through the transformation of these arts into a colorful spectacle which imitated the qualities of the spatial arts. We have already referred to the literary debate in Spain about how poetry should imitate the spatial, three-dimensional appearances of nature, and how this injunction was conflictingly understood. It is no coincidence that in this same period the opera and ballet were originated as new expressive genres: both take music and add it, the first to dramatic tableau, the second to the dance, and thus create new marriages of space and time realized artistically. Of all genres, however, the drama itself was the medium that best expressed the Baroque agony, since it was the one medium that combined space and time completely. In the first place, the drama is a visual medium, an infinite series of pictures. As Tirso himself claimed, the Spanish drama also 'painted' in words; hence in multiple senses, space, tableau and composition may be appropriately applied to describe it. Conversely, the drama is a temporal medium, since it runs about two hours in performance,[10] has

---

9. See William Fleming, "The Element of Motion in Baroque Art and Music," *JAAC,* 5, no. 2 (Dec., 1946), 121-28, at p. 124.

10. In his article, " 'Lo fingido verdadero,' y la escenificación en el Siglo de Oro," *Boletín del Instituto Español de Londres,* 7 (Feb., 1949), 7-11, J. M. García Lora draws attention to the words of Carino in Lope's play to the effect that a *comedia* lasted about one and a half hours in performance, and some two hours total when the music, interludes and final dance were added.

pace and movement in plot, rhythm and meter in its language and cannot be understood without reference to the evolution of events in time, however compressed. One should also add that all Spanish dramatists freely employed song, music and dance in the drama, while some of Calderón's late works are *libretti* rather than *comedias* in the old sense.[11] Thus the drama, not only in its subject matter but in its very essence as a medium, satisfied the craving of the Spaniard to be shown his world as he felt it to be. In the light of these remarks, moreover, one may appreciate that the exhausting controversies on the Unities of Place, Time and Action were not the academic quibbles they might appear, but urgent issues in a world sensing its 'unity' to be disintegrating and acutely aware of space and time as never before in Western civilization.

Tirso and Velázquez

In view of what has been said so far, it will be clear that a comparison of Tirso's work to the painting of Diego de Silva Velázquez (1599-1660) is very far from capricious or arbitrary. Apart from extrinsic similarities,[12] they each in their different media translate the Baroque *Zeitgeist* by analogous experiments with aesthetic 'space' and 'time' and the skeptical interplay of these to set up a conflict-filled, illusory reality. Both strove to disconcert the onlooker and set his critical intellect at variance with the spontaneous feelings of trust and aesthetic acceptance experienced through the senses, notably the sight. Our precise interest lies in examining how Velázquez realizes aesthetic

---

11. Music became an increasingly important integral part of Calderón's *autos* and late mythological plays. For an early use, see N. D. Shergold, "The first performance of Calderón's *El mayor encanto amor*," *BHS*, 35 (1958), 24-27. *La púrpura de la rosa* and *El golfo de las sirenas* were entirely set to music, although Calderón had misgivings about the public's willingness to "... sufrir toda una comedia cantada." On Calderón's views about music and for other settings, see Jack Sage, "Calderón y la música teatral," *BH*, 58 (1956), 275-300, and "Texto y realización de *La estatua de Prometeo* y otros dramas musicales de Calderón," in *Hacia Calderón* (Berlin: Gruyter, 1969), 37-42. On a more modern musical setting, see Theodore S. Beardsley Jr., "Manuel de Falla's Score for Calderón's *Gran teatro del mundo*: the Autograph Manuscript," *KRQ*, 16, no. 1 (1969), 63-74.

12. Tirso and Velázquez were contemporaries, and it is hard to imagine that they had not met in Madrid by the 1620's or 1630's. Both were frank, even brutal, realists, and both brilliantly developed the traditions of an existing school (Tirso in following Lope, Velázquez in following the Venetian school).

'time' in a static medium like painting (*Las hilanderas*) and how Tirso realizes aesthetic 'space' in a dynamic medium like the drama (*El vergonzoso*), producing in each form that sense of antagonistic elements in competition for the same metaphysical 'space', which is the key to the Baroque. Such a comparison is not, however, the slavish imposition of Wölfflin's categories on literature, but an attempt to expose the affinities between art forms that all but consciously strove to be like one another.

Velázquez was first called an impressionist by R. A. M. Stevenson, a cousin of the English novelist.[13] Although the term was in vogue in the nineteenth century to describe the work of contemporary artists, Stevenson had sensed intuitively that Velázquez's overall impact created a multiple impression in the onlooker's mind, rather than a clear outline. Stevenson's biographer has referred to the art critic's precocious insight as follows: "Thus his emphasis upon Velázquez's ability to fuse different fields of vision in one composition, which is evident in the master's latest works, anticipates one of the main theories outlined by Heinrich Wölflin [sic] in his *Principles of Art History* (1915), namely that multiplicity of vision occurred with the Baroque and that a distinction can be made between 'das Lineare und das Malerische.' "[14] Numerous critics have concurred in the notion that Velázquez's canvases are painterly, and analyzed the master's use of color, light, space and depth to demonstrate the fact.[15] The more

---

13. See R. A. M. Stevenson, *Velázquez,* ed. Denys Sutton and T. Crombie (London: Bell, 1962). This is a modern reprint of the original, epoch-making study of the 1890 s.

14. See the biographical study by Denys Sutton in Stevenson, *Velázquez,* at p. 40.

15. Stevenson devoted considerable space to a discussion of Velázquez's 'impressionist' use of color and the sense of extemporization or of capturing moments in the Spanish painter's work. See also the more modern studies by Diego Angulo Iñiguez, "Las hilanderas," *Archivo Español de Arte* (Jan.-March, 1948), and his longer study, *Velázquez: Cómo compuso sus principales cuadros* (Seville, 1947); José Camón-Aznar, "El concepto del espacio en Velázquez," in *Varia Velazqueña,* vol. I (Madrid, 1960); and Emilio Orozco Díaz, *El barroquismo de Velázquez* (Madrid: México, 1965). In the last named work, the author writes: "Cuando Wölfflin, al fijar sus conceptos fundamentales, contraponía en el arranque los principios de lo *lineal* y lo *pictórico* como definidores de dos actitudes o visiones correspondientes a los siglos XVI y XVII, esto es, a lo clásico y lo barroco, distinguía como ejemplo expresivo en la pintura neolatina el caso de Velázquez, que pareaba en contraste con el Bronzino" (p. 30).

urgent issue is to see how agonizing metaphysical disintegration led Velázquez to suggest a corresponding multiplicity of vision on a plane surface, and to the representation of aesthetic time in paint.

Taking, as one must, religious conflict and a shifting world view as his point of departure, Orozco Díaz accords to Lafuente the realization that the Baroque aspects of Velázquez's art were fundamentally spiritual in inspiration:

> Es el primero de esa estética que él ha llamado de *salvación del individuo,* que frente al ideal renaciente que *aspira a la belleza ideal del arquetipo,* exalta, como valor máximo, la existencia del hombre concreto de carne y hueso, pero de alma inmortal. Esa estética, como arrancando de una actitud ante el mundo en la que se agudiza la conciencia de lo temporal, determina una decisiva transformación temática y un cambio de punto de vista del pintor ante el hombre y las cosas — sin selecciones ni jerarquías —, viéndolo todo en la próxima y concreta realidad del espacio, aire y luz en que viven, cuya apariencia se traslada al lienzo como aspirando a eternizar un momento de su existencia. (op. cit., pp. 31-32. Orozco's italics)

Orozco observes that the Baroque painter did not conceive his composition so much as a distribution of forms and colors in one plane, but as a distribution of elements within the profundity of space. Velázquez, he argues, pursued as a central aspiration the paradox that the picture should not in fact be a picture; that the picture should offer ". . . un ámbito espacial con *aire ambiente,*" imparting a sense of depth to the onlooker and stimulating him actually to penetrate the painting or, conversely, give him the impression that the persons who inhabit the picture could actually walk out of their world and enter his. There is in the well-attested sense of 'projection outwards' conveyed by Velázquez's work, an implicit notion that the spectator is himself a living component of the picture with which he is communicating; that he is, as I have said in connection with Tirso's theory of the drama, an active participant in the scene before him. Sñr. Orozco insists, I think rightly, that a vision or sense of continuous space and the form in which the sense of the temporal is made plastic and visible are central elements of the Baroque.

Las hilanderas (see fig. 2) is Velázquez's ultimate expression of temporal continuity. Thanks to the essential elucidations of Diego Angulo Iñiguez,[16] we now know that the subject of the painting is the

---

16. See his article "Las hilanderas," in *Archivo Español de Arte* (Jan.-March, 1948), pp. 1 et seq.

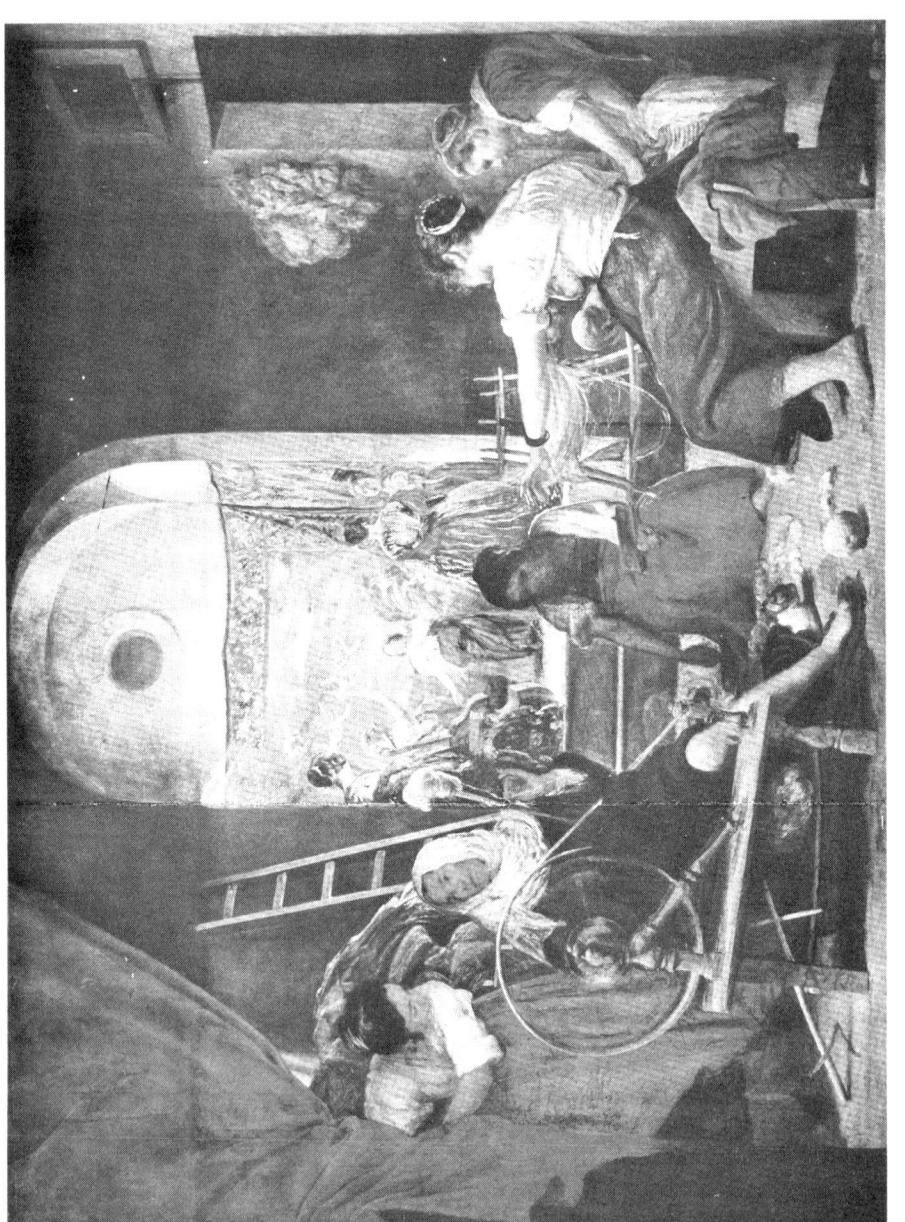

Fig. 2 *Las hilanderas* of Velázquez (1647-57)

Fig. 3 *The Rape of Europa* by Titian (c. 1560-61)

story of Pallas and Arachne from the sixth book of Ovid's *Metamorphoses*. As in many of his mythological canvases, however, Velázquez provides us with at least two time references, since the Classical scene in the central recess is set within the larger foreground of a contemporary spinners' workroom in Madrid. The connection between the two scenes is much more than a Chinese box pattern though, as we shall see. *Las hilanderas* is perhaps the most 'literary' work that Velázquez ever produced. As regards the master's humanist culture, this should cause little surprise; he possessed a personal library of some hundred and fifty-four titles, including the *Metamorphoses* in the Italian of Doles and possibly, according to Angulo, in the Spanish translation of 1542 by Jorge de Bustamante.[17] In Ovid's account of this legend, Arachne was a Lydian woman so skilled in weaving that she openly rivaled Pallas Athene (or Minerva according to native Roman tradition) in the handicrafts of needlework and tapestry, the domain proper of the goddess. Arachne (the Greek for 'spider'), not content with this indiscretion, depicted the sundry infidelities of Zeus — executed as a bull, swan or shower of gold — in tapestries which were the admiration of the women of Lydia. Pallas, warning Arachne against this *laesa majestas*, was challenged to a competition by the mortal, and when the goddess destroyed her web, Arachne, according to some accounts, hanged herself. Pallas at all events changed her into a spider.

Velázquez's painting shows a palace tapestry workshop, traditionally held to have been the one in the Calle Santa Isabel. The central recess, strikingly illuminated by rays of sunlight from the left against the gloomier foreground, shows a completed tapestry in which we see the martial Pallas, her arm upraised to strike or metamorphosize Arachne, standing against an even more blurred scene. This ultimate background was identified by Angulo Iñiguez as *The Rape of Europa* of Titian (see fig. 3) in a copy of Rubens known to Velázquez. In the original, Europa is being borne off by the lustful Zeus in the form of a bull. Thus the tapestry in the palace workshop not only portrays the imminent fate of the hapless tapestry weaver, but portrays within it the tapestry of Zeus and Europa, the occasion of her offense, 'quoted' by Velázquez from a Titian original copied by Rubens.

Within the recess of Velázquez's painting, ladies admire the Spanish

---

17. See F. Sánchez Cantón, *Cómo vivía Velázquez* (Madrid, 1942), at p. 1, and also his "La librería de Velázquez," in *Homenaje a Menéndez Pidal* (Madrid, 1925).

tapestry, just as the women of Lydia admired the tapestries of Arachne. To the left is a double-bass instrument lying against a chair, the significance of which was long held to be obscure. Angulo showed that this musical suggestion obviously referred to the old superstition that music was an antidote to the bite of the tarantula. The claim was repeated by numerous authorities of the sixteenth century, including the commentary on Discorides by Andrés de Laguna. These hints of harmony and cure from tarantula bite are indeed reduplicated in the tapestry scene, since Velázquez has chosen not to depict the wrathful destruction of Pallas, but the moment before Arachne's metamorphosis, which is both non-violent and also incidentally the 'cure' to the virulence of Arachne's indiscretions.

Angulo suggests, in the light of the complexity of Velázquez's conception, that the young woman spinning thread in the right foreground may also be Arachne and the old woman to the left swathed in a headscarf, Pallas in disguise. The Spanish critic also observes the following concerning the master's prepossession with a reduplication of scenes within scenes in this fashion: "El deseo de ligar con la escena principal del cuadro otras complementarias o aclaratorias es preocupación constante en Velázquez desde su juventud hasta sus últimos años, desde el recurso de primitivo de introducir en el fondo diversos episodios en que se repite la figura del protagonista del *S. Antonio* y el *S. Pablo,* hasta el más complicado de *Marta y María* o de *las Meninas.*"[18] As to Angulo's "complementary and explanatory scenes," we may say that the subject of Velázquez's painting is Arachne, who is herself the subject of the tapestry. She is a 'spider' who spins and weaves a web, just as the contemporary women spin and weave in the foreground, and she is finally turned into a real spider by Pallas. Velázquez has placed a picture (the Titian) within a picture (the tapestry) within a picture (*Las hilanderas*), and in so doing compressed five chronological moments into a single plane surface. These events are in order: the incident of Europa's actual rape by Zeus, Arachne's weaving of her tapestry of this scene, the imminent metamorphosis of the unfortunate girl by Athene, the

---

18. See Angulo Iñiguez, loc. cit. at p. 16. The painting of St. Anthony and St. Peter, also in the Prado, shows several scenes from the life of the hermit saint in different parts of the canvas. The protagonists appear, therefore, three or four times over in one framework. This kind of painted hagiography was not unknown in Medieval iconography, but acquires in the context of the Baroque a special meaning for Velázquez's artistic vision.

eventual weaving of the Spanish tapestry of this third event, and finally the present moment captured by Velázquez in his painting of the tapestry in the contemporary workshop. Thus we see that the ideas of weaving, web, spinning, spider and the rest all resonate to and fro and backwards and forwards throughout the picture in both space and time. As has been stated before, the spectator *must* participate with his whole consciousness, both aesthetic and intellectual, in order to bring out the significance of the picture and its deepest ironical or self-reinforcing statements. While the picture is gradually understood, the mind feels a sense of marvelous complexity, vertigo and a loss of grip on reality.

The final *tour de force* in *Las hilanderas* lies in Velázquez's deliberate attempt to fuse or confuse the various orders of reality within one aesthetic space and by this ambiguity leave the onlooker in a permanent state of doubt. The most brilliant patch in the picture is the paved floor of the recess flooded by sunlight from a hidden window to the left. If we look carefully, we perceive that though a decorative border runs round three sides of the tapestry, it is surpressed on the lower edge near the floor, either hidden by the dresses of the court ladies or simply missing completely. Pallas and Arachne seem, then, to be standing on the paving stones of the background among the ladies, with the whole tapestry as a background to themselves. As if this *trompe l'oeil* were not enough, Pallas can actually be seen to throw a *shadow* from the light of the window. Thus the mythological figures, by the suppression of the border and the addition of the shadow, appear to enter the world of the court ladies. The ladies of court, meanwhile, by their admiring attitudes, seem to enter the mythological world as the Lydian women. Velázquez, therefore, has succeeded in raising the tapestry scene to a plane of semi-reality by his ambiguous representation of the same aesthetic space, and this conflict never resolves itself. The most striking object in the foreground, a modern spinning-wheel, reassures one of a less insecure, mundane reality and acts as a second focus to the brilliant patch of stone. As the spectator's eye is forced to move between these two foci, he will suffer the optical illusion of seeing the spinning-wheel actually appear to be moving — an extraordinary feat of brushwork! If he stares at the wheel, it seems still; only when the eye catches it by surprise does it appear to move, i.e. when the eye itself is moving. Thus space, time and movement merge in scores of ways into a single, brilliant and dizzying performance of temporal continuity.

Earlier I called this painting the most literary of Velázquez because of its constant quotations and self-reference; Velázquez even quotes two modern painters. When Orozco Díaz feels bound by *Las hilanderas* to think of the Spanish theater, we cannot feel this second literary connection to be far-fetched. He says:

> Aquí, en *Las hilanderas,* donde todo es acción, nos hace pensar más en el teatro dentro del teatro. Y al decir esto pensamos no en el sentido de apariencia de sala y escenario, según anotó Justi, sino en que aquí Velázquez ha procedido en varios sentidos como en nuestro teatro barroco: presentando un acontecer extraordinario, de ficción o fábula, que tiene lugar y desarrollo dentro del plano de la realidad cotidiana, o con la duplicidad que supone las acciones paralelas de amos y criados en la comedia de capa y espada, o incluso en el hecho de presentar la representación teatral dentro de la escena, como en *El gran teatro del mundo* de Calderón. (op. cit., pp. 108-09)

... Calderón, one would agree, and certainly Tirso, who used the play-within-the-play device not just systematically, but almost obsessively. These plays-within-plays are not the "Mousetrap" of Hamlet or the distribution of roles within Calderón's *auto,* but scenes or parts of scenes that grow in complexity as they proceed in time and finally dissolve into new orders of reality or become subsumed in higher orders of illusion.

Tirso and the Play-within-the-Play

We have already noted in a previous chapter how fond Tirso's protagonists are of producing theatrical tableaux to influence other characters and how adeptly they assume spurious roles to mystify and manipulate opponents. Such play-acting was seen as a complex of goal-directed energy, will and practical intelligence that often led to a splitting of personality into two or three personae. But we have yet to analyze such performances from the dupes' point of view as complex illusions involving several people; as plays-within-plays. Though feeling superior to the play's victims, a Tirsian audience still comprehends the dramatic situation from their point of view in order to follow the action. Perspectivism in drama of this kind, however, can only be achieved with reference to time. Observable phenomena first seen from a given standpoint (physical appearances, characters' actions and reactions) may prove in time to be more or less than what they seemed. Conversely, deliberate illusions may be dismantled to reveal a truth always hidden to certain eyes. Thus objects occupying physical and aesthetic 'space' in the play will alter in significance as dramatic time elapses, or assume a quite new significance depending on the standpoint of the observer. Such practices also test the playgoer's agility and teach him at first hand the skeptical lesson that appearances may be deceptive.

In the minor love plot of *El vergonzoso en palacio* revolving around Doña Serafina and Don Antonio, we discover the most remarkable scenes of masquerade and play-acting.[19] Of interest here is the perspectivistic complexity of play-within-play achieved by Tirso and the Velázquez-like recession of succeeding levels of illusion into and inside each other. Significantly for the play's organic unity and Tirso's fascination with the manipulation of aesthetic space in the drama, painting itself assumes prime importance both as symbol and reality.

Antonio (II, ix) has contrived to remain in the palace to pursue his passion for Serafina, and through the connivance of his cousin Doña Juana, arranged to watch Serafina dressed as a man rehearsing a play for Carnival, *La portuguesa cruel*. He will be hidden among the bushes in a garden, in the company of a painter commissioned to sketch Serafina's likeness and subsequently work this sketch into a portrait. Juana is really the situation initiator of this scene (II, xiv), since she has engineered the presence of the hidden onlookers, whereas Serafina believes they are alone. Thus Antonio and the painter become spectators, while Juana's status is between that of spectator and participant. She makes this status clear when deceiving Serafina with the truth by her reference to ". . . un pintor que está escondido/ por copiarte en el jardín" (II, xiv, 468). After a tense moment, Juana explains that this painter is actually Love, hidden on Cyprus (the abode of Venus) to draw her, a statement both true and false. Juana, therefore, retains control over the situation, and we the audience surveying the scene within the scene have been reduced to spectators of a second order. Meanwhile the painter has been instructed to draw the transvestite Serafina as a man not a woman.

As Serafina acts out her role of jealous lover in *La portuguesa cruel*, not only is the tirade convincing but, using Juana as a mock rival suitor of the fictive Celia, she genuinely succeeds in arousing the girl's terror. During the ensuing reconciliation scene with Juana (now become 'Celia'), Serafina grows so amorous that she actually goes to embrace her companion physically and Juana recoils. Thus Juana has lost her manipulative status and become Serafina's victim and, far from semi-spectator, has been turned willy-nilly into an actress in the play-within-

---

19. For a discussion of aspects of play-acting within this play, see Joaquin Casalduero, "Sentido y forma de *El vergonzoso en palacio*," *NRFH* 15 (1961), 198-216; Francisco Ayala, "Erotismo y juego teatral en Tirso," *Insula*, 19, no. 214 (Sept., 1964), pp. 1 and 7; and Richard F. Glenn, "Disguises and Masquerades in Tirso's 'El vergonzoso en palacio,' " *BCom*, 17, no. 2 (Fall, 1965), 16-21.

the-play. As Francisco Ayala says, when Serafina starts to perform in this fashion, we in the audience have become spectators of a third order.

The *tour de force* comes in Serafina's third set piece. Announcing she will play the role of a madman, she in fact starts to play several roles at once. She no longer needs Juana, who has now been demoted to full spectator, but takes some six parts in succession – Sastre, an old man; Pinabel, a curate; Hernán Alonso, Celia, Fabio, etc. Since the play-acting is now confined to Serafina playing against herself, by the process of successively deepening illusions described by Ayala, we now become spectators of the fourth order. We end up, in fact, with an identical structure of receding degrees of illusion as in *Las hilanderas*. In each case the live spectator surveys a scene created by the artist (first order). The hidden men in the garden watching the two women are like the spinners in Velázquez's foreground aware of the recess behind (second order). When Juana becomes the participant-cum-spectator of Serafina she resembles the ladies of court admiring the tapestry (third order). When Serafina splits her identity six ways and takes over all the roles of *La portuguesa cruel* at once, she is like the tapestry which by superimposing one scene on another, is split between the cherubs, bull and maiden of the *Rape of Europa*, and the figures of Pallas and Arachne standing before it. Put another way, Serafina and the tapestry both contain their own illusions that are divided against themselves (fourth order).

When the episode is over and the women leave the palace garden, Tirso has not finished with 'painting' illusions. The painter asks Antonio if the portrait should show Serafina dressed as a man? Yes, replies the other, but the ill-omened black shades should be altered to gold. Antonio, therefore, is not content to see Serafina as what she was *not* (i.e. as a man), he now introduces his own fantasizing and changes even the appearance of the illusion. When Serafina (III, xi) rejects Antonio's love, he throws the finished portrait at her feet and leaves in a fury. On picking it up, deceived by the male dress and its gold color but struck by the subject's similarity to herself, the narcissistic Serafina actually falls in love with her own portrait:

> Un retrato!
> (Alzale.)
> Es de un hombre, y me parece
> que me parece de modo,
> que es mi semejanza en todo.

> Cuanto el espejo me ofrece,
> miro aquí: como en cristal
> bruñido mi imagen propia
> aquí la pintura copia
> y un hombre es su original.
> ¡Válgame el Cielo! ¿Quién es?
> (III, xii, 484)

Apart from the irony, humor and psychological insight of this twist, Tirso has now pushed the reduplication of illusion even further. What was an illusory portrait of an illusion, now deceives Serafina into believing that what she sees is the representation of an objective reality. In this sense, the completely fictive male in the painting who has stirred the co-heroine to passion represents an order of reality five times removed from the starting point: Serafina as a woman, Serafina as a man in black, Serafina as a man in gold, Serafina as a portrait of a man in gold, Serafina as a man in gold in the mind of Serafina!

Tirso's most elaborately conceived illusion within a play occupies the bulk of Act II of *El rey don Pedro en Madrid*.[20] Without exaggeration, one may say that all the characters in the play become actors to varying degrees in the king's carefully staged spectacle. The ostensible purpose of this play-within-a-play is to humiliate the fractious Infanzón de Illescas and his accomplice, Cordero. Of greater technical interest, the inner illusion objectifies the king's internal spiritual division, and also presents us with a use of dramatic space and imaginary progress designed to drag out psychological (and hence dramatic) time to the utmost. The space through which the offenders pass is not so much three-dimensional as mental.

King Pedro, who died by his brother's hand at Montiel in 1365, fascinated many Spanish dramatists; he appears in plays by Lope, Tirso, Calderón, Claramonte, Moreto and others.[21] Pedro's historically dual

---

20. *El rey don Pedro en Madrid* has been challenged in its attribution to Tirso. Cotarelo (cf. his *Catálogo razonado*, *BAE*, vol. 9 at p. xlv) thought it to be Lope's work, but Doña Blanca zealously defended its Tirsian paternity in her edition. The themes of double identity, division of personality, fraternal strife, the plain but gripping dialogue, the use of illusions, apparitions and play-within-play are all so overwhelmingly Tirsian, that only the most overscrupulous hesitation could deny Tirso the attribution. It is with the doubters, at least, that the burden of definitely assigning the play's authorship to another playwright must rest.

21. Apart from this play, Tirso treats a refugee relative to the king, also called Pedro, in his *Amor y celos hacen discretos* set in Italy. In *Siempre ayuda la verdad*, his Castilian namesake is invoked by the contemporary King Pedro of Portugal, a cha-

nature appealed profoundly to Tirso's sense of drama. The twin soubriquets of *cruel* and *justiciero* provided Tirso with a readymade combination of two 'roles' within a single 'part.' Here was a king divided against himself: cruel, vengeful and impetuous on the one hand, justicer and upholder of law and order on the other. As Hesse and McCrary have pointed out,[22] it was not Tirso's purpose to decide which label suited Pedro better, but brilliantly to consider him both. The duality of the king's nature, then, is the fundamental datum of the play and this fact influences the play's structure and Baroque technique. Pedro's identity conflicts achieve their most striking expression in Act II, since the ego's flight from direct action here makes others the instruments of the manipulative will and presents the king as protagonist in his own illusion.

The necessity for the palace masquerade has been established in Act I. Tello García, the overweening feudal baron, and his servant Cordero have committed rape against the persons of Elvira and Ginesa, two peasant girls, and the Infanzón against that of Leonor also. Tello's contempt for regal authority creates a graver political problem, however, compounded by the princeling's taunts (I, viii) against the personal worth and valor of the king directed to Acebedo (actually Pedro in disguise). Tello even challenges the king to single combat. The elaborate games of Act II are planned to inflict a humiliating revenge on the upstart for all these offenses, then, but while subordinate to this end, the masquerade technique itself is what interests us here.

Elvira's question: "Traernos de Leganés/ el Rey, y mandar vestirnos/

---

racter in the Inés de Castro legend. Tirso also refers approvingly to Pedro in his *Historia general de la Merced* (II, folio 267 v.). Lope brings Pedro into *La niña de plata* and he plays essential roles in Calderón's *El médico de su honra,* Andrés de Claramonte's *De esta agua no beberé* and Moreto's *El valiente justiciero.*

22. See E. W. Hesse and W. C. McCrary, "La balanza subjetiva-objetiva en el teatro de Tirso: ensayo sobre contenido y formas barrocos," *Hispanófila,* 3 (1958), 1-11. Speaking of the plays *Don Gil* and *El rey don Pedro,* the authors write that: "Es esta técnica de múltiples perspectivas cambiantes, proyectadas en dos planos de percepción dramática, lo que da la forma característicamente barroca de ambas obras..." (p. 9). For a discussion of King Pedro's dual character in Calderón's play, see Irvine A. Watson, "Peter the Cruel or Peter the Just? A reappraisal of the role played by King Pedro in Calderón's *Médico de su honra,*" in *RJ,* 14 (1963), 322-46; D. W. Cruickshank, "Calderón's King Pedro: just or unjust?" *Spanische Forschungen der Görresgesellschaft,* 25 (1970), 113-32, and Frank P. Casa, "Crime and Responsibility in *El médico de su honra,*" in *Homenaje a William L. Fichter* (Madrid: Castalia, 1971), 127-37.

desta suerte, ¿qué será?" (II, v, 133), early establishes the theatrical quality of these scenes. Pedro's decision to dress the women in new costumes, Elvira in aristocratic finery, Ginesa tricked out as a "dueña ridícula," indicates that the peasant girls are to become actresses in the king's play. Don Juan and Don Alonso, courtiers armed with keys, and Fortún act the role of masters of ceremonies obeying the wishes of an invisible regal director. The balance of characters, Rodrigo, Leonor, Tello and Cordero, remain confused about the king's intentions. Tello and his lackey, lured to the court by a summons, have first been made to enter the palace by the postern gate — a slight staged with deliberate care. His bodyguard is then forcibly removed by Fortún acting on the king's orders. When Tello draws his sword to defend himself against Rodrigo, both have their weapons removed and the latter is arrested. The eye imagery of the following exchanges effectively underscores Pedro's role as an all-seeing, but unseen guiding force: "DON JUAN. A los ojos de su Alteza/ ¡ital atrevimiento! DON RODRIGO. Agravios/ en todo parte se vengan./ FORTUN. Ya el Rey lo ha visto. Quitadles/ las espadas" (II, x, 135).

Now disarmed and alone, the villains feel apprehensive of a trap. The masquerade continues as Alonso, knowing full well who he is, asks which of the pair is the Infanzón? Kafka-like, he leads them from the chamber to a second room and locks them within. After a pause, two courtiers enter with Elvira who is propelled in an unreal, somnabulant trance across the stage and disappears, having feigned the while not to notice the Infanzón. Fortún enters next with new orders from the king; they are led into a third room and again locked in. Cordero, beginning to understand these manoeuvres, exclaims: "Mas, ¿que nos encierran/ en otra pieza? A recados/ nos castigan" (II, xiv, 137). Tello, starting to feel awe for the unseen majesty of the king, confesses to his servant: "Esta majestad que ves,/ es la que los hombres tiemblan,/ que por sí solos son hombres/ los reyes; mas la grandeza/ los pasa a divinidades." (II, xv, 137). Maintaining the theatrical symmetry, Ginesa, the comic heroine of the parodic subplot, now walks across the villains' line of vision, uttering obscure warnings and concluding on the very Tirsian line: "Quien tal hace, que tal pague" (II, xvi, 138).

Thoroughly unnerved, Tello and Cordero are ushered into a fourth room — the royal chamber — where they await the king. The magnificent, consciously postponed entry of Pedro into his own domain, accompanied by his retinue, overwhelms the pair and Tello realizes with horror that Pedro is none other than the Acebedo to whom he had so violently abused the king's name on the previous day. When they abase themselves at King Pedro's feet, he pretends not to notice them but protracts the play-acting by attending to petitions and royal business instead. Even after repeated submissions, Pedro will only say absentmindedly: "¿Sois vos ... Esta es de la Reina .../ Tello García?" (II, xviii, 139). Maintaining the pose, Pedro asserts with sarcasm how pleased he is to see the man who could only offer a lowly footstool to his king. When Tello shams that he has always recognized Pedro as his king, the latter finally drops all masquerading and catalogues his crimes to Tello's face. Reaching a climax on the issue of *laesa majestas,* Pedro also reveals the deeper reasons for his fury: his doubts about his true worth as a man (II, xviii). The tirade finished, Pedro drags Tello by the scruff of the neck to a doorway, beats him about the head and leaves with his entire retinue.

Thus we see that Pedro has been throughout the invisible director of an interpolated drama designed to harrow his victims into fear and submission. For the most part, the king's will is carried out by his attendants and his scorn the more effective by being remote and indirect. Though the offended heroines and courtiers also function like puppets under the king's control, the main purpose is to put Tello and Cordero through a vast, Baroque carnival as unwilling participants, using the entire palace as a four-dimensional stage. The king appears in his own play-within-the-play, pretending first about the petitions, then dropping all pretenses to deliver his final blows, both psychological and physical. Though we must not subordinate the overall purpose of humiliating the arrogant to the play-in-play technique, we must recognize that here as so often in Tirso, the protagonist's inner illusion is used to create doubt and confusion in the minds of other characters, and it is through illusion that important changes of attitude or emotional condition are brought about. The noteworthy circumstance is how Tirso (through Pedro) uses space to this end, for the successive apartments and movements within the palace do not achieve any real progress in a horizontal sense, but merely bring the offenders psychologically nearer and nearer the king and to the appropriate state of mind for a subject-monarch confrontation.

The Aberration of the Senses

By examining play-in-play from the dupes' point of view, we have appreciated how characters can be made to suffer. Their fate at the hands of the manipulator variously excites in them confusion, a partial understanding of their situation or serious judgmental error. When dramatic illusion is pushed to extremes, however, the victim may pass through two last phases: mistaken certainty and total mystification. This final stage is often compared to madness and such chronic states of doubt and confusion often seem the ultimate goal of a Tirsian *enredo*: to leave a point of security and achieve in drama an objective correlative for contemporary skeptical anguish as soon as possible. A confused character, echoing the spiritual plight of the seventeenth century, cries out that he cannot trust his organs of perception, that nothing makes sense, that his very senses have deserted him. This malaise may extend by active participation to the onlooker; complex illusion and multiplicity of vision force him to subject his world to a more fundamental scrutiny than before, thus generating that impalpable 'extra' effect always produced by the finest Baroque art.

André Nougué, referring to this aspect of Tirsian drama as far as the victims are concerned, terms their condition an "aberration of the senses." With regard to three lighter comedies, Nougué writes: "On a souvent remarqué, en effet, que Tirso fonde bien souvent l'intrigue de ses comédies sur la mystification d'un personnage; il s'agit de lui faire croire que ce qu'il voit n'est pas ce qu'il croit voir; il faut jeter le trouble dans son esprit et le persuader qu'il se trompe; il faut l'obliger à reconnaître lui-même qu'il est victime de ses sens abusés."[23] Nougué notes that in *En Madrid y en una casa, Por el sótano y el torno* and *Los balcones de Madrid,* substantially the same device is exploited with similar results. In the first play, one room in a house is joined by a trapdoor and a secret staircase to a lower apartment beneath; in the second, a chateau apartment and a convent are joined by a secret tunnel; while in the third two neighboring house are joined by a kind of catwalk between two balconies.[24] In each case, the secret connection enables young lovers to meet clandestinely and so outwit the girl's guardian, prospective husband, etc. and in the process precipitate in the guardian figure an experience of aberration of the senses.

What Tirso is doing in these comedies is certainly to make the victim

---

23. See A. Nougué. "Le thème de l'aberration des sens dans le théâtre de Tirso de Molina," *BH,* 58 (1956), 23-35 at p. 23.

24. For a discussion of the symbolic meanings attached by Tirso to the tunnel and the revolving dumb-waiter in the convent (*el torno*), see Dr. Premraj Halkhoree's insightful article "Satire and Symbolism in the Structure of Tirso de Molina's *Por el sótano y el torno," FMLS,* 4, no. 4 (1968), 374-86.

a vehicle of high humor, but this is achieved by literally playing with space. As far as the victim is concerned, things no longer fit, for how can one object occupy two different places or spaces at the same time? The object seems to reduplicate and reality itself to multiply in a way that negates the fidelity of perception. The best example in *Los balcones de Madrid* falls in Act III, and draws on the *comedia* (or play-within-play) as a point of reference since Alonso, the father, is the victim of an elaborately staged hoax in which four other people cooperate to fool him. The enraged father (III, xii) has seen his daughter, Elisa, with her lover Juan but covered by a kerchief over her face. When Elisa reaches her own room via the catwalk where her maid is waiting, the problem is to dispose of the kerchief in order to dispel suspicion. After rejecting several options, Elisa suggests hiding it in her sleeve: "En la manga. LEONOR. Mal consejo,/ que en una comedia vi/ que le escondieron ansí,/ y todas las oye el viejo./ ELISA. Mira, pues, que sube. LEONOR. Aguarda,/ verás un ardid bisoño./ Metámosle en este moño" (III, xiv, 1150). Thus rejecting the precedent offered by the *comedia* (acting unpredictably and *unlike* a character in a play), Leonor hides the kerchief inside the wire frame of her bouffant hairstyle.

When Alonso rushes in only to find Elisa in her own room, he feels not merely that he is going mad, he is encouraged to feel that he is going mad. He acts predictably as if he were in a play (which he is twice over) by looking for the kerchief in Elisa's sleeve:

    ELISA'   ¡Señor!, pues ¿a qué otra vez?
    DON ALONSO. ¡Jesús, Jesús!, mi vejez
                       el seso me precipita.
                       (Mira y tienta todas las paredes, y la alcoba.)
                       ¿Por dónde pudiste entrar
                       en esta pieza?
    ELISA.   ¿Qué dices?
                       ¿Qué buscas en los tapices?
                       ¿Qué por la cama?
    DON ALONSO.   ¿Engañar
                       mis advertencias pensabas?
                       ¿Qué es del manto que traías?
    ELISA.   ¡Manto! ¿Cuándo? Desvarías.
    DON ALONSO. Cuando con don Juan estabas.
    LEONOR.   ¡Ay desdichada de mí!
                       Señor, ¿ha perdido el seso?
    ELISA.   ¡Yo, con don Juan!
    DON ALONSO.   De tu exceso,
                       liviana, evidencias vi.

> Despejad las dos las mangas,
> (Míraselas.)
> manifestad faldriqueras.
> LEONOR. O está sin seso de veras,
> o viene de caza de gangas.
> (III, xv, 1150-51).

In all three plays, the process is the same: to force the victim to admit an error where none exists. One character appears to be in two places at once and by visual illusion provokes in the dupe an acute skeptical crisis which borders on insanity. While this crisis is comic, it is also serious inasmuch as it raises the gnawing epistemological problem of how any object can be known, once for any reason having admitted the imperfection of the senses? In *Los balcones de Madrid,* Don Alonso is obliged to admit the imperfection or aberration of his senses when no such admission is necessary: hence the comedy.

A splendid example of a character brought to the edge of madness through very little fault of his own is Federico in *La mujer por fuerza.* While the earlier work is similar in plot and conception to *Don Gil de las calzas verdes,* Count Federico suffers greater skeptical anguish than Martín. Although the former has caused less offense, he has, in a moment of rash overflorid courtesy, offered to marry Finea, the sister of his host Alberto, without ever having seen her. Finea then pursues Federico to Naples dressed as a man, alienates his fiancée Florela through jealousy, allows everyone to think she has been abducted by the Count and finally convinces her brother that Federico has killed her. From Federico's point of view, however, the whole nightmarish situation makes no sense at all. Everyone believes he has in fact been responsible for Finea's disappearance, which in an ironical way is true, and since Finea is his page Celio in disguise, his sincere claims never to have seen her are, in a way, untrue. By the same token, Finea as Celio can swear by mental reservation to have this knowledge or not, as the occasion demands.[25]

Federico has sensed the nature of his dilemma in an aside when he

---

25. There is a good example of this when Federico (II, iv) calls on Finea-Celio to support his own version of the truth. When he asks her awkward questions point-blank, the inherent ambiguity of the situation and her clever casuistry absolve her of direct lying: "CONDE. Pues hago elección de ti,/ yo sé que sabrás por mí/ defender mi noble intento./ ¿No conociste en Hungría/ a Alberto? FINEA. ¿Yo? Sí, señor./ CONDE. ¿Pues quién le hablará mejor,/ Celio, en la inocencia mía? / Nó sabes tú que he venido/ solo? FINEA ¡Y cómo si lo sé! " (II, v, 524).

says: ". . . que a un hombre le culpe/ la ajena imaginación,/ es la mayor novedad/ que se ha visto ni se ha oído" (II, v, 523). His plight grows worse as the soundness of Federico's senses is increasingly put in question. Alberto, having glimpsed his sister in female dress at the Neapolitan court, asks Federico how he can deny what everyone else sees with their own eyes:

> Federico, si tenemos
> ojos, si razón, si ley,
> si trato humano, ¿qué es esto?
> ¿Como niegas a los ojos
> lo que con los ojos vemos?
> ¿Por qué a la razón la pena?
> ¿Por qué a la ley el derecho?
> ¿Por qué al trato humano el ser
> con que se vive en concierto?
> Tienes a mi hermana aquí,
> y en deshonor y en desprecio
> suyo y mío, y aun del Rey
> que a los dos nos está oyendo
> ¿niegas que jamás la viste?
> (III, viii, 540).

While Tirso extracts the maximum comic effect and ambiguity from Alberto's words, the questions themselves do also raise the wider epistemological issue. This problem assumes truly philosophical proportions when Federico's lackey Clarín answers his master's incipient doubts about his own sanity in the following terms: "Señor, señor, yo no digo/ que lo he visto ni lo creo,/ sino que lo dicen todos" (III, x, 541). Clarín in other words is suggesting that truth is not necessarily in the eye of the beholder, but in the consensus of a majority – one of the most perturbing conclusions a skeptic can reach. When Finea-Celio pretends to believe her master is mad, this is the last straw for Federico – he genuinely believes his reason has snapped:

> Acabóse fortuna; yo estoy loco;
> no tengo que esperar, pues un lacayo
> y un paje tienen mi valor en poco.
> ¡Abrase esta mujer, del cielo un rayo!
> Pero, por Dios, que a veces me provoco,
> si bien me causa tan mortal desmayo,
> presumir de que debe de ser cierto,
> y que se queja con razón Alberto.
> *Así deben de estar los que enloquecen*
> *como yo ahora, no creyendo nada,*

a quien varias imágenes se ofrecen,
nubes de confusión, alma turbada.
(My italics. III, xii, 542).

The *octavas* in italics express, I would submit, the very essence of seventeenth-century man's desolation, the "misère de l'homme" of which Pascal left such a sublime testimony in the *Pensées*: a desolation essentially spiritual and metaphysical, a state of doubt in which clouds of confusion offer various, undifferentiated images of an unstable world to man's disbelieving senses and through such aberration fill his soul with anguish. For Tirso, the image before the sight can often barely be trusted, least of all in the field of human relations. His theater constantly strives to portray this confused image in as many ways as possible simultaneously; hence the confusion becomes more precisely postulated, but also more pregnant with secondary meanings and potential ambivalence. The devices of illusion and play-acting are used to this end, and the center of this skepticism lies in the faculty of sight. This is one reason why Tirso has constant recourse to painting as the highest expression of manmade, visual illusion. Thus, as I have maintained *ad nauseam,* Tirsian comedy at its best, while remaining comic, reaches down for enlightenment into the nether depths of understanding about the human situation.

What we have called the Baroque in Tirsian drama depends above all on the playwright's skill in creating confusion by a subtle and illusory representation of space and time, often in terms of each other. We have tried to show that space-time confusions and world view are connected; such an inversion forms a constituent of the whole panorama of the world upside down (*el mundo al revés*) which both perturbed and delighted Baroque artists. As Mikhail Bakhtin maintains in his study of Rabelais,[26] the Renaissance had already shifted the center of the medieval cosmos downwards. The concept expressed in Hermes Trismegistes that God is a sphere whose center is everywhere and whose circumference is nowhere, leads inevitably to the conclusion that all centers are therefore equal; the underworld, the center furthest from God in medieval cosmogeny, became an underground womb pregnant with riches, the other face of heaven.

This downward movement expresses itself in carnival and travesty

---

26. See Mikhail Bakhtin, *Rabelais and his World,* tr. Helene Iswolsky (Cambridge, Mass.: MIT Press, 1968), especially his sixth chapter, "The Material Bodily Lower Stratum."

but also in an inversion of spiritual topography. In medieval thought, the visible model of the earth was essentially vertical; the notions of 'upper' or top were contrasted with the 'lower' or bottom, and hence their sense of space was related to real values. By contrast, the horizontal held no fascination for the medieval mind since it implied no change or rise. Since this hierarchical movement ignored the horizontal plane, it also ignored time since time was not necessary for ascent; progress in one sense (a movement forward in time on a horizontal plane) did not exist. Columbus' westward crossing of the Atlantic could be viewed as an early expression of the breakdown of such a hierarchy. By Rabelais' time, according to Bakhtin, the leading role had been transferred to horizontal lines, to movement forward in real space and historical time. Hence in comic representations of experience, the inside is out; the top and bottom change places. The mixing of hierarchical levels enables the observer to discover the core of the object's concrete reality, free it from its shell and show, in the Russian critic's phrase, its material bodily aspect.

Important for comedy in this new world picture, is Bakhtin's concept of 'positive negation': the description of an object by stating what it is not — a device beloved of Góngora among others. As he states: "... that which stands behind negation is by no means nothingness, but the 'other side' of that which is denied, the carnivalesque upside down . . . . The object that has been destroyed remains in the world but in a new form of being in time and space; it becomes the 'other side' of the new object that has taken its place" (op. cit., p. 410). We have already seen how the Baroque took this process a stage further, for if the artistic breakthrough of the Renaissance was the discovery of the third dimension — perspective —, the artistic breakthrough of the Baroque was the discovery of the fourth dimension, time. Not only this, the Baroque endeavored to blur space and time by expressing them in terms of each other and pursued as deliberate aesthetic goals the ambivalences that space-time inversions and perceptual confusions gave rise to. As a playwright, Tirso is perhaps less interested in the "varias imágenes" of nature as objects under the scrutiny of a philosopher, than as ambivalent *human* phenomena. What delights him is to take a single event (the kissing of a hand for example) and show how many meanings the 'event' (an object in space in the widest sense) may have when viewed from a multiplicity of points of vantage. The game with reality is pure comedy, pure drama and a pure questioning, in which events and objects are posited, negated and restated in complex new syntheses.

The theme of *el mundo al revés* is not, of course, limited to Tirso's theater in seventeenth-century Spain; it appears as the theme of Quevedo's *La hora de todos,* is treated in Gracián's *Criticón*[27] and inasmuch as Sancho is the inversion of Don Quijote, provides a running dialectical debate throughout Cervantes' masterpiece, etc. Tirso specifically addressed himself to the theme in *El pretendiente al revés* and *La república al revés,* but the concept pervades his whole theater. To close the present chapter on the Baroque in Tirsian drama as a portrait of a confused world view, we may conclude that the Spanish Baroque brought to the surviving medieval and Renaissance elements in its culture a greater understanding of human life than had been achieved previously. With a prodigious capacity for harmonizing the irreconcilable and with marvelous artistic mastery, the writers of the Spanish Counter Reformation achieved one last tenuous synthesis before theocracy finally collapsed before the triumph of human institutions and became a memory. As to the Spanish theater itself, one notorious theoretician of historical processes has suggested that: "History acts fundamentally and goes through many phases when it carries obsolete forms of life into the grave. The last phase of the universal historic form is its comedy."[28] Marx was probably right.

27. Gracián (*Criticón,* pt. 1, Crisi VII) writes for example: "... un día saliera el sol por el poniente y caminara al oriente y entonces fuera España cabeza del mundo, sin contradicción alguna, que no hubiera quien viviera con ella. Y es cosa de notar que, siendo el hombre persona de razón, lo primero que ejecuta es hacerla a ella esclava del apetito bestial. De este principio se originan todas las monstruosidades. Todo va al revés, en consecuencia de aquel desorden capital: la virtud es perseguida; el vicio, aplaudido; la verdad, muda; la mentira, trilingüe; los sabios no tienen libros y los ignorantes librerías; los libros están sin doctor y el doctor sin libros; la discreción del pobre es necedad y la necedad del poderoso es celebrada..." Quoted from Ion T. Agheana, *The Situational Drama of Tirso de Molina* (Madrid: Plaza Mayor, 1972), pp. 60-61, n. 29.

28. Karl Marx and F. Engels, *Collected Works,* vol. 1, p. 418. Quoted by Bakhtin, op. cit., p. 436.

V

TIRSO'S PRISMATIC USE OF LANGUAGE

> "...que nos ahorremos de todas esas zarandajas de circunloquios cuando en un solo vocablo hallamos significación proporcionada a nuestro intento sin ofender ni al *dialecto*, ni al común modo de hablar de nuestra patria...."
>
> Dedication of the *Quinta parte*.

Thus far, our remarks concerning the Baroque in Tirso have been confined to an analysis of its overall impact in the theater and its relation to a contemporary world picture. In the second half of our definition of the Baroque, it was claimed that the work of art resulting from an internal spiritual conflict is forced to elaborate a form that can contain multiple, possibly antagonistic, elements within the same aesthetic space. Now clearly in drama, it is the words themselves that constitute the aesthetic space of a work. To illustrate the definition fully, we must now turn to the question of Tirso's language, and specifically to his success in forcing multiplicity of effect into single words and phrases. This practice I have termed a prismatic use of language, since a single term may fragment into a plurality of connotations or meanings within its context. For clarity's sake, the essay is divided into conflation of time, image and semantic wordplay.

The natural exuberance and playfulness of Tirso's language has often been noted by critics, but mostly in general terms. Agustín Durán wrote in his *Talía española* (Madrid, 1834), that Tirso's talent lay in his "... estilo natural, versificación armoniosa y abundante, en su audacia y oportunidad para el manejo del idioma, en la riqueza de sus rimas, en su caudaloso y rápido diálogo, en su modo travieso e ingenioso de contrastar las ideas, en sus sales picantes y epigramáticas, y, en fin, en su expresión, llena de gracia, soltura y amenidad."[1] Mesonero Romanos

---

1. This quotation and those immediately following are taken from the "Florilegio crítico" in José Sanz y Díaz's *Tirso de Molina* (Madrid: C. B. E., 1964), pp. 211-20.

spoke of Tirso's "gracejo peculiar en el decir y admirable conocimiento de la lengua patria . . ."; others sometimes found that his daring quips degenerated into obscenity, while Hurtado y González Palencia claimed that: "Tirso es insuperable en la naturalidad, verdad y gracia del diálogo, el primero entre nuestros dramáticos en cuanto al lenguaje y estilo, gustando mucho de formar verbos de nombres, y fue defensor siempre del teatro nacional."

While these commendations of Tirso's naturalness, effortless command of Spanish and propensity for verbal ingenuity are accurate, there has been little done to study *how* precisely he achieves these effects. At first glance, mention of verbal ingenuity may remind one of the new modes of diction established by Góngora and Quevedo. But whereas Tirso consciously rejected and satirized *culteranismo*,[2] his own verbal exuberance is obviously of a piece with it and in some plays of the mid-sixteen twenties, Tirso's dialogue displays patent gongoristic influence.[3] What always saves Tirso's theater from banality and obscurity, however, is the fact that his verse remains first and foremost dramatic. The dialogue had to be intelligible at a first and single hearing, so that even when mannered or ingenious the dramatic meaning behind the verbal acrobatics could shine through.

What all the styles have in common, however — *culteranismo, conceptismo,* the crowded poetic exuberance of Tirso's *habla llana* —, is a desire to compress. That is, by the use of metaphor, extended metaphor, symbolism, puns, quibbles and cruces of every kind, to force

---

2. In the *Cigarral segundo*, Tirso praises those who handle the Spanish language with exquisite polish and naturalness, and says of the *culteranistas*: "Pero aquellos escabrosos en la primera digestión que necesitan de gramáticos intérpretes, obligando a construir Erasmos romancistas, desacomodando con violencia los adjetivos de sus sustantivos, y echando los verbos por contera de la oración, merecen, mientras sus autores no cantan la palinodia, ridículas inventivas, como él que, convidando a curiosos huéspedes les da guisadas las aves con sus plumas y las frutas con sus cáscaras, para que primero que entren en provecho al ingenio, se quiebren en ella los dientes del entendimiento: éstos vitupero y esotros reverencio y alabo." Quoted by Cotarelo, *NBAE*, vol. IV, p. xl.

3. A good example of Tirso's gongoristic diction is the opening of *El amor y la amistad*, where a mountain is apostrophized as an "Alta presunción de nieve,/ pirámide de diamante,/ encelado que gigante/ al primer zafir se atreve,/ el sol en tus cimas bebe/ espíritus de candor;/ y apenas su resplandor/ sale con luz pura y mansa,/ cuando en tus hombros descansa,/ por ser el sitial mayor." One may also point to the increasingly 'Calderonian' diction of plays from the 1620's, such as the exchanges of Hernando and Laura in *La huerta de Juan Fernández*, I, ii.

more associations, connotations and meanings into a word than it would normally bear. The total effect of this continuous desire for compression is to produce a sense of strain and nervous vigor, a prismatic style that refracts in language the sense of strain that we have claimed is the essence of the Baroque as a spiritual phenomenon. With the rise of rationalism, unperspicuous language fell into disfavor; words were chosen for their clarity, precision and, above all, their lack of ambiguity. In the Baroque, however, it was precisely the maximization of ambiguity as an expression of multiple perspectives that exercized the poet's ingenuity and delighted the quick-witted audience; for, as Professor Otis Green reminds us, Cervantes had rightly proclaimed the theater-going populace of Madrid to be *discreto*.[4]

Ambiguity arises linguistically in many ways, but in our analysis of Tirso's use of dramatic language, we have distinguished three categories illustrating the manner in which words may acquire a new sense: (a) when two points in time are brought together, (b) when images begin to project outwards by subtle repetition, and (c) when words acquire ambiguity through forced playing on semantics. The reader will inevitably draw comparisons with other Spanish dramatists; these remarks are not intended to be exclusive. Nor are they, in the light of modern linguistics, more than a primitive study, but one must begin somewhere.

Tirso's Anticipation and the Compression of Time

As in music, time and timing lie at the very heart of drama; without its diachronic component, we cannot conceive of theater at all. In the simplest form of representation, a story is acted out following the events in the order they occur, and each event is self-contained, providing a logical chain down to the play's close. In the hands of a more ambitious dramatist such as Tirso, however, an attempt is made to interlink events out of the particular synchronic moment of their occurrence in the play. This practice not only imparts a more vital organic unity to the total effect, it also heightens the impact of particular events by careful preparation, ironical hindsight and so on. Anticipation is understood here, then, as any dramatic device whereby a state of mind proper to judging a given situation is induced or provoked in the

---

4. See Otis H. Green, "Se acicalaron los auditorios: An aspect of the Spanish Literary Baroque," *HR*, 27 (1959), 413-22.

audience *before* that situation actually occurs. The dramatic obverse of anticipation is retrospect, a device also frequently employed; such simultaneity of reference to two separate events in the same play is what I have termed compression of dramatic time.

The most obvious way by which anticipation may be achieved is in the very choice of playtitle, a technique that in the mature *comedia* was elevated almost to an art in its own right. Tirso's playtitles fit four main categories: simple or descriptive, paradoxical, proverbial, and the global metaphor. The simple title states the business of the play (e.g. *La vida y muerte de Herodes*) or is eponymous (e.g. *Antona García, Mari-Hernández la gallega*).[5] A much larger and more characteristic group is that containing paradoxical titles, where the masthead is a mystifying proposition and the play the illustration or resolution of the inherent paradox. Obvious examples of this group are *El cobarde más valiente, El pretendiente al revés, La celosa de sí misma,* etc. In such cases, the spectator will have begun to wrestle with the title in an effort to grasp the paradox *before* the story unfolds the elements contributing to the paradoxical master situation. Tirso's contemporaries used this device too, as Calderón's *El alcaide de sí mismo,* Lope's *El castigo sin venganza* and Gaspar de Avila's *El familiar sin demonio* all demonstrate.

Where Tirso is in his element, is in the choice of paradoxical titles that only reveal their full import as the play progresses. His best known play is called *El burlador de Sevilla y convidado de piedra.* A spectator not knowing the plot would certainly be intrigued by the subtitle, but the main title also comes to radiate paradox and irony through its seemingly plain facets. Apparently the play deals with a trickster or deceiver from Seville: a simple, identifying title of our first group. As the play proceeds, however, the word *burlador* starts to grow in complexity. He is a trickster, as the *burlas/veras* antithesis familiar in the *comedia* would suggest. In Tirso's context, though, *burlar* rapidly acquires its second meaning of libertinage and *sexual* deception. And as the trail of Don Juan's other victims grows to include men as well as women, aristocrat and lackey, the word *de* in the title acquires a second

---

5. Despite these simple titles, however, *Antona García* may have suggested the contemporary litigation in which the descendants of the heroine of the Beltraneja war were involved over royal privileges. Similarly, Mari-Hernández would instantly acquire certain characteristics in the popular mind by being called *gallega,* for the *gallego* had been a stock figure of fun in the Spanish theater since the days of Lope de Rueda.

new dimension, signifying 'of' rather than 'from', i.e. Don Juan is the deceiver *of* Seville, the man by whom all picaresque Seville is itself tricked. In this light, the word *burlador* has gained a fresh tinge, since the second meaning of *de* has restored the verbal force latent in *burlar* and made *Sevilla* accusative rather than ablative. As the play reaches its climax, the title implicitly acquires a final, didactic dimension. Tirso might well have called this play *No hay quien de Dios se burle* without damaging its message. But even so, the fate of Don Juan, specifically demonstrating that God cannot be fooled even by eleventh-hour recantations, adds to the title the inevitable predicate, *El burlador de Sevilla (sí, mas de Dios, ¡ no!*). Hence an apparently simple title increases its complexity in succeeding moments of dramatic time, without itself having been altered.

The next group of titles we must consider, those which draw on proverbs, is a large one and highly characteristic of Tirso. Once again, he is not alone in the choice of a *refrán* as a title, as Lope's *El perro del hortelano,* Calderón's *Guárdate de agua mansa* and Alarcón's *Las paredes oyen* amply indicate. Where Tirso is unique is in the frequency with which he employed proverb lore and proverbial characters, and the accomplishment with which he did so. F. C. Hayes has stated that the playwright who most successfully used *refranes* in the Siglo de Oro drama was Tirso de Molina.[6] The same critic correctly observes that while resorting frequently to proverbs, Tirso escaped the dangers of being used *by* the proverb, namely of restricting a play's interest by sticking rigorously to the literal possibilities proposed by a given *refrán.* Hayes continues: "No doubt much of his success is due to this practice of poetic freedom. His accomplishments in the use of proverbs surpass those of any of his contemporaries" (p. 317).

There are many explanations for Tirso's attraction to the *refranero* as dramatic raw material, and one of them is the obvious case of anticipation and compression of time it offered, in that a proverbial title provided the audience with a basis of reference before the play had even begun. Even if the *corrales* had not widely advertised the playtitle in advance, it was known just before the performance got under way, and set up expectations to be fulfilled later or ingeniously inverted by novel

---

6. See F. C. Hayes, "The Use of Proverbs as Titles and Motives in the Siglo de Oro drama: Tirso de Molina," *HR,* 7 (1939), 310-33. I am indebted throughout this section to Prof. Hayes' article.

twists.[7] Of eighty-eight extant titles in the Tirsian canon, some twenty-two of them are wholly or partly paroemiological. Whole proverbs include *Amor y celos hacen discretos, No le arriendo la ganancia, Quien calla, otorga* etc. In fourteen cases, Tirso is content to quote the proverb only in part, as in "Los amantes de Teruel, tonta ella y tonto él," "Háblame en entrando marido, que tengo miedo (que estoy merendando)," "Ventura te dé Dios, hijo, que el saber poco te basta," "Palabras y plumas, las lleva el viento." In the case of *El castigo del penseque,* Tirso created a phrase suggesting proverbial usage on the model of stock expressions of foolishness such as *un creíque, asnéque.* Needless to say, proverbs occur by the score in the text of the plays, mostly in the mouth of *gracioso*.

The play called *Marta la piadosa* provides an excellent example of dramatic anticipation through the use of a paroemiological title. There are numerous proverbs concerning Marta, most of them ironical: "Marta la piadosa, que daba el caldo a los ahorcados (mascabo el vino a los enfermos, mascaba la miel a los dolientes)." There also exists the expression, "mentir Marta, como sobrescrito de carta." In other words, by evoking the proverbial Marta, Tirso pre-establishes in the audience's mind the idea that the heroine is not *piadosa* at all. This proves to be exactly the case, since Marta feigns a vow of chastity to avoid marrying her suitor Urbina, adopts penitentially severe clothing, performs acts of 'piety' including taking her lover Felipe into her father's house to cure him of palsy. Tirso's Marta is indeed one of the earliest stage hypocrites, though the dramatist never paints her in the obnoxious fascinating colors of Molière's Tartuffe.

A little examined aspect of the play *Don Gil de las calzas verdes* is the proverbial character of Don Gil as a pursuer or tormented spirit. The improbably rustic quality of the name Gil is noted from the start by Caramanchel and Inés, but as the play draws to its close in Act III, Tirso fulfills the original expectations of the audience by lending Juana the dimension of a persecutor. Martín and the credulous Caramanchel come to believe that she is some hobgoblin, ideas suggested by the pro-

---

7. Professor C. A. Soons, during his discussion of *Antona García* in, "Two historical comedies and the question of 'manierismo,'" *RF,* 73 (1961), 339-46, draws attention to the widely held learned view of the Renaissance that "... the peasantry had preserved in their lore the remnants of primordial wisdom." For a cultivated man like Tirso, proverb lore held the attraction of popular poetry as well as archetypal wisdom.

verb, "que nunca falta un Gil que nos persiga." At the very end (III, xviii), moments before his arrest, Martín satisfies our long primed anticipation in a fine, fully orchestrated soliloquy consisting of four *octavas* which use the proverb as an *estribillo*. The set-piece quality of this speech is emphasized by Tirso in his metrical contrasts. The speech follows directly from a scene in *redondillas* and the play continues in a *romance* in a-a. An extract from the third stanza will illustrate the point:

> A Doña Inés adoro. ¿Eso merece
> el castigo invisible que me asombra?
> ¿Qué Don Gil mis deseos desvanece?
> ¿Por qué, fortuna, como yo se nombra?
> ¿Por qué me sigue tanto? ¿Es porque diga
> *que nunca falta un Gil que me persiga*?
> (III, xviii, 1759. My emphasis).

The idea that Juana (presumed dead in childbirth) is a soul in torment now haunting Madrid, may well have been suggested by yet another proverbial character, "Juan de las calzas blancas," who according to Correas was "un difunto que salía de la sepultura."[8] When Caramanchel appears in the last scene, weighed down with the paraphernalia of exorcism, his words corroborate this association textually and again fulfill a well prepared expectation: "¿Hay quien rece por el alma/ de mi dueño, que penando/ está dentro de sus calzas?" (III, xxiii, 1762).

The fourth group in which Tirso's playtitles fall is that of the global metaphor, but since an examination of structural metaphor and anticipatory imagery belongs more properly to a discussion of imagery as such, I shall include this group in a general consideration of those matters further on. Suffice it to add at this point that the characteristic dramatist's habit of repeating the play's title in the closing scenes (often two or three times) was an obvious attempt to hammer home in retrospect the full implications of the original caption. Hearing the title again (now with all its ironies and double meanings) inspires the hearer with a sense of superiority and strange satisfaction that never fails. This trick, involving looking back in time, achieves compression and pregnancy and also incidentally explains why titles so often were octosyllables (or heptasyllables in the case of *agudos*) in order to facilitate their being dovetailed into the final lines.

---

8. See Gonzalo Correas, *Vocabulario de refranes* (Madrid, 1924), p. 322.

Tirso's Use of Prophecy and the Ominous

Before leaving the question of dramatic anticipation, a few words on prophecy and omens are called for. Both clearly secure the effect of referring the spectator forwards in time; prophecy by explicit prediction, and omens by a more covert prognostication. Both were used by Greek dramatists, by Seneca and the neo-Senecan playwrights of Spain, notably Juan de la Cueva and to some extent Rojas Zorilla.[9] The parental imprecation and the dramatic curse belong to the same tradition and also prime the spectator's expectations.

Gabriel Téllez delighted in almost all these traditional devices and worked certain techniques into Tirsian stylistic fingerprints (notably the ominous recurrent line and hand-clasping). One of the best examples of Tirso's use of prophecy is the ghost in *El rey don Pedro en Madrid*. The ghost reminds the king of his past violence, hints at his possible murder by his brother at Montiel (III, xiii) and makes an ambiguous prophecy about Pedro's fate "por hombre/ que ha de ser piedra en Madrid" (II, xxvi, 146). The king surmises he shall be stone through his immortal works and renowned justice (III, ii), but eventually discovers that he is to build a monastery in Madrid for St. Dominic, both to expunge his own crimes and to release the cleric's soul from purgatory (III, xiii). In *La mejor espigadera* (II, vi), Ruth's slave companion Alva predicts through a prophetic dream that her mistress will mary Boaz, although a gentile, and figure in the direct genealogy of the Jewish Messiah. The courtship and marriage of Ruth and Boaz come to pass in act three. In *El condenado por desconfiado* (I, iii), Paulo has a prophetic dream wherein Death fires arrows into his body. In the play's climax, Paulo does indeed die transfixed, Sebastian-like, by the arrows of secular justice (III, xx).

Tirso is also fond of the recurring *leitmotif* or heavy repetition of certain key words. Undoubtedly the most famous case of the repeated line is Don Juan's "¡Tan largo me lo fiáis!", which in some printed versions became the play's actual title.[10] The image of a bond not due

---

9. In this regard, see Raymond R. MacCurdy, *Francisco de Rojas Zorrilla and the Tragedy*. Univ. of New Mexico Publications in Language and Literature, no. 13 (Albuquerque: Univ. of New Mexico Press, 1958), esp. the second chapter and the same author's *Francisco de Rojas Zorrilla* (New York: Twayne, 1968), pp. 136-40.

10. Doña Blanca de los Ríos reprinted this slightly different version of the play in her Aguilar edition, vol. II, 585-633, before *El burlador*. An edition of *Tan largo*

till far into the future gains, by a sort of inversion of prophecy, a tremendous dramatic impact when fate finally overtakes Don Juan. The motif then appears for the last time, sung by an off-stage chorus: "Mientras en el mundo viva,/ no es justo que diga nadie:/ ¡Qué largo me lo fiáis,/ siendo tan breve el cobrarse! " (III, xx, 684). Similarly, the final act of *La venganza de Tamar* is full of recurrent tags and prophecies, giving it a static, surreal effect. Laureta, the village sybil, distributes flowers as portents like Shakespeare's Ophelia, and predicts that Absalom will one day be "en alto por los cabellos" (III, xi). The phrase recurs thrice in the remaining scenes. Similarly Tamar repeats three times to Amnon (III, xiii): " ¡Qué amigo sois de forzar! ", an enigma treated by Amnon as a prophecy. The phrase "la venganza de Tamar" recurs increasingly, and there is a retrospective reminiscence of Amnon's sonnet (II, xi) in the phrase spoken ironically by David, "la sangre hierve sin fuego" (III, xvii). In *El vergonzoso en palacio,* the word *vergonzoso* recurs nine times in the third act alone.

As regards omens proper, they may be spoken portents, good or bad; ominous songs, voices, tableaux or visual symbols. The most omen-ridden play of Tirso is beyond doubt *Los amantes de Teruel.* This dramatic legend of star-crossed lovers bears obvious resemblances to *Romeo and Juliet,* and shares with Shakespeare's play a pervading sense of preordained doom and chances missed. The *refrán* from which the title is derived, "Los amantes de Teruel, tonta ella y tonto él" indicates that a common verdict on the lovers' fate was to lament their stupidity. Tirso, however, by loading the play with ominous elements, has endeavoured to suggest inherent self-destructive impulses that bring about the separation and *Liebestod* of two people seemingly meant for each other from earliest childhood.

The Omen, then, with Time and the Sea, is one of the three basic motifs of the play. Apart from the *ostinato* repetition of terms like *fortuna, dicha, estrella, hado, agüero, hechizo,* etc., Tirso changes the time allowed Marsilla to make his fortune, from the five years in the original legend, to the more menacing *plazo* of three years and three days. Tirso adds portents such as inkblots on a love-letter (I, 1360),[11]

me lo fiáis, attributing the play to Calderón de la Barca, was published by Prof. Xavier Fernández as recently as 1967 in *Revista Estudios* (Madrid). See Gerald E. Wade, "The Fernández Edition of *Tan largo me lo fiáis.* A Review Article," *BCom,* 20 (Fall, 1968), 31-42.

11. These references to *Los amantes de Teruel* are complete; there are no scene divisions in Doña Blanca's edition of the play.

salt-spilling (II, 1372) and a broken mirror (III, 1395). When Isabel opens books from a basket at random (II, 1379), she lights on Boscán's version of the tragic Hero and Leander story, Vergil's account of the death of Dido, and a retelling of the life and death of Pyramus and Thisbe. When Gonzalo, Marsilla's rival for the love of Isabel, five times curses the hapless lover (I, 1370), all the maledictions subsequently befall him, though not always as Gonzalo (or the audience) might have imagined. Isabel herself curses Juan, the treacherous harbinger of Marsilla's 'death' (II, 1380-81), and the hero curses the mysterious Caminante of act three. The Caminante himself sings a prophetic song (III, 1386): "Vengo de la guerra,/ niña, por verte;/ hállote casadita;/ quiero volverme." By these and similar devices, then, Tirso charges the preknown story and its notorious climax with drama. He could not cheat the audience by changing history, so the play contains no event that has not already been ominously prefigured or does not acquire ironic impact in retrospect. What the tale loses in suspense through its familiarity, Tirso restores by his search for anticipatory foreboding and the cross-references in dramatic time.

Lastly, we may mention the ominous tableau, such as that displaying three dishes with crown and a noose, sword and wimple, and stones bathed in blood, presented by Jezabel to Naboth in *La mujer que manda en casa* (III, xii, 613), all signifying future options. In the same play, the live dogs of the first scene are mute, visual symbols portending the Queen's eventual death as carrion eaten by dogs. In countless plays, Tirso's visual use of the touch or clasp of a hand is highly characteristic. With such phrases as *dame la mano, dadme la mano, dame esa mano,* the speaker signifies that he or she who takes the proffered hand is about to fall under the power of the speaker. If a woman accepts a man's hand, this generally indicates imminent sexual intimacy, if not seduction. If a woman clasps the hand of a man or another woman, this signifies that she has succeeded in duping or manipulating the other. If a man takes a man's hand, it may signify duplicity, a bargain, or in the case of divine emissaries (the Comendador in *El burlador,* the dead galán in *La Santa Juana* pt. III, the cleric's ghost in *El rey don Pedro*) the potent wrath of God. The cases of ironic or ominous songs, sung on or offstage, are so legion in Tirso and the other exponents of the *comedia* that detailed commentary here would be superfluous.

Tirso's Imagery

Imagery in the seventeenth-century drama might well be called "la peinture de la pensée."[12] It is a kind of netherworld of subliminal reference, sitting under the bare story or sense of a play, which adds color, plastic life and impressionistic significance to the entire dramatic poem, beyond the moment of speech. When images recur regularly in a given play, they carry much of the emotional impact of a situation with them and in the hands of a master, imagery assuming an obsessive stature, or appearing in regularly associated clusters, can actually convey articulate statements about the play's themes and meaning.[13]

As I shall endeavour to show, Tirso handles his images with consummate skill, and even when his effects are not striking, the constant workmanlike dècoration of the thought conveys to Tirso's theater an unfailing, nervous intricacy redeeming even his mediocre comedies from banality. In his finest achievements, it is not an exaggeration to say that, through recurrent and clustered imagery and saturation of the subconscious, Tirso sets up a subliminal dialogue with his audience. If the brittle shape of a play's storyline has faded, it is still often possible to surround a title with a whole nexus of remembered feelings, elicited at the moment of reading or viewing, by the cumulative effect of the poetry; feelings which one would be hard pressed to clarify in words. Those recollections would immediately become explicit on a second perusal if undertaken in search of the text's interior décor. In what degree the overall effects or imagistic felicities were intentional or unintentional, however, seems to me a dead-end, academic question.

It is not easy to say, of course, what one means by an 'image.' One evidently does not mean a mental representation, but a diffuse category of literary figure, related most strongly to metaphor and simile. Of

---

12. The phrase is Pascal's, quoted by Morris W. Croll in his essay "The Baroque Style in Prose," from *Style, Rhetoric, and Rhythm*, ed. J. Max Patrick et al. (Princeton: Princeton Univ. Press, 1966), 207-33, first published in *Studies in Honor of Frederick Klaeber*, ed. K. Malone and M. B. Ruud (Minneapolis: Univ. of Minn. Press, 1929).

13. In her study *Shakespeare's Imagery and what it tells us* (Cambridge: Cambridge Univ. Press, 1935), Caroline Spurgeon wrote: "It is a curious thing that the part played by recurrent images in raising, developing, sustaining and repeating emotion in the tragedies has not so far as I know, ever yet been noticed. It is a part somewhat analogous to the action of a recurrent theme or 'motif' in a musical fugue or sonata, or in one of Wagner's operas" (p. 309). Does not this observation still hold broadly true in the case of Tirso?

these, the former makes, to quote R. A. Lanham, an "... assertion of identity, rather than, as with simile, likeness."[14] Dr. Stephen Ullmann, taking the distinction further, stresses that: "We possess several criteria which enable us [...] to distinguish between imagery and other expressions of similarity or analogy. In the first place, there can be no question of an image unless the resemblance it expresses has a concrete and sensuous quality. A comparison between two abstract phenomena, however acute and illuminating [...], will not constitute a real image. Secondly, there must be something striking and unexpected in every image: it must produce a surprise effect due to the discovery of some common element in two seemingly disparate experiences."[15] In the light of these remarks, I would offer the following compact definition of an image: 'any non-literal, unexpected representation of the concrete world in a poetic (or literary) comparison.'[16]

As far as I have been able to judge, Tirso's procedure is to select three base images, predicated in the actual story to be dramatized, and work the imagery of the whole play around them. As we saw, the base images of *Los amantes de Teruel* were the Ominous, Time and the Sea. Since the medieval story concerned star-crossed lovers separated by a *plazo* of five years (Time) and the hero's campaigns abroad (across the Sea), the choice of those ideas as base images is a logical one. Tirso develops the base image in two ways: by extracting all its double meanings and lexical ambiguities, and by extending the 'field' of the base image into closely related images, which then begin to constitute a cluster. Again, in *La venganza de Tamar,* blood, eating and flowers form the three base images, derived from the storyline elements of 'blood' kinship, Amnon's feigned lack of appetite and the half-sister's 'defloration.' But blood is extended by its association with passion, blood 'boiling,' incest, and, finally, bloodshed. The two other base images are similarly expanded and extended into repetitive clusters.

---

14. See Richard A. Lanham, *A Handlist of Rhetorical Terms* (Berkeley: Univ. of California Press, 1969), p. 66.

15. See Stephen Ullmann, *Language and Style. Collected Papers* (Oxford: Blackwell, 1964), p. 178.

16. The notion that great tragedy is impossible in a world that has rejected poetry as a medium forms part of the thesis of George Steiner's *The Death of Tragedy* (London: Faber, 1961). When we refer to the poetic imagery of Aeschylus, Shakespeare or Tirso, we are certainly tempted to feel that modern drama, in prose, using realistic scenery to do the work of imagination, has set itself an automatic upward limit of excellence.

The shedding of blood at a banquet illustrates a fourth principle at work in Tirso's handling of imagery: the crossing or combination of base images. As is clear, the associations of feast, banquet, guest and host are derived from the image of eating; when the hero Amnon is transfixed amid blood, slumped across the banquet table, the two images are actually fused. Tirso presents this scene in one of his famous tableaux, so the effect is clearly consciously calculated.

Finally, it should be noted that Tirso often succeeds in making two or more base images cross in the playtitle. This, the fourth category of titles distinguished by us earlier, thus becomes the global metaphor of the play and in a sense anticipates the rich, imagistic interplay to come. To illustrate this principle and those outlined above, I have selected *Palabras y plumas,* a comedy of undoubted authenticity based on Boccaccio's ninth story from the fifth day of the *Decameron.* It is a *comedia palaciega* with a happy ending, and will thus serve to indicate that Tirso's methodology in plays of a lighter vein is the same, as regards imagery, as in the more dense and harrowing tragedies.

Briefly, the story concerns the steadfast love of Iñigo, a Spaniard, for Matilde, Princess of Salerno, who spurns him for the vapid and effete Próspero. Iñigo, through lavish jousts, feasts and serenades designed to win Matilde's affection, precipitates his own financial ruin and retires to one remaining small estate, where he subsists by hunting. In the course of the play, Iñigo saves Matilde from drowning, rescues her from a successful arson by her enemy Rugero, and houses her when dispossessed of her estates and exiled. When Matilde is reinstated in the King of Naples' favor, Iñigo expresses his joy by rewarding the messenger of these glad tidings with his last and most precious possession, the gun by which he scrapes a bare existence. This ultimate and supreme act of love finally wins Matilde's heart and she marries him.

We have seen that *Palabras y plumas* quotes the first half of a proverb which continues "el viento las lleva (las tumba)," thus the full idea of wind or air is inseparable from the title. The *refrán* is quoted in full by Próspero (I, xiv, 1306) and Iñigo at the very end of the play. Now words, since they are articulated by breath, and feathers, since they enable birds to fly, make all the images evoked by the title pertain to the element air. Words, being abstract and not sensuous, do not constitute an image in the strict terms of our definition, but certainly form a *leitmotif.* Tirso varies the motif of 'words' as being fine words, empty words, the word as a promise, the word as against silent action or *obrar callando,* as Matilde says (II, vii, 1315). *Palabras* occurs at least once every hundred lines throughout the play.

The *plumas* of the title well demonstrate Tirso's habit of multiplying secondary meanings and building up an image cluster. In the sense of plumes, we are presented with the base image visually from the very beginning, where the foppish Próspero enters "bizarro, con muchas plumas." Thereafter the base image is regularly associated with his vanity and 'feather-weight' constancy. Iñigo, by punning on the idea of the pin feathers of a bird which enable it to fly, accuses Próspero of cowardice to his face (I, vi, 1300) when he says: "Paso, que sé ser/ hombre, que a pesar de sumas/ de ducados, corto plumas,/ y las habréis menester/ para volar, si me enojo." Gallardo, the *gracioso,* puns on *pluma* in the sense of a pen. In an anecdote, he explains how his mother urged to him earn his bread by learning to write. Now that he sells his master's hunting catch (including gamebirds) for their survival, he can say: "... pero ya conozco, en suma,/ si llevo caza a vender,/ que he de ganar de comer,/ sin escribir, por la pluma" (II, v, 1312). Similarly, the oars of a boat are described as the "plumas de sus alas" (I, v, 1299); a loquacious lover is described as a "papagayo de amor" (II, viii, 1316) and Laura in the same scene continues to criticize Próspero saying: "... toda ave de mucha pluma/ tiene poco que comer./ Un cisne en la consonancia,/ música y plumas, alegra;/ mas es de poca importancia,/ pues su carne dura y negra...."

As regards the global metaphor, the feathers of the title point clearly to the one main event of the original story which Tirso has omitted to mention. In Boccaccio and Lope's earlier dramatization, *El halcón de Federico,* the story's climax hinges on the falcon by which the impoverished hero earns his living from hunting. The heroine, whose son is sickening of the desire to possess the falcon, goes to dinner with Federigo in the hope of persuading him to give up the bird. The hero, having nothing left to offer her, roasts the falcon for Madonna Giovanna to eat. Now whereas Iñigo's gun replaces the bird in the Tirso version, it is the original falcon of the story which provides the main base image of the play, developed in countless ways. Moreover, the three base images of the proverb (word-feather-wind) also provide an image entry into the other three elements: of earth, fire and water.[17]

---

17. Ullmann, *Language and Style,* p. 176, quotes Gaston Bachelard's theory that metaphors should be classified according to the four elements. He directs the

Early in the play (I, iii, 1295), Iñigo establishes this relationship. Returning from the joust where Matilde has taken one of Próspero's feathers as a mark of favor instead of Iñigo's ring, the hero tells his servant to burn his finery: "... arroja esas galas viles/ en el fuego, su elemento;/ esparce plumas al viento,/ mudables como sutiles." The element of fire then is extended to the 'fire' of passion, flames, smoke and the like. Even more important, the three non-air elements provide Iñigo with the occasion to prove his love thrice over. Once he saves Matilde's life from the element of water (I, ix, 1302), providing the *gracioso* with the opportunity to multiply sea and fish images (*humano batel, merluzas, cangrejo, besugo, abadejo, pulpo* etc.). On a second occasion he saves her from the element of fire (I, xix, 1307), and when she is stripped of her lands and has no safe 'ground' in exile, Iñigo again comes to her rescue. That this is no accident may be seen clearly in Matilde's sonnet railing against the cowardice of Próspero:

> Prueba tu amor el mar cuando me anego,
> tu cobardía saca a plaza el fuego,
> y hasta el favor me niegas de la tierra.
> Tres elementos, bárbaro, han mostrado
> que eres cobarde, ingrato y avariento;
> en el cuarto tu amor solo has cifrado ...
> (II, iv, 1310).

In a real sense, Iñigo through his constancy and deeds rather than empty words, eventually saves her from herself and the element of air as well.[18]

Tirso's Wordplay

If recurrent images can refract a spectrum of connotations within one word, then wordplay delights in fusing two or more words into a complex meaning. Like the other devices considered in this chapter, wordplay can perform a crucial role in drama by endowing the *dramatis*

---

reader to C. G. Christofides, "Gaston Bachelard's Phenomenology of the Imagination," *RR*, 52 (1961), 36-47.

18. Among the most basic of sensuous images are colors themselves. The fact that colors possessed strong, traditional connotations in Tirso to convey specific emotional states, was first made clear by S. G. Morley in 1917 in "Colour Symbolism in Tirso de Molina," *RR,* 8 (1917), 77-81. Applying the findings of H. A. Kenyon to Tirso's theater, Morley showed that *morado* indeed represented love, *verde* hope, *azul* jealousy, *amarillo* despair, *leonado* (i.e. tawny) anguish, *naranjado* constancy, *negro* mourning, *pardo* grief, *blanco* innocence and purity etc.

personae with three-dimensionality. As Molly M. Mahood has written: "Wordplay is one of the most effective means towards the interplay between character and creator which is the essence of drama. It may be anticipatory or retrospective, may imply a difference of values between what the speaker is allowed to say for himself and what the writer and his audience think, or it may simply intensify or widen the speaker's meaning to give it significance beyond the moment of speech."[19] The same writer is surely correct when she points (p. 30) to the wanton or aggressive nature of most witty wordplay, and its scope as an outlet for skepticism about authority or relief from emotional tension. In the *comedia* these functions devolve generally, though by no means exclusively, on the *gracioso*, who by his punning succeeds in grafting comic interludes and commentary onto the play's storyline. Though the pun is held nowadays to be the lowest form of wit, the seventeenth-century audience esteemed the pun for its humor, capacity to uncover sudden, arcane relationships, the exuberance and vivacity it lent to dialogue and the *agudeza* of the writer thereby revealed. A brief, descriptive catalogue of Tirso's wordplay must include double and triple puns (homonyms), words that differ in meaning but not in spelling (homographs), accidental similarities of sound in words derived from different roots (homophones), metaplasmic deformations and grotesque neologisms.

Let us look first at plays on sound or paronomasia. Strict paronomasia in Spanish depends on a similarity between words differing only by an accented or unaccentuated vowel (e.g. *lago/lego*). Leonora's words (II, 1094):[20] "Mira que ya son *hojas/ ojos* de Argos, que nos ven/ deste jardín," provide an example of this type. Armesinda's "¡Tálamo! Mejor dijeras/ túmulo, Violante mía" (I, 276), offers a looser example involving some metathesis. Modern criticism, however, has extended the use of paronomasia to include all playing on sound similarities. Homonymic puns which exploit secondary meanings in words (and hence are identical in sound and spelling) abound in Tirso. When Isabela comments on partner switching in a country house and exclaims: "¿Qué *quinta tercera* ha sido/ de aficiones descompuestas? " (II, 1131), we think of 'house' and 'go-between' but are also reminded necessarily of

---

19. See Molly M. Mahood, *Shakespeare's Wordplay* (London: Methuen, 1957 and 1968), p. 41.
20. For this section only, since our study is linguistic not interpretative, references have been simplified to the volume and page number of the Aguilar edition. The words containing the pun or quibble have been italicized throughout.

the ordinal numbers. Similarly Próspero, commenting on Rugero's cowardly flight (I, 1329), puns: "¡Qué buenas fugas hiciera,/ a ser músico, el cobarde!" The quibble involving 'fugues' then releases a veritable flurry of puns: "Pudiera/ ser músico de interés,/ según *pasacalles* canta;/ que hacen *pasos de garganta*/ las *gargantas* de sus *pies*."

The homograph usually occurs when a verb form renders a word identical to another in sound and spelling. Thus when Naboth states (I, 612): "Crisella me ha dado aviso,/ que Vuestra Alteza me *llama*," Jezabel can hint: "Nabot, si es fuego esa *llama*,/ deciros mis *llamas* quiso." Gallardo's reply: "Mas no *nada* para vos" (I, 1301), to Próspero's words "que amor vuela, mas no *nada*," exploits the resemblance of the verb 'to swim' and 'nothing.' The homophone, a recourse beloved of Quevedo as well as the playwrights, exploits words of the same sound but different meaning and written form. Tirso has the popular *hierro/ yerro* (I, 1304), *cazar/ casar* (I, 1586) and a more novel one in Boaz's words apostrophizing Ruth: "... segando mis esperanzas/ a *ciegas* mis dichas *siegas*" (I, 1018). More Tirsian still are the Mercedarian's emetic Portuguese-Castilian homophonic puns in *El amor médico* (II, 986). There Tello is told that *cagados* will be served at dinner (Sp. feces, Port. fresh-water turtles). The housekeeper then tells him: "tracei-me [...]/ do jardin unas boninas;/ olhai, e un ramo de cravos." The *gracioso* then misunderstands *olla* (Sp. cooking-pot, Port. *olhai*-look), *boñigas* (Sp. cowdung, Port. *boninas* – English daisies) and *clavos* (Sp. tumors on a horse's fetlock, Port. *cravos* – carnations), and fetches the Spanish articles!

A play on words in Tirso occasionally depends on a conceptual link. For example Tomasa quips (III, 612): "En Yepes [...]/ donde muere el vino moro,/ porque allá no le bautizan,/ me criaron...", and water, although not mentioned, provides the connection between 'wine' and 'Moor' by its association with dilution and baptism. The type of pun which combines sound play *and* this kind of concept juggling, thus forcing a multiplicity of effects into the words, has been dubbed in this century a 'portmanteau' word for obvious reasons. When Rodrigo uses the verb *prestar* in the subjunctive to his servant (i.e. *preste*), Chinchilla lets loose this pyrotechnical display:

> ¿*Preste* aquí? ¡Vocablo extraño!
> Los negros lo entenderán,
> que sirven al *Preste*-Juan,
> Un *preste* hace tanto daño
> como tiña o pestilencia.

> De *peste* a *preste* verás
> que hay una letra no más.
> En tan poca diferencia
> nadie se querría *apestar*
> por *prestar.*
> (I, 677).

A similar, portmanteau crowd of meanings is extracted from *doblón, doble, doblado, dos caras, falso, moneda* to serve an aggresive purpose, when Gastón attacks his friend's supposed duplicity (I, 300-01).

Chinchilla's jest on *peste/preste* brings us to the category I have broadly termed metaplasm, or the remolding of words by moving letters or syllables from their natural place. Tirso's prowess at fracturing words is on occasion so extreme and ingenious that terms do not really exist to describe it. One trick is to break a word in half and pun on the two fragments, as when Tamayo in a comic scene replies to Rosela's summons, "Oiga, hidalgo" (I, 279), with the phrase "Yo soy *ese*/ y *clavo* de vuesaucé" (= *esclavo*). Again, when Gallardo explains to Laura why the destruction of his master's house by fire has forced him to sell buttons for a livelihood, he continues: "... y no siendo *camaleones,*/ aunque le pese a la llama,/ he de buscar provisión;/ que aun para ser *'cama-león',*/ me quemó el fuego la *'cama'*" (I, 1317). In another exchange (II, 1451-52), the *gracioso* caps his irreverences about his master's fascination with a veiled girl's hand by a triple fragmentation:

> MELCHOR. Este es un *dedal* de plata.
> VENTURA. *De-dallo* fue su embeleco.
> MELCHOR. Este es un *devanador.*
> VENTURA. Los tuyos son *devaneos.*
> MELCHOR. Y es *de ébano.*
> VENTURA.   De Eva, no;
> que Eva, en fin, andando en cueros,
> no te engañara tapada.

In another case, Tirso resorts to spelling a word backwards! Adam, fallen from Grace, laments that he now is nothing, saying: "Ya mi dignidad pasada/ lo mismo que nada es,/ que soy Adán, y al revés/ lo mismo es Adán que nada" (I, 1967).

Elsewhere (I, 292-93), a *gracioso,* hidden in a trunk, rhymes in echoes eight times over on the final syllables of his mistress's words; Tabaco descends into onomatopoeic gibberish on his own name:

> ... que no es mal ensayo
> que *Don* Tabaco me nombren,
> aunque los *dones* me asombren

>   de haber hecho un *don* lacayo.
>   Mas tantos los *dones* son
>   que aun las campanas los *dan,*
>   pues si tañe el sacristán,
>   pronuncia *dan, dan, don, don.*
>   Y si *dan don,* desde hoy quiero
>   un *don,* aunque sea trabajo;
>   que un *don dado* de un badajo,
>   bien está en un majadero.
>   (II, 1051).

Metaplasmic puns on proper names are legion: *Serafina/ será fin* (I, 457), *Amón/ amo, Tamar/ amar* (III, 382), *Penamacor/ péname el corazón* (III, 418), *mal/ Málaga* (III, 604).[21]

Tirso was criticized in his own day for his habit of forging new verbs from nouns or simply inventing neologisms as he saw fit. This criticism was repeated by Cotarelo in 1906 when he complained of Tirso's "... conceptismo mitigado y el empleo de algunos neologismos no todos admisibles, por su tendencia a convertir los substantivos en adjec-

---

21. In *Amor y celos hacen discretos*, III, vii, Tirso pulls off a prosodic truncation which is an extraordinary piece of virtuosity and for which it is impossible to find an adequate category. The Duchess of Malfi, in her provocative attempts to arouse the sexual interest of the self-effacing Pedro, makes him read a sonnet in hendecasyllables apparently addressed to the inept Carlos (for whom Pedro, like Cyrano de Bergerac, has been composing amatory verses). In fact, it is addressed to Pedro himself, an ambiguity made possible by the omission of the first three syllables of every line. The two versions are here juxtaposed for easier comprehension. The *Mariscal* of reference is Carlos; Victoria is the Duchess's sister:

>   Mariscal,   Si sois cuerdo, en esta empresa,
>   amando,   mucho vuestra dicha gana.
>   Estimad   Los favores de mi hermana
>   pues que no   dan digusto a la Duquesa.
>   Proseguid,   Y pues veis lo que interesa
>   con ella   vuestro amor, la pena vana
>   que tenéis,   olvidad de la tirana
>   voluntad   que vuestra alma tiene presa.
>   Mirad que,   Si os preciáis de agradecido,
>   eterna   fama y triunfo desta gloria
>   gozoso   ganaréis contra el olvido.
>   Acordaos,   A vuestra alma haced memoria
>   que siempre,   de que sois de mí querido
>   me acuerdo,   mucho más que de Victoria.

tivos y en verbos..." (*NBAE,* vol. IV, p. xxxviii, n. 5).[22] Tirso, however, forestalled this charge in the Dedication of the *Quinta parte.* There he mocks those who would be miserly purists concerning verbal wit. He points out that Castilian is descended from Latin, contains Arabic, Greek, Italian and Carribean-Indian loan words and hence contains a large number of available synonyms (e.g. *comboyes* for *municiones, vivres* for *bastimientos*). There is no reason, he argues, why Spanish should not take advantage of new linguistic possibilities. The word *paralelo*, for example, has a long history in the language and to derive a verb from a noun is a common grammatical practice. Why not then use the verb *paralelar* to mean 'to liken two things,' since the usage is not stylistically offensive? We should not bother with cumbersome, redundant expressions when we can convey our full meaning neatly in a single word, he continues, provided we do not do violence to the normal conventions of Spanish and its word order. This finally leads Tirso to attack his critics for their own solecism in matters of prosody, mistaken Greek etymologies, crass hyperboles and the construction of ludicrous couplets merely to secure a given rhyme...

Such a clear indication of Tirso's linguistic sensitivity should serve to emphasize the underlying theme that has unified all the remarks in this chapter: our attempt to show how words, phrases and sometimes whole speeches are loaded by the dramatist with a maximum of meaning, sometimes to the breaking point, such that his *language* reflects that same prismatic dislocation of significance as was observable in his handling of character and his overall picture of seventeenth-century experience. Tirso's language, always tense with anticipation, hindsights, repetitions, expanding and recurrent imagery, sometimes becomes an almost plastic entity with which the master juggler projects his crowded and exuberant dramatic vision out at us across the centuries.

---

22. Though Tirso seems to satirize neologisms borrowed from French (*Privar contra su gusto,* II, viii, 1092-93), his own list is a very long one. Here is a brief selection: *protolacayo* (I, 274), *enlacayado* (I, 450), *enceleminara* (I, 275), *filosofisticamos* (I, 306), *embragué* (I, 455), *desasnóse* (I, 1550).

CONCLUSION

> Quien sus pasiones reprime
> no tenga amor, pise estrellas ...
> *El Aquiles,* II,i.

In this study, we have attempted to show that, while religious division in the sixteenth century and the problem of freedom created a universal need in Western civilization for drama, Spain differed from the rest of Europe in presenting a monolithic façade of Catholic unity and reaffirmation towards the world and communicated this spirit outward on the stage. Since the ideas of Spanish, Christian and Catholic were virtually synonymous to the Spaniard of the Counter Reformation, the drama became an ideal medium for the reaffirmation of popular national values. Under the stimulus of attack from the northern Protestant reformers, the *comedia* could provide an outlet for the public debate of urgent, controversial issues at a popular level and from a Catholic point of view. Dramatic treatments, even the most deeply serious, were generally optimistic in that the ultimate implications of tragic plots were 'retracted' in the plays' ingenious, frequently evasively subtle endings. Thus, while providing an opportunity for debate, fundamental values were scrutinized under stress and then triumphantly reaffirmed.

The labyrinthine divisions and spiritual convulsion that lay behind the monolithic Counter-Reformation façade, however, were both explicitly stated in the neo-Scholastic theology of Spain and implicitly conveyed via its intellectual methods. The atmosphere of muted debate that provided the need for plays also provided the subjects for discussion in the plays' themes: *inter alia,* free will and salvation, the defense of the sacrament of the Eucharist in the *autos sacramentales,* the canonical legality of duelling, the sacramental validity of clandestine marriage, doubt as a probabilistic principle in moral theology and doubt as a principle of metaphysics and epistemology. The neo-Scholastic mode of thinking largely defined Tirso de Molina's methodological approach to drama in a) dramatic theory itself b) the concept of personality, behavior and ethics, and c) poetic style. The mood of barely contained strain found expression under his hands in an exuberant, compressed and prismatic use of language which we have termed Baroque.

What neo-Scholastic theology and the drama shared in common was the hair-splitting accomodation of principle to meet new necessities of life. True monolithic unity had ceased to exist when Luther split Christendom on the doctrine of justification by faith alone. The idea of the One's splitting into two led to a proliferation of subsidiary splits of which the split in Spain on the difference between efficacious grace and sufficient grace was the major model. The split extended to opinions in a new-born, moral theology and their tenability's being assessed according to degrees of probability, and from thence to division upon division within that system down to the mere authority of a single theologian.

If one note has been sounded more than another in the appraisal of Tirso's theological and philosophical perspectives, it is undoubtedly the concept of the will; this is the faculty which, either conceptually or dynamically, seems to lie beneath most of Tirso's major assumptions and to provide his thought with a strongly unified and harmonious logic. We saw in the debate on grace and free will that Tirso followed the Mercedarian theologian Zumel. The attenuated Thomism of Zumel, rejecting negative antecedent reprobation and stressing human perseverance, made greater room for the will in the question of personal salvation than in the system of Báñez and his allies. Tirso clearly does not elevate the free will to the privileged position accorded to it by the Molinists, but his dramas demonstrate that free will does play an influential part in the attainment of glory.

Will thus had several meanings. In its sense of free will (*liberum arbitrium*), we have demonstrated its central importance to the *De auxiliis* controversy. As *voluntas,* will figured in the topology of Scholastic "faculty" psychology. Memory, reason and imagination made up the rational soul for Thomas Aquinas. Will's place within this topology was variously conceived. Synonymous roughly with the modern word 'desire,' will could be viewed as good or bad depending on the perspective of the theologian. Luther regarded will as a slave; Ambrose saw it as the seat of evil. St. Augustine and St. Thomas subordinated will to reason and sought to *know* God via the latter; Duns Scotus and Ockham saw will as superior to reason, and the medium by which man should *love* God. The tradition of Duns Scotus, Ockham and other orthodox theologians was upheld by the Franciscans, whose founder had given the Order the imprint of his own universally loving soul. The

Mercedarians, founded in the allied spirit of loving intercession represented by the Mother of God, stood close to the Franciscans in their own Marian emphasis on the inarticulate forces of the human soul. For the Mercedarian Tirso, it seems to have been the highest faculty, the basis of the human *raison d'être*.

Tirso investigates the freedom of the individual in the pursuit of personal goals. This subordination of intellect, energy and ethical nicety to the attainment of an end determined by the individual will may be termed an ethical voluntarism. The human being is shown free to master circumstances successfully, but only at the price of a controlled disintegration of personality and the assumption of bogus personae. Tirsian *voluntad* desires ends and employs manipulative, intelligent cunning to obtain that end. He shows the need for disciplining the degenerative aspects of ethical voluntarism by discretion and prudence. The doctrine of the direction of intention ultimately exonerates the machinations of the will's expedient measures. Tirsian thought falls a good way short, however, of the Machiavellian principle that the ends justify the means.

As an artist, Tirso claims the freedom to alter history and to violate the neo-Aristotelian unities in the name of poetry and psychological verisimilitude. He proclaims the freedom of the individual artist to elect through the will how to make ultimate decisions about the fitness or unfitness of aesthetic choices. He thus makes sovereign will (*la reina voluntad*) the highest principle of the creative process in art. All the faculties serve this sovereign will and if the latter is not infallible in its choices, it always remains disciplined by its aesthetic direction of intention: the perpetual love of the good.

Tirso's dramatic theory as reconstructed here is really an eclectic *mélange* of several theories: the mimetic, the pragmatic and the expressive. His theory thus embraces a juxtaposition of sub-systems displaying the same lack of mononuclear coherence that is reflected in contemporary lack of coherent, theological resolution. The Unities of Action, Time and Place (or space) also convey a sense of splitting or breaking down. Unity of Action is split in double plots; fusion is attempted by the synthesis of discrete genres, the tragic and the comic, into a hybrid *comedia nueva*. Tirso attempts to mix the coördinates of time and place (or space) and express them in drama in terms of one another. This after-the-fact search to recreate a global, "Catholic" unity replacing an essential, monolithic unity that no longer existed results in a Baroque art form. Tirso's world view delights in space-time confusion wherein the vertical, medieval space/value coördinates clash with horizontal, Renaissance space/value coördinates and Counter-Reformation Spain lies caught in the confusion between the two.

According to Tirso, the play is an imitation of itself (*una imagen y representación de su argumento*), a concept which creates a kind of internal cohesion. It permits paradoxes of self-reference and a series of mirror-like recessions within recessions occupying the same aesthetic space. But just as the play represents itself, the theologians in their rationalizations and accomodations were representing a true image of *themselves* (i.e. not of God). Both theological rationalizations and dramatic complexities (the Baroque world view, disintegrating personality, prismatic use of language) finally end up representing humanness in an internal/external complexity beyond the divisive categorizations of theology and art. For the intellectual mood of Spain rested on an equivocation. How could one be human within a prohibitive context? Within an often theologically prohibitive context? Tirso teaches us how wilful desire may walk safe and free through a minefield and reach the other side unscathed. Don Juan Tenorio, Paulo the hermit and Queen Jezabel were a few of the casualties.

SELECTED BIBLIOGRAPHY

Abrams, Fred. "Una nueva teoría sobre el origen del seudónimo Tirso de Molina." *Duquesne Hispanic Review*, 6 (1967), 21-29.
Abrams, M. H. *The Mirror and the Lamp: Romantic Theory and the Critical Tradition.* New York: Oxford Univ. Press, 1953.
— "Poetry, Theories of." *Encyclopedia of Poetry and Poetics.* Ed. Alex Preminger et al. Princeton: Princeton Univ. Press, 1965.
Addison, Joseph. "On the Pleasures of the Imagination." *Spectator Essays.* London, 1834.
Agheana, Ion T., and Henry W. Sullivan. "The Unholy Martyr: Don Juan's Misuse of Intelligence." *Romanische Forschungen*, 81 (1969), 311-25.
— *The Situational Drama of Tirso de Molina.* New York: Plaza Mayor, 1972.
Alonso, Dámaso. *Poesía española.* Madrid: Gredos, 1966.
Angulo Iñiguez, Diego. *Velázquez: Cómo compuso sus principales cuadros.* Seville, 1947.
— "Las hilanderas." *Archivo español de arte.* Jan.-March, 1948.
— "La fábula de Vulcano, Venus y Marte." *Archivo español de arte.* April-Sept., 1960.
Ashcom, B. B. "Concerning 'La mujer en hábito de hombre' in the Comedia." *Hispanic Review*, 28 (1960), 43-62.
Ayala, Francisco. "Erotismo y juego teatral en Tirso." *Insula*, 19 (Sept., 1964), 1-7.
Bakhtin, Mikhail. *Rabelais and his World.* Tr. Helene Iswolsky. Cambridge: Massachusetts Institute of Technology Press, 1968.
Bances Candamo, Francisco. *Theatro de los Theatros.* Ed. Duncan W. Moir. London: Tamesis, 1970.
Barrera y Leirado, C. A. *Catálogo bibliográfico y biográfico del teatro antiguo español.* Madrid, 1860.
Beardsley Jr., Theodore S. "Manuel de Falla's Score for Calderón's *Gran teatro del mundo*: the Autograph Manuscript." *Kentucky Review Quarterly*, 16, no. 1 (1969), 63-74.
— *Hispano-classical Translations Printed Between 1482 and 1699.* Pittsburgh: Duquesne Univ. Press, 1970.
Bentley, Eric. "The Universality of the *Comedia.*" *Hispanic Review*, 38 (1970), 147-62.
Bennetton, N. A. *Social Significance of the Duel in Seventeenth-Century French Drama.* Baltimore: Johns Hopkins Press, 1938.
Bettenson, Henry, ed. *Documents of the Christian Church.* Oxford, 1943.
Bonet, Alberto. *La filosofía de la libertad en las controversias teológicas del siglo XVI y primera mitad del XVII.* Barcelona, 1932.
Bravo-Villasante, Carmen. *La mujer vestida de hombre en el teatro español.* Madrid, 1953.

Brodrick, James. *The Origin of the Jesuits.* London, 1940.
— *The Progress of the Jesuits: 1556-1579.* London, 1946.
Bryson, Frederick R. *The Sixteenth-century Italian Duel.* Chicago: Univ. of Chicago Press, 1938.
Bullón y Fernández, Eloy. *Los precursores españoles de Bacon y Descartes.* Salamanca, 1905.
Bushee, Alice H. "The Five 'Partes' of Tirso de Molina." *Hispanic Review,* 3 (1935), 89-102.
— *Three Centuries of Tirso de Molina.* Philadelphia, 1939.
Calderón de la Barca, Pedro. *Aprobación* to the *Quinta parte* of Tirso, July 16, 1635.
— *Dramas. Obras completas,* vol. I. Ed. A. Valbuena Briones. Madrid: Aguilar, 1966.
— *Comedias. Obras completas,* vol. II. Ed. A. Valbuena Briones. Madrid: Aguilar, 1956.
— *Autos sacramentales. Obras completas,* vol. III. Ed. A. Valbuena Prat. Madrid: Aguilar, 1956.
— *La vida es sueño.* Ed. Albert E. Sloman. Manchester: Manchester Univ. Press, 1961.
Camón Aznar, José. "El concepto del espacio en Velázquez." *Varia velazqueña,* vol. I. Madrid, 1960.
Camus, Albert. "Le don juanisme." *Le Mythe de Sisyphe.* Paris, 1942.
Cansinos Assens, R. "El mito de Don Juan." *Evolución de los temas literarios.* Santiago de Chile, 1936.
Casa, Frank P. "Crime and Responsibility in *El médico de su honra.*" *Homenaje a William L. Fichter.* Madrid: Castalia, 1971.
— "Retraction in Golden Age Drama." Lecture delivered at Univ. of Illinois, Chicago Circle, February 23, 1973.
Casalduero, Joaquín. *Contribución al estudio del tema de Don Juan en el teatro español.* Smith College Studies in Modern Languages XIX, nos. 3, 4. Northampton, Mass., 1938.
— "Sentido y forma de *El vergonzoso en palacio.*" *Nueva revista de filología española,* 15 (1961), 198-216.
Castro, Américo. "Algunas observaciones acerca del concepto del honor en los siglos XVI y XVII." *Revista de filología española,* 3 (1916), 1-56; 357-86.
— "Noruega, símbolo de la oscuridad." *Revista de filología española,* 6 (1919), 184-86.
— ed. *El vergonzoso en palacio y El burlador de Sevilla.* Madrid: Clásicos castellanos, 1932.
— "Las complicaciones del arte barroco." *Tierra firme,* 1 (1935), 161-68.
— "El Don Juan de Tirso y de Molière como personajes barrocos." *Hommage à Ernest Martinenche.* Paris, 1939.
— *De la edad conflictiva, I: El drama de la honra en España y en su literatura.* Madrid, 1961.
Chaytor, H. J. *Dramatic Theory in Spain.* Cambridge, 1925.
Christofides, C. G. "Gaston Bachelard's Phenomenology of the Imagination." *Romanic Review,* 52 (1961), 36-47.

Cioranescu, Alexandre. "La Biographie de Tirso de Molina. Points de repère et points de vue." *Bulletin Hispanique,* 64 (1962), 175-92.
Clark, Barrett H. *European Theories of the Drama.* New York, 1919.
Correas, Gonzalo. *Vocabulario de refranes* (1627). 2nd. ed. Madrid, 1924.
Cotarelo Y Mori, Emilio. *Tirso de Molina. Investigaciones bio-bibliográficas.* Madrid, 1893.
— *Sobre el origen y desarrollo de la leyenda de los Amantes de Teruel.* Madrid, 1903.
— *Bibliografía de las controversias sobre la licitud del teatro en España.* Madrid, 1904.
— ed. *Comedias de Tirso de Molina. Nueva biblioteca de autores españoles,* vols. IV, IX. Madrid, 1906-07.
Covarrubias y Orozco, Sebastián. *Tesoro de la lengua castellana o española* (1611). Ed. Martín de Riquer. Barcelona, 1943.
Croll, Morris W. "The Baroque Style in Prose." *Style, Rhetoric, and Rhythm.* Ed. J. Max Patrick et al. Princeton: Princeton Univ. Press, 1966.
Cross, Frank L., ed. *The Oxford Dictionary of the Christian Church.* London: Oxford Univ. Press, 1966.
Cruickshank, D. W. "Calderón's King Pedro: just or unjust?" *Spanische Forschungen der Görresgesellschaft,* 25 (1970), 113-32.
Cueva, Juan de la. *Ejemplar poético* (1609). Ed. Francisco A. de Icaza. Madrid: Clásicos castellanos, 1965.
Curtius, Ernst Robert. *European Literature and the Latin Middle Ages.* Tr. Willard R. Trask. Princeton, 1953.
David-Peyre, Yvonne. "Un cas d'observation clinique chez Tirso de Molina." *Les Langues Neo-Latines,* 4 (1971), 9-22.
Delaney, J. J. and J. E. Tobin, eds. *Dictionary of Catholic Biography.* London: Hale, 1962.
Delgado Varela, Jacomé. "Psicología y teología de la conversión en Tirso." *Estudios,* 5 (1949), 341-77.
Descartes, René. *Oeuvres et Lettres.* Ed. André Bridoux. Paris, Gallimard, 1953.
Devesa O.M., Juan. *El monasterio del Puig y su virgen.* Valencia, 1968.
Edwards, Paul, ed. *The Encyclopedia of Philosophy.* 8 vols. New York: Macmillan, 1967.
Empson, William. *Seven Types of Ambiguity.* 3rd ed. London, 1963.
Entrambasaguas y Peña, Joaquín. *Lope de Vega y los preceptistas aristotélicos.* Madrid, 1946-47.
Espasa-Calpe editores. "Probabilismo." *Enciclopedia universal ilustrada,* vol. XLVII. Madrid & Barcelona, 1922.
Estudios (Order of Mercy). "Tirso de Molina. Ensayos sobre la biografía y la obra del P. M." *Revista Estudios.* Madrid, 1949.
Fernández, Xavier, ed. *Tan largo me lo fiáis.* Madrid: Revista Estudios, 1967.
Flasche, Hans, ed. *Calderón de la Barca.* Wege der Forschung, vol. CLVIII. Darmstadt: Wissenschaftliche Buchgesellschaft, 1971.
Fleming, William. "The Element of Motion in Baroque Art and Music." *Journal of Aesthetics and Art Criticism,* 5, no. 2 (Dec., 1946), 121-28.
Fries, Heinrich. *Conceptos fundamentales de teología.* Madrid, 1967.

Foss, Michael. *The Founding of the Jesuits, 1540.* London, 1969.
Fucilla, Joseph G. "On the Mirror Symbols in Tirso's *El Aquiles.*" *Bulletin of the Comediantes,* 9, no. 1 (1957), 4-5.
Fülöp-Miller, René. *The Jesuits: A History of the Society of Jesus.* New York: Capricorn, 1963.
García Lora, J. M. " 'Lo fingido verdadero' y la escenificación en el siglo de oro." *Boletín del Instituto Español de Londres,* 7 (February, 1949), 7-11.
Gendarme de Bévotte, Georges. *La légende de Don Juan.* Vol. I. Paris, 1911.
Gicovate, B. "Observations on the Dramatic Art of Tirso de Molina." *Hispania* (California), 43 (1960), 328-37.
Gilman, Stephen. "An Introduction to the Ideology of the Baroque." *Symposium,* 29 (1946), 82-107.
— "The 'Comedia' in the Light of the New Criticism." *Bulletin of the Comediantes,* 12, no. 1 (1960), 1-9.
Gilson, Etienne. *Etudes sur le Rôle de la Pensée Médiévale dans la Formation du Système Cartesien.* Paris: Vrin, 1951.
Glenn, Richard F. "Disguises and Masquerades in Tirso's 'El vergonzoso en palacio'." *Bulletin of the Comediantes,* 17 (Fall, 1965), 16-21.
González y Palencia, Angel. "Quevedo, Tirso y las comedias ante la Junta de Reformación." *Revista de la Real Academia Española,* 117-118 (1946), 43-84.
Grabmann, Martin. "Die Disputationes Metaphysicae des Franz Suarez in ihrer methodischen Eigenart und Fortentwicklung." *Mittelälterliches Geistesleben.* Vol. I. Munich, 1926.
Gracián, Baltasar. *Oráculo manual y arte de prudencia.* Ed. M. Romera-Navarro. Madrid: CSIC, 1954.
Green, Otis H. "Notes on the Pizarro Trilogy of Tirso de Molina." *Hispanic Review,* 4 (1936), 201-25.
— "New Light on Don Juan: A Review Article." *Hispanic Review,* 7 (1939), 117-24.
— "Se acicalaron los auditorios." *Hispanic Review,* 27 (1959), 413-22.
— *Spain and the Western Tradition.* 4 vols. Madison: Wisconsin Univ. Press, 1963-66.
Guastavino Gallent, Guillermo. "Notas tirsianas." Tirada aparte de *Revista de Archivos, Bibliotecas y Museos,* 67, no. 2 (1959).
— "Más sobre el nacimiento de Tirso." *Revista de Archivos, Bibliotecas y Museos,* 69 (1961), 817-20.
Guerra y Ribera, Manuel de. *Aprobación* to the *Verdadera Quinta parte de las Comedias del célebre Don Pedro Calderón de la Barca.* Ed. J. Vera Tassis y Villaroel. Madrid, 1682.
— *Apelación al tribunal de los doctos.* Ed. Gonzalo de Xaraba. Madrid, 1752.
Gurlitt, Cornelius. *Geschichte des Barockstils in Italien.* Stuttgart, 1887.
Hafter, Monroe Z. *Gracián and Perfection.* Cambridge: Harvard Univ. Press, 1966.
Halkhoree, Premraj. "Satire and Symbolism in the Structure of Tirso de Molina's *Por el sótano y el torno.*" *Forum for Modern Language Studies,* 4, no. 4 (1968), 374-86.
— "Social and Literary Satire in the Comedies of Tirso de Molina." Doctoral Thesis. Edinburgh, 1969.

Halstead, F. G. "The Attitude of Tirso de Molina toward Astrology." *Hispanic Review*, 9 (1941), 417-39.
- "The Optics of Love: Notes on a Concept of Atomistic Philosophy in the Theater of Tirso de Molina." *Publications of the Modern Language Association*, 58 (1943), 108-21.
Hamilton, B. *Political Thought in Sixteenth-century Spain*. Oxford, 1963.
Hatzfeld, Helmut. *Estudios sobre el barroco*. Madrid: Gredos, 1964.
Havelock Ellis, Henry. *The Soul of Spain*. London, 1897.
- *The Colour Sense in Literature*. London, 1931.
Hayes, F. C. "The Use of Proverbs as Titles and Motives in the Siglo de Oro drama: Tirso de Molina." *Hispanic Review*, 7 (1939), 310-33.
Hazard, Paul. *La crise de la conscience européenne*. Paris, 1963.
Hesse, Everett W. "Catálogo bibliográfico de Tirso de Molina (1648-1948)." *Revista Estudios*, 5 (1949), 781-889.
- With W. C. MacCrary. "La balanza subjetiva-objetiva en el teatro de Tirso: ensayo sobre contenido y formas barrocos." *Hispanófila*, 3 (1958), 1-11; 13 (1961), 23-32.
- *La comedia y sus intérpretes*. Madrid: Castalia, 1972.
Highet, Gilbert A. *The Classical Tradition: Greek and Roman Influences on Western Literature*. Oxford, 1949.
Horatius Flaccus, Quintus. *Horace on Poetry: The 'Ars Poetica.'* Ed. C. O. Brink. Cambridge: Cambridge Univ. Press, 1971.
Hornedo S.J., Rafael M. de. " 'El condenado por desconfiado' no es una obra molinista." *Razón y Fe*, 120 (May, 1940), 18-34.
- "La tesis escolástico-teológica de 'El condenado por desconfiado'." *Razón y Fe*, 138 (1948), 633-46.
Huerta, Eleazar. "Tirso el vergonzoso." *Ateneo*, 89 (1948), 317-86.
Hughes, Philip. *The Church in Crisis: A History of the General Councils*. New York, 1961.
Hume, Martin. *The Court of Philip IV*. London, n.d.
Iriarte, I. *Kantesischer oder Sanchezischer Zweifel*. Bonn, 1935.
Jones, Royston O. *A Literary History of Spain. The Golden Age: Prose and Poetry*. London: Ernest Benn, 1971.
Jonson, Ben. *Selected Works*. Ed. Harry Levin. New York, 1938.
Kennedy, Ruth Lee. "On the Date of Five Plays by Tirso de Molina." *Hispanic Review*, 10 (1942), 183-214.
- "Certain Phrases of the Sumptuary Decrees of 1623 and Their Relation to Tirso's Theater." *Hispanic Review*, 10 (142), 91-115.
- "Studies for the Chronology of Tirso's Theater." *Hispanic Review*, 11 (1943), 17-46.
- " 'La Prudencia en la Mujer' and the Ambient that Brought it Forth." *Publications of the Modern Language Association*, 63 (1948), 1131-190.
- "The Madrid of 1617-1625." *Homenaje a Archer M. Huntington*. Wellesley, Mass., 1952.
- "Notes on Two Interrelated Plays of Tirso: *El amor y la amistad* and *Ventura te dé Dios, hijo.*" *Hispanic Review*, 28 (1960), 189-214.

- "Tirso's *No hay peor sordo*: Its Date and Place of Composition." *Homenaje a Rodriguez-Moñino.* Vol. I. Madrid, 1966.
- "A reappraisal of Tirso's Relations to Lope and His Theater." *Bulletin of the Comediantes,* 17 (Fall, 1965), 23-34; 18, (Spring, 1966), 1-13.

Kerr, Walter. *Tragedy and Comedy.* New York: Simon and Schuster, 1967.

Lanham, Richard A. *A Handlist of Rhetorical Terms.* Berkeley: University of California Press, 1969.

Lea, Henry C. *A History of Auricular Confession.* Vol. II. Philadelphia, 1896.

Leavitt, Sturgis E. "Striptease in Golden Age Drama." *Homenaje a Rodríguez-Moñino.* Vol. I. Madrid, 1966.

López, Angel. *El cancionero popular en el teatro de Tirso de Molina.* Madrid, 1958.

Lucas, F. L. *Tragedy: Serious Drama in Relation to Aristotle's Poetics.* London: Hogarth, 1957.

MacClelland, Ivy L. *Tirso de Molina: Studies in Dramatic Realism.* Liverpool, 1948.

MacCluhan, Marshall and Harley Parker. *Through the Vanishing Point: Space in Poetry and Painting.* New York and Evanston: Harper, 1969.

MacCrary, William C. "The Authorship of *Próspera y adversa fortuna de Don Alvaro de Luna." Bulletin of Hispanic Studies,* 35 (1958), 30-40.
- See Hesse, Everett W.

MacCready, Warren T. *Bibliografía temática de estudios sobre el teatro español antiguo.* Toronto: Univ. of Toronto Press, 1966.

MacCurdy, Raymond R. *Francisco de Rojas Zorrilla and the Tragedy.* Univ. of New Mexico Publications in Language and Literature, no. 13. Albuquerque: Univ. of New Mexico Press, 1958.
- *Francisco de Rojas Zorrilla.* New York: Twayne, 1968.

MacDonald, William J., ed. *The New Catholic Encyclopedia.* 15 vols. New York: McGraw-Hill, 1967.

Madariaga, Salvador de. *Don Juan y la donjuanía.* Buenos Aires, 1936.

Mahood, Molly Maureen. *Shakespeare's Wordplay.* London: Methuen, 1957.

Márquez Villanueva, Francisco. *Espiritualidad y literatura en el siglo XVI.* Madrid and Barcelona: Alfaguara, 1968.

Maurel, Serge. *L'Univers dramatique de Tirso de Molina.* Poitiers, 1971.

May, T. E. *"El condenado por desconfiado.* 1. The Enigmas. 2. Anareto." *Bulletin of Hispanic Studies,* 35 (1958), 138-56.

Menéndez y Pelayo, Marcelino. "De los orígenes del criticismo." *Ensayos de crítica filosófica.* Madrid, 1918.
- "Tirso de Molina." *Estudios y discursos de crítica histórica y literaria.* Ed. nacional, vol. III. Madrid: CSIC, 1941.
- *Historia de las ideas estéticas en España.* Ed. nacional, 5 vols. Madrid: CSIC, 1946-47.
- *La ciencia española.* 3 vols. Santander, 1953.

Menéndez Pidal, Ramón. "Sobre los orígenes de 'El convidado de piedra'." *Estudios literarios.* Madrid, 1920.

Metford, J. C. J. "Tirso de Molina's Old Testament Plays." *Bulletin of Hispanic Studies,* 27 (1950), 149-63.
- "The Enemies of the Theatre in the Golden Age." *Bulletin of Hispanic Studies,* 28 (1951), 76-92.

- "Tirso de Molina and the Conde-Duque de Olivares." *Bulletin of Hispanic Studies*, 36 (1959), 15-27.
Moir, Duncan W. "The Classical Tradition in Spanish Dramatic Theory and Practice in the Seventeenth Century." *Classical Drama and its Influence: Studies Presented to H. D. F. Kitto.* London, 1965.
- See Bances Candamo, Francisco.
Molina S.J., Luis de. *Concordia liberi arbitrii cum gratiae donis* (1588). Antwerp, 1595.
Montaigne, Michel de. *The Essays of Montaigne.* New York and London: Oxford Univ. Press, 1948.
Morby, Edwin S. "Portugal and Galicia in the Plays of Tirso de Molina." *Hispanic Review*, 9 (1941), 266-74.
Moreau, Joseph. "Doute et savoir chez Francisco Sánchez." *Aufsätze zur portugiesischen Kulturgeschichte.* 1st series, vol. I. Münster in Westfalen: Portugiesische Forschungen der Görresgesellschaft, 1960.
Morley, S. Griswold. "El uso de las combinaciones métricas de las comedias de Tirso de Molina." *Bulletin Hispanique*, 16 (1914), 177-208.
- "Colour symbolism in Tirso de Molina." *Romanic Review*, 8 (1917), 77-81.
- "Character Names in Tirso de Molina." *Hispanic Review*, 27 (1959), 222-27.
Muñoz, V. "Zumel y el molinismo." *Estudios*, 9 (1953), 345-86.
Muñoz Peña, Pedro. *El teatro del maestro Tirso de Molina.* Valladolid, 1885.
Muratori, Ludovico. *Della Perfetta Poesia Italiana.* 2 vols. Modena, 1706.
Nelson, Robert. *Play within a Play.* New Haven, Conn.: Yale Univ. Press, 1966.
Newels, Margarete. *Die dramatischen Gattungen des Siglo de Oro.* Wiesbaden, 1959.
Nougué, André. "Le thème de l'aberration des sens dans le théâtre de Tirso de Molina." *Bulletin Hispanique.* 58 (1956), 23-35.
- "Compte rendu du livre de M. Penna." *Bulletin Hispanique*, 60 (1958), 250-52.
- " 'La venta de las Pavas' chez Tirso de Molina." *Bulletin Hispanique*, 62 (1960), 326-30.
- "A propos de l'auto-imitation dans le théâtre de Tirso de Molina." *Bulletin Hispanique*, 64 (1962), 559-66.
- *L'Oeuvre en prose de Tirso de Molina.* Paris, 1962.
Oppenheimer, Max. "The Baroque Impasse in the Calderonian Drama." *Publications of the Modern Language Association*, 65 (1950), 1146-165.
Orozco Díaz, Emilio. *El barroquismo de Velázquez.* Madrid: México, 1965.
- *El teatro y la teatralidad del barroco.* Barcelona: Planeta, 1969.
Ortúzar O.M., Martín. " 'El condenado por desconfiado' depende teológicamente de Zumel: nueva aclaración." *Estudios*, 5 (1949), 321-36.
Panofsky, Erwin. *Problems in Titian, Mostly Iconographic.* New York: New York Univ. Press, 1969.
Parker, Alexander A. "Santos y bandoleros en el teatro español del Siglo de Oro." *Arbor*, 13 (1949), 395-416.
- "Reflections on a new definition of Baroque Drama." *Bulletin of Hispanic Studies*, 30 (1953), 142-51.
- "The Approach to the Spanish Drama of the Golden Age." *Diamante*, no. 6. London, 1957.

- "History and Poetry: the Coriolanus theme in Calderón." *Hispanic Studies in Honour of I. González Llubera.* Oxford, 1959.
- ed. "The Meaning of 'Discreción' in 'No hay más fortuna que Dios': The Medieval Background and Sixteenth- and Seventeenth-Century Usage." *No hay más fortuna que Dios.* 2nd ed. Manchester: Manchester Univ. Press, 1962.
- "Towards a Definition of Calderonian Tragedy." *Bulletin of Hispanic Studies,* 39 (1962), 222-37.
- "The Father-Son Conflict in the Drama of Calderón." *Forum for Modern Language Studies,* 2 (1966), 99-113.
- "Los amores y noviazgos clandestinos en el mundo dramático-social de Calderón." *Hacia Calderón: Segundo coloquio anglogermano, Hamburg.* Berlin and New York: Gruyter, 1970.

Parker, Jack Horace. "Tirso de Molina, defensor de la comedia nueva." *Revista de la Univ. de San Carlos.* 12 (1948), 39-48.
- *Breve historia del teatro español.* México, 1957.

Paterson, A. K. G. "Tirso de Molina: An Edition of *La venganza de Tamar* with bibliographical, textual and literary criticism." Doctoral Thesis. Cambridge, 1966.
- "Tirso de Molina: Two Bibliographical Studies." *Hispanic Review,* 35 (1967), 43-68.
- ed. *La venganza de Tamar.* Cambridge: Cambridge Univ. Press, 1969.

Penna, Mario. *Don Giovanni e il mistero di Tirso.* Turin: Rosenberg and Sellier, 1958.

Pereira, Gómez. *Antoniana Margarita, opus nempe physicis, medicis, ac theologis non minus utile, quam necessarium.* Medina del Campo, 1554.

Pérez, Luis C. and F. Sánchez Escribano. *Afirmaciones de Lope de Vega sobre preceptiva dramática.* Madrid: CSIC, 1961.

Pérez Pastor, Cristóbal. *Documentos para la biografía de Calderón.* Madrid, 1905.
- *Bibliografía madrileña.* 3 vols. Madrid: RABM, 1907.

Peristiany, J. G., ed., *Honour and Shame: The Values of Mediterranean Society.* London, 1965.

Peyton, Myron. "Some baroque aspects of Tirso de Molina." *Romanic Review,* 36 (1945), 43-69.

Popkin, Richard H. *The History of Scepticism from Erasmus to Descartes.* Assen: Van Gorcum, 1960.
- "Sánchez, Francisco" and "Scepticism." *The Encyclopedia of Philosophy.* Ed. Paul Edwards. Vol. VII. New York: Macmillan, 1967.

Powicke, F. M. and C. R. Cheney. *Councils and Synods.* Oxford, 1964.

Prado O.M., Norberto del. *A un académico de la Española sobre* El condenado por desconfiado. Vergara, 1907.

Preminger, Alex et al. eds. *The Encyclopedia of Poetry and Poetics.* Princeton: Princeton Univ. Press, 1965.

Quevedo Villegas, Francisco de. *Política de Dios. Govierno de Christo.* Ed. James O. Crosby. Madrid: Castalia, 1966.

Quiñones Benavente, Luis de. *Burlas veras, o represión moral* (1645). Ed. Cayetano Rosell. Madrid, 1872.

Rackham, H. *Aristotle: The Nicomachean Ethics.* 2nd ed. London: Loeb Classical Library, 1934.
Rank, Otto. *Die Don Juan-Gestalt.* Vienna, 1924.
Reichenberger, A. G. "The Uniqueness of the *comedia.*" *Hispanic Review,* 27 (1959), 303-316.
Rennert, H. A. *The Spanish Stage in the Time of Lope de Vega.* New York, 1909.
Rice Pereira, Irene. *The Nature of Space: A Metaphysical and Aesthetic Inquiry.* New York, 1956.
Ríos Lampérez, Blanca de los. *El enigma biográfico de Tirso de Molina.* Madrid, 1928.
– ed. *Tirso de Molina: Obras dramáticas completas.* 3 vols. Madrid: Aguilar, 1946-58.
Rivers, Elias L. *Renaissance and Baroque Poetry of Spain.* New York: Scribner's 1966.
Roaten, D. H. and F. Sánchez Escribano. *Wölfflin's Principles in Spanish Drama: 1500-1700.* New York: Hispanic Institute, 1952.
Romero-Navarro, M. "Las disfrazadas de varón en la comedia." *Hispanic Review,* 2 (1934), 269-86.
– "Lope de Vega y las unidades dramáticas." *Hispanic Review,* 3 (1935), 190-201.
– "Querellas y rivalidades en las academias del siglo XVII." *Hispanic Review,* 9 (1941), 494-99.
– *La preceptiva dramática de Lope de Vega.* Madrid, 1958.
Sabuco, Miguel. *Nueva filosofía de la naturaleza del hombre.* Madrid, 1587.
Sage, Jack. "Calderón y la música teatral." *Bulletin Hispanique,* 58 (1956), 275-300.
– "Texto y realización de *La estatua de Prometeo* y otros dramas musicales de Calderón." *Hacia Calderón.* Berlin: Gruyter, 1969.
Sánchez, Francisco. *Quod nihil scitur.* Lyons, 1581.
– *Que nada se sabe.* Intro. by M. Menéndez y Pelayo. Buenos Aires, 1924.
Sánchez, Francisco (El Brocense), tr. and ed. *Epicteto.* Madrid, 1612.
Sánchez, José. *Academias literarias del Siglo de Oro español.* Madrid: Gredos, 1961.
Sánchez S.J., Thomas. *Opus morale in praecepta decalogi sive summa casuum conscientiae.* Paris, 1617-22.
– *Disputationum de Sancto Matrimonio Sacramento.* Antwerp, 1617.
Sánchez Canton, F. J. "La librería de Velázquez." *Homenaje a Menéndez Pidal.* Madrid, 1925.
– *Cómo vivía Velázquez.* Madrid, 1942.
– *Las Meninas y sus personajes.* Barcelona, 1943.
– "La Venus del espejo." *Archivo español de arte.* Madrid, April-Sept., 1960.
Sánchez Escribano, F. and A. Porqueras Mayo. *Preceptiva dramática española.* 2nd ed. Madrid: Gredos, 1972.
Sanz y Díaz, J. *Tirso de Molina.* Madrid: CBE, 1964.
Shergold, N. D. "The first performance of Calderón's *El mayor encanto amor.*" *Bulletin of Hispanic Studies,* 35 (1958), 24-27.
Shepard, Sanford. *El Pinciano y las teorías literarias del Siglo de Oro.* Madrid, 1962.
Schumaker and Longsdorf, eds. *The Cyclopedic Law Dictionary.* 3rd ed. Chicago, 1940.

Sidney, Sir Philip. *The Defense of Poesy.* Ed. Albert S. Cook. Boston, 1890.
Solana, Marcial. *Historia de la filosofía española: Epoca del renacimiento, siglo XVI.* 3 vols. Madrid, 1941.
Soons, C. A. "Poetic elements in the plots of Tirso's novels." *Bulletin of Hispanic Studies,* 32 (1955), 194-203.
— "Two historical comedies and the question of 'manierismo'." *Romanische Forschungen,* 73 (1961), 339-64.
Spitzer, Leo. "En lisant 'El Burlador'." *Neophilologische Mitteilungen,* 35 (1935), 282-90.
Spingarn, Joel E. *Literary Criticism in the Renaissance.* New York: Harcourt, 1963.
Spurgeon, Caroline. *Shakespeare's Imagery and what it tells us.* Cambridge: Cambridge Univ. Press, 1935.
Steiner, George. *The Death of Tragedy.* London: Faber, 1961.
Stenchelstrup, Andreas. *Dissertatio de duellis.* Hafnia, 1677.
Stevenson, R. A. M. *Velázquez.* Ed. D. Sutton and T. Crombie. London: Bell, 1962.
Suárez S.J., Francisco de. *Disputaciones metafísicas* (1597). Ed. and tr. S. Rábade Romeo et al. 6 vols. Madrid: Biblioteca hispánica de filosofía, 1960–.
— Selections from three works of —. *De legibus ac Deo legislatore,* 1612. *Defensio fidei catholicae, et apostolicae, adversus anglicanae sectae errores,* 1613. *De triplici virtute theologica, fide, spe et charitate,* 1621. 2 vols. Oxford, 1944.
— *Varia opuscula theologica. Opera omnia,* vol. X. Venice, 1741.
Sullivan, Henry W. See Agheana, Ion T.
— "Two hundred years of Calderonian criticism, 1681-1881." Doctoral Thesis. Harvard, 1970.
— "Was Gaspar Lucas Hidalgo the Godfather of Tirso de Molina?" *Bulletin of the Comediantes,* 26, no. 1 (1974), 5-11.
— "Tirso de Molina, the Arias Dávila Family and Other Curiosities." *Bulletin of the Comediantes,* 28, no. 1 (1976), 1-11.
— With Ion T. Agheana. 'Der unheilige Märtyrer: Don Juans Missbrauch der Intelligenz." *Don Juan: Darstellung und Deutung.* Ed. Brigitte Wittmann. Wege der Forschung, vol. CLXXXII. Darmstadt: Wissenschaftliche Buchgesellschaft, in press.
— "Tirso de Molina: dramaturgo andrógino." *Actas del V Congreso Internacional de Hispanistas.* Bordeaux: Centre d'Etudes Hispaniques, in press.
Sypher, Wylie. *Four Stages of Renaissance Style.* Garden City, N.Y.: Doubleday, 1955.
Taylor, Jeremy. *Ductor Dubitantium.* London, 1659.
Tejedor, José I. *Calderón de la Barca.* Madrid: CBE, 1967.
Téllez, Gabriel. *Los cigarrales de Toledo.* Ed. Victor Said Armesto. Madrid, 1913.
— *El bandolero.* Ed. Luis Carlos Viada y Lluch. Barcelona, 1915.
— *Vida de Santa María de Cervellón.* Ed. Duque de Fernán-Núñez. Madrid, 1930.
— *Obras dramáticas completas.* Ed. Blanca de los Rios. 3 vols. Madrid: Aguilar, 1946-59.
— *Don Gil de las calzas verdes.* Ed. I. Manuel Gil. Madrid, 1964.
— *El melancólico.* Ed. Jacomé Delgado Varela. Madrid, 1967.
— *El monasterio del Puig y su virgen.* Ed. Juan Devesa O.M. Valencia, 1968.
— *Poesías líricas de Tirso de Molina.* Ed. Ernesto Jareño. Madrid: Castalia, 1969.

– *Historia general de la Orden de Nuestra Señora de las Mercedes.* Ed. Manuel Penedo Rey. 2 vols. Madrid: Revista Estudios, 1973.
Templin, E. H. *The Exculpation of 'Yerros por amores' in the Spanish Comedia.* Berkely: Univ. of California Press, 1933.
– "Another Instance of Tirso's Self-Plagiarism." *Hispanic Review,* 5 (1937), 176-80.
– "The Encomienda in *El condenado por desconfiado* and other Spanish works." *Hispania* (Baltimore), 15 (1940), 465-82.
– "The 'burla' in the Plays of Tirso de Molina." *Hispanic Review,* 8 (1940), 185-201.
– "Night Scenes in Tirso de Molina." *Romanic Review,* 41 (1950), 261-73.
Tirso de Molina. See Téllez, Gabriel.
Tolnay, C. D. "Las pinturas mitológicas de Velázquez." *Archivo español de arte.* Jan.-March, 1961.
Ullmann, Stephen. *Language and Style: Collected Papers.* Oxford: Blackwell, 1964.
Vacant, A. et al. eds. *Dictionnaire de Théologie Catholique.* Vols. IX and XIII. Paris, 1936.
Valbuena Prat, Angel. *Historia del teatro español.* Barcelona, 1956.
Valencia, Pedro de. *Academica, sive de judicio erga rerum ex ipsis primis fontibus* (1596). Ed. F. Cerda y Rico. *Clarorum Hispanorum opuscula selecta.* Madrid, 1781.
Vega Carpio, Félix Lope de. *Arte nuevo de hacer comedias* (1609). Ed. Juana de José Prades. Madrid: CSIC, 1971.
Vidart, Luis. *La filosofía española: indicaciones bibliográficas.* Madrid, 1866.
Villanova, A. "Preceptistas españoles de los siglos XVI y XVII." Ed. G. Díaz-Plaja. *Historia general de las literaturas hispánicas.* Vol. III. Barcelona, 1953.
Vossler, Karl. *Lecciones sobre Tirso de Molina.* Madrid: Taurus, 1965.
Wade, Gerald E. "Tirso's self-plagiarism in plot." *Hispanic Review,* 4 (1936), 55-65.
– "Notes on Tirso de Molina." *Hispanic Review,* 7 (1939), 69-72.
– "El escenario histórico y la fecha de 'Amar por razón de estado'." *Estudios,* 5 (1949), 657-70.
– "Tirso de Molina." *Hispania* (Baltimore), 32 (1949), 131-40.
– "Adición a 'Three Centuries of Tirso de Molina' de A. H. Bushee." *Nueva revista de filología española,* 5 (1951), 414-17.
– "La dedicatoria de Matías de los Reyes a Tirso de Molina." *Estudios,* 8 (1952), 589-93.
– "The Literary Sources of *El castigo del penseque* of Tirso de Molina." *South Atlantic Studies for Sturgis E. Leavitt.* Washington, 1953.
– "On Tirso's Don Gil." *Modern Language Notes,* 74 (1958), 609-612.
– "Notes on two of Tirso's plays." *Bulletin of the Comediantes,* 12, no. 2 (1960), 1-6.
– "The Year of Tirso's Birth." *Hispanófila,* 19 (1963), 1-9.
– "Tirso's *Cigarrales de Toledo*: some clarifications and identifications." *Hispanic Review,* 33 (1965), 246-72.
– "Tirso's Friends." *Bulletin of the Comediantes,* 19, no. 1 (1967), 1-6.
– "Tirsiana." *Romance Notes,* 9 (1967), 95-101.
– "The authorship and date of El burlador de Sevilla." *Hispania,* 32 (1968), 1-22.

- "The Fernández Edition of *Tan largo me lo fiáis*: A Review Article." *Bulletin of the Comediantes,* 20, no. 2 (1968), 31-42.
Wardropper, B. W. *Introducción al teatro religioso del siglo de oro.* Madrid, 1953.
- "Lope's *La dama boba* and Baroque Comedy." *Bulletin of the Comediantes,* 13, no. 2 (1961), 1-3.
Watson, Anthony I. "Peter the Cruel or Peter the Just? A reappraisal of the role played by King Pedro in Calderón's *Médico de su honra.*" *Romanistisches Jahrbuch,* 14 (1963), 322-46.
Weinstein, Leo. *The Metamorphoses of Don Juan.* Stanford, 1959.
Weisbach, Werner. *Der Barock als Kunst der Gegenreformation.* Berlin, 1921.
Wellek, René. "The Concept of Baroque in Literary Scholarship." *Journal of Aesthetics and Art Criticism,* 5 (1946), 77-109.
Wilson, E. M. "Las 'Dudas curiosas' a la aprobación del Maestro Fray Manuel de Guerra y Ribera." *Estudios escénicos,* 6 (1960), 47-63.
Wilson, W. E. "Tirso's *Privar contra su gusto*: A Defense of the Duke of Osuna." *Modern Language Quarterly,* 4 (1943), 161-66.
- "Did Tirso hate the Girones?" *Modern Language Quarterly,* 5 (1944), 27-32.
Wilson, W. Margaret. "The Last Play of Tirso de Molina." *Modern Language Review.* 47 (1952), 516-28.
- "'La próspera fortuna de Don Alvaro de Luna': an Outstanding Work by Mira de Amescua." *Bulletin of Hispanic Studies,* 33 (1956), 25-36.
- ed. *Antona García.* Manchester: Manchester Univ. Press, 1957.
- *Spanish Drama of the Golden Age.* Oxford: Pergamon, 1969.
Wölfflin, Heinrich. *Kunstgeschichtliche Grundbegriffe: Das Problem der Stilentwicklung in der neueren Kunst.* Munich, 1915.

Index

The following index is basically an onomastic one and uses the word-by-word method of alphabetization. It contains all historical personages and authors mentioned in the text, plays by authors other than Tirso, all titles of relevance to earlier *comedia* theory and literary critics up to the year 1860 only. Modern critics are cited in the footnotes and Selected Bibliography. All mythological and apocryphal figures are omitted, as well as play characters, except where the latter are also Spanish historical personages. References to Tirso's works are not separately filed and should be consulted under "Téllez" and the relevant genre subheading (e.g. WORKS – DRAMA).

A secreto agravio, secreta venganza, 67
Addison, Joseph, 99
Aeschylus, 160n16
Alcaide de sí mismo, El, 152
Alciati, Andrea, 107
Apologética de las comedias españolas, 72
Aristotle, 16, 31, 53, 55, 64, 73, 74, 74n6, 76, 79, 81, 83, *90-93,* 94n26, 99, 171
Ars Poetica, 85n17, 86n18
Arte nuevo de hacer comedias, 71, 71n1, 72, 74, 75, 78n8, 81
Avila, Gaspar de, 152
Azor S. J., Juan, 40
Azpilcueta, Martín, 40

Bacon, Francis, 54n41
Bances Candamo, Francisco, 64n52, 65, 66
Bandello, Mateo, 88
Bañez, O. P., Domingo, *30-32,* 35, 36, 36n23, 38-40, 170
Bañecists, *See previous entry*
Barclay, Alexander, 88
Basta callar, 26
Bauny, S. J., Etienne, 41
Bayle, Pierre, 54
Beltraneja, Juana la, 45, 152n5
Boccaccio, Giovanni, 88, 161, 162
Bodmer, Johann Jakob, 99
Boil, O. M., P. Francisco, 47
Boscán Almogáver, Juan, 158
Breitinger, Johann Jakob, 99
Bronzino, Il (pseud. Agnolo Tori), 128n15
Bruno, Giordano, 17
Bustamante, Jorge de, 132

Caesar, Gaius Julius, 58
Calderón de la Barca, Pedro, 9, 9n1, 21, 22n7, 23, 24,26, 26n12, 43, 43n28, 44, 60, 61, 61n49, 61n51, 62, 65, 65n55, 65n56, 66-68, 68n58, 83, 84, 84n15, 90n23, 101, 106, 106n5, 127, 127n11, 135, 138, 139n21, 150n3, 152, 153, 157n10
Calvin, Jean, 17, 28-30
Calvinists. See previous entry
Camargo S. J., Ignacio de, 65
Cano O. P., Fr. Melchor, 20
Caramuel y Lobkowitz, Juan, 43
Carneades, 52n37, 58
Casa con dos puertas, mala es de guardar, 68
Casas, Cristóbal de las, 104n4
Cascales, Francisco, 72
Castelvetro, Lodovico, 74, 74n6
Castigo sin venganza, El, 67, 74n5, 152
Castro y Bellvís, Guillén de, 64
Cerda y Rico, F., 58n46
Cervantes Saavedra, Miguel de, 14, 88, 148, 151
Céspedes y Meneses, Gonzalo de, 88
Charles I of England, 84n16
Charles V of Spain, 16, 22
Charles IX of France, 22
Cicero, Marcus Tullius, 73, 74
Cintio, Giraldi, 74n6, 88
Claramonte, Andrés de, 138, 139n21
Clavius (Christoph Klau), 55, 55n43
Clement VIII, Pope, 31, 36
Clitomachus, 52n37
Coleridge, Samuel Taylor, 76, 113
Columbus, Christopher, 147
Copernicus, Nicolas, 46, 62
Córdoba, Antonio de, 26n13
Corral de la Cruz, 14
Corral del Príncipe, 14
Correas, Gonzalo, 155, 155n8
Covarrubias y Horozco, Sebastián de, 104n4, 105, 107, 108
Cueva, Juan de la, 119n19, 156

Dama duende, La, 68
De esta agua no beberé, 139n21
Defense of Poesy,The, 89n20, 90n24
Del rey abajo ninguno, 84, 85
Descartes, René, 17n2, 54, 54n41, 56n45, 61, 61n51, 62, 125n8
Devoción de la cruz, La, 67
Diana, P. Antonino, 43, 43n28
Discorides, 133
Doles, 132

Don Quijote de la Mancha, Pt. I, 72
Donatus, 73
Duchess of Malfi, The, 25
Durán, Agustín, 118, 149

Ejemplar poético, 119n19
Elizabethan drama, 7, 14
En esta vida, todo es verdad y todo mentira, 68, 83
Engels, Friedrich, 148n28
Epictetus, 59, 59n47
Epicurus, 59
Erasmus of Rotterdam, Desiderius, 16, 28, 29, 56n45, 83, 109n10, 150n2
Esclavo del demonio, El, 66
Estatua de Prometo, La, 68, 127n11
Estrella de Sevilla, La, 85
Euclid, 55
Every Man in his Humour, 97n28
Expostulatio Spongiae, 72

Falla, Manuel de, 127n11
Familiar sin demonio, El, 152
Ferdinand V of Aragón, 16
Fianza satisfecha, La, 66
Fingido verdadero, Lo, 68, 126n10
Fomperosa S. J., Pedro, 65
Freud, Sigmund, 114
Fuenteovejuna, 44, 67

Galán fantasma, El, 68
Galileo Galilei, 17, 46, 46n31, 125n8
Goethe, Johann Wolfgang von, 126
Golfo de las sirenas, El, 127n11
Góngora y Argote, Luis de, 72, 147, 150, 150n3
Gracián S. J., Baltasar, 108, 109, 109n9, 148, 148n27
Gragnano, Antonio di, 26
Gran teatro del mundo, El (auto), 60, 127n11, 135
Gryphius, Andreas, 7, 99
Guárdate de agua mansa, 153
Guerra y Ribera, Fray Manuel de, 65, 65n56
Gustos y disgustos no son más que imaginación, 68, 83
Gutiérrez, Juan, 26n13

Halcón de Federico, El, 162
Hamlet, 135, 157
Hebreo, León (Jehudah León Médigo Abravanel), 95n27
Heliodorus, 88
Henry IV of Castile, the "Impotent," 44
Henry IV of France, 84n16
Henry VIII of England, 62

Hermes Trismegistes (apocryphal), 146
Herrera S. J., Augustín de, 65
Herrera Sotomayor, Juan de, 82
Höffding, Harald, 27n14
Horace (Horatius Quintus Flaccus), 85, 85n17, 86n18
Hurtado S. J., Gaspar, 26n13

Isabella I of Castile, 16, 45

Jacobean drama, 14, 21
James I of England, 84n16
Jones, Inigo, 97n28
Jonson, Ben, 97n28

Kafka, Franz, 140

LaCroix S. J., François de, 42
Laetius, 59
Laguna, Andrés de, 133
Laínez S. J., Pedro (second General of Jesuit Order), 20
Ledesma O. P., Pedro de, 25
Leibniz, Gottfried Wilhelm, 125n8
Leitanus, 24
León, Fray Luis de, 30
Leonardo de Argensola, Bartolomé, 60, 60n48, 61
Leonardo de Argensola, Lupercio, 60, 60n48, 61
Lessius S. J., Leonardus, 32
Longinus, 89n20
López O. P., Luis, 40
López de Aguilar, Francisco, 89, 89n21
Luis Pérez el gallego,23, 67
Luther, Martin, 13, 18, 20, 28, 29, 31, 39, 62, 170
Lutherans. *See previous entry*

Machiavelli, Niccolò, 85, 108, 118, 171
Mágico prodigioso, El, 67
Mal casados de Valencia, Los, 64
Manichaeans, 28, 28n15, 33
María de Molina (Queen Regent of Castile), 107, 111, 111n12
Mariana S. J., Juan de, 85
Marx, Karl, 148, 148n28
Mayor encanto amor, El, 127n11
Mayordomo de la Duquesa de Amalfi, El, 25
Médico de su honra, El, 45, 67, 139n21
Medina O. P., Bartolomé de, 40, 40n26, 41
Melanchthon (Philipp Schwarzerd), 28
Méndez Pinto, Fernán, 88
Merino O. M., Fray Pedro, 36
Mesonero Romanos, Ramón de, 118, 149
Milhard, Pierre, 41

Mira de Amescua, Antonio, 44, 65n55, 66
Molière (pseud. Jean-Baptiste Poquelin), 122n3, 154
Molina S. J., Luis de, 30-32, 32n17, *33, 34,* 34n18, 35n19, 35n20, 37, 39, 40, 111, 170
Molinists. *See previous entry.*
Montaigne, Michel de, 54, 56, 57, 107, 107n6
Montemayor S. J., Prudencio, 30
Morales, Ambrosio de, 48
Moreto y Cabaña, Agustín, 138, 139n21
Muratori, Ludovico, 99

Nadie fíe su secreto, 26
Navarro O. P., Pedro, 40
Neo-Aristotelians. *See* Aristotle
Newton, Sir Isaac, 125n8
Niña de plata, La, 139n21
No hay más fortuna que Dios (auto), 106, 106n5
Nuñez O. P., Fray Diego, 30
Nuñez, Hernán, 104n4

Ockham, William of, 93, 170
Origen, 28
Othello, 85
Ovando, Fray Francisco de, 26n13
Ovid (Publius Ovidius Naso), 132

Padilla S. J., Antonio, 30
Palacios, Fray Miguel de, 26n13
Paredes oyen, Las, 153
Pasajero, El, 72
Pascal, Blaise, 48, 146, 159n12
Paul III, Pope, 22
Paul V, Pope, 31
Pedraza O. P., Juan, 40
Pedro of Castile and León, the "Cruel," 47, 98, 115, 138, 138n21, 139, 139n21, 140, 141
Pelagius, 29n15, 30
Pelagians. *See previous entry*
Peñarrosa, Gerónimo, 43n28
Pereira, Gómez, 52, 53
Peribañez, y el Comendador de Ocaña, 45, 67
Perro del hortelano, El, 153
Philip II of Spain, 16, 19
Philip IV of Spain, 98
Pinciano, El, 64n52
Pintor de su deshonra, El, 26, 67
Plato, 52n37, 55, 64, 65, 68, 90
Poetics, 73, 74, 74n6, 91, 93
Ponce de León (Augustinian), Basilio, 25

Postrer duelo de España, El, 22, 26
Pound, Ezra, 78n8
Pruebas del segundo Adán, Las (*auto*), 65n55
Purgatorio de San Patricio, El, 66
Puritans, 63
Púrpura de la rosa, La, 127n11
Pyrrho, 52n37, 58, 83

Quevedo y Villegas, Francisco Goméz de, 15, 148, 150, 165
Quiñones Benavente, Luis de, 82, 82n13

Rabelais, François, 146, 146n26, 147
Ravaillac, François, 84n16
Reinar después de morir, 26
Remón O. M., Fray Alonso de, 44, 65n55
Robortelli, Francesco, 74, 74n6, 89n20
Rojas Zorilla, Francisco de, 14, *84*, 156, 156n9
Romeo and Juliet, 157
Rubens, Peter Paul, 132
Rueda, Lope de, 152n5
Ruiz de Alarcón, Juan, 104n4, 153
Russell, Bertrand 64

Saber del mal y del bien, 61
Sabuco, Miguel, 52, 57, 58
Sabuco de Nantes Barrera, Oliva (pseud.), 57
St. Alphonse Liguori, 41n27, 42, 43
St. Ambrose, 170
St. Anthony, 133n18
St. Augustine of Hippo, 28, 93, 170
St. Bruno (founder of Carthusian Order), 35n21
St. Chrysostom, 28
St. Dominic (founder of Dominician Order), 156
St. Francis of Assisi (founder of Franciscan Order), 170
St. Francis Xavier, 118n17
St. Genestus (San Ginés), 68
St. Ignatius Loyola (founder of Jesuit Order), 15, 34n18, 49n33
St. Paul, 59n47
St. Peter, 133n18
St. Thomas Aquinas, 16, 28, 31-33, 36, 36n23, 37, 40, 40n26, 93, 103n3, 108, 170
Salmerón S. J., Alfonso, 20
San Ambrosio, María de, 86
Sánchez S. J., Thomas, 25, 40, 42
Sánchez de Brozas, Francisco, 52, *59*, 59n47, *60*
Sánchez de Moratalla, 72
Sánchez of Toulouse, Francisco, 52, *54*, 54n42, *55*, *56*, 56n44, 56n45, *57*
Scotus, Duns, 26n13, 93, 117, 170
Seneca, 156
Servet, Miguel, 17

Sextus Empiricus, 52n37, 53
Shakespeare, William, 9, 85, 99, 104n4, 157, 159n13, 160n16, 164n19
Sidney, Sir Philip, 89n20, 90n24
Sixtus V, Pope, 35n21, 90
Socrates, 55
Solomon, 59n47
Soto O. P., Domingo de, 20, 40
Spinoza, Baruch, 45n30, 125n8
Spongia, 72
Stenchelstrup, Andreas, 23, 24n9
Stevenson, Robert Louis, 128
Stoics, 58, 59n47
Struvius (Georg Adam Struve), 24, 24n9
Suárez S. J., Francisco de, 15, 16, 17n2, 27, 34n18, 41, 62
Suárez de Figueroa, Cristóbal, 72
Sulzer, Johann Georg, 99

Tablas poéticas, 72
Tartuffe, 154
Taylor, Jeremy, 41
Téllez O. M., Fray Gabriel, *passim*
  WORKS – DRAMA:
  Amantes de Teruel, Los, 154, *157,* 157n11, *158,* 160
  Amar por arte mayor, 71
  Amar por razón de estado, 45, 67
  Amor médico, El, 13, 94n26, 98, 103, 165
  Amor y celos hacen discretos., 71, 94n26, 138n21, 154, 167n21
  Amor y la amistad, El, 150n3
  Antona García, 45, 67, 73n3, 152, 152n5, 154n7
  Arbol del mejor fruto, El, 35n21
  Aquiles, El, 169
  Balcones de Madrid, Los, 68, 112, *142-144*
  Bellaco sois, Gómez, 103
  Burlador de Sevilla, El, 35, *39,* 67, 81, 102, 102n1, 115, 122n3, *152, 153,* 156n10, 157, 158
  Castigo del penseque, El, 154
  Cautela contra cautela, 105
  Celos con celos se curan, 71
  Celosa de sí misma, La, 71, 152
  Celoso prudente, El, 87
  Cobarde más valiente, El, 152
  Cómo han de ser los amigos, 110n11, 113
  Condenado por desconfiado, El, 34n19, 35, 35n20, *37-39,* 67, 81, 111, 112, 156
  Dama del Olivar, La, 35n21
  Don Gil de las calzas verdes, 68, 103, 104, 107, 115, 144
  Elección por la virtud, La, 35n21, 90, 91n25
  En Madrid y en una casa, 68, 142

Fingida Arcadia, La, 48, 49, 71, 80, *95-97,* 98, 112
Habladme en entrando, 154
Huerta de Juan Fernández, La, 103, 150n3
Madrina del cielo, La (auto), 35n21
Mari-Hernández la gallega, 152, 152n5
Marta la piadosa, 118n18, 154
Mayor desengaño, El, 35n21, 67
Mejor espigadera, La, 156
Mujer por fuerza, La, 50, 51n35, 67, 68, 101, *104,* 106, 121, *144-146*
Mujer que manda en casa, La, 76n7, 80n9, 112n12, 158
Ninfa del cielo, La (comedia), 35n21
No le arriendo la ganancia, 154
Palabras y plumas, 154, *161-163*
Por el sótano y el torno, 68, 142, 142n24
Pretendiente al revés, El, 25, 148, 152
Privar contra su gusto, 115-117, 168n22
Prudencia en la mujer, La, 97, 98n29, 107, 111
Quien calla otorga, 154
Quien no cae, no se levanta, 35, 37
Reina de los reyes, La (attrib. dub.), 35n21
República al revés, La, 112n12, 148
Rey don Pedro en Madrid, El, 98, 115, 121, *138,* 138n20, *139-41,* 156, 158
Santa Juana, La, Pt. III, 35n21, 158
Santo y sastre, 35n21
Siempre ayuda la verdad, 138n21
Tan largo me lo fiáis (same as *Burlador*), 156n10
Tanto es lo demás como lo de menos, 35n21
Venganza de Tamar, La, 81, 157, *160, 161*
Ventura te dé Dios, hijo, 154
Vergonzoso en palacio, El, 71, 73, 75, 78, 86, *90-95,* 109, 110, 121, 122n3, 128, *136,* 136n19, *137, 138,* 157
Vida y muerte de Herodes, La, 45-47, 67, 81, 112n12, 152
WORKS – PROSE:
Bandolero, El (third novel of *Deleitar aprovechando*), 88
Cigarrales de Toledo, Los, 71, 75, 77, 86, 87, 90, 150n2
Dedication of *Deleitar aprovechando,* 87, 88
Dedication of the *Tercera parte,* 71, 89, 89n21
Dedication of the *Quinta parte,* 71, 149, *168*
Deleitar aprovechando, 71, 85, 87, 88
Historia general de la Orden de Nuestra Señora de las Mercedes, 35, 36n22, 47, 139n21
Tesoro de la lengua castellana, 105, 107
Thomists. *See* St. Thomas Aquinas
Timon, 52n37, 55
Timoneda, Juan de, 21
Tirso de Molina. *See* Téllez O. M., Fray Gabriel
Titian (Tiziano Vecellio), 108, 108n7, 132, 133

Torres Rámila, 72
Turia, Ricardo del, 72

Valdivielso, José de, 21
Valencia O. P., Gregorio de, 40
Valencia, Pedro de, 52, *58, 59*, 60n48
Valiente justiciero, El, 139n21
Vázquez S. J., Gabriel, 40
Vega Carpio, Félix Lope de, 14, 21, 23, 25, 44, 64n52, 66-68, 71, 71n1, 72, 74, 74n5, 77, 78n8, 80, 81, 85, 90n23, 98, 99, 101, 112, 114, 126n10, 127n12, 138, 138n20, 139n21, 152, 162
Velázquez, Diego de Silva, 118n19, 121, 127, 127n12, 128, 128n13, 128n14, 128n15, 129, *132*, 132n17, *133-37*
Vélez de Guevara, Luis, 26
Vergil (Publius Vergilius Maro), 158
Vida es sueño, La, 61, 61n50, 62, 67, 68, 83
Vitelleschi S. J., Muzio (sixth General of Jesuit Order), 42
Vondel, Joost van den, 7, 99

Wagner, Richard, 159n13
Webster, John, 25

Zoroaster, 28n15
Zumel O. M., Fray Francisco, 30, 34, 35, 35n20, *36*, 36n23, 37, 39, 170
Zumelists. *See previous entry*
Zwingli, Ulrich, 28